How to
Help Your Child
Have a
Spiritual Life

How to Help Your Child Have a Spiritual Life:

A Parent's Guide to Inner Development

ANNETTE HOLLANDER, M.D.

A & W Publishers, Inc.
New York

Published by
A & W Publishers, Inc.
95 Madison Avenue
New York, New York 10016

Text Design by Fran Miskin

Library of Congress Cataloging in Publication Data
Hollander, Annette, 1941-
    How to help your child have a spiritual life.

    Bibliography: p.
    Includes index.
    1.   Children—Religious life.   I.   Title.
BV4571.2.H64   649.7   79-28074
ISBN 0-89479-061-7

Printed in the United States of America

To my husband, Myron Kaplan, and our children, Eve and Amelia. And to the men and women who spent hours contributing to this book out of their love for other parents and children.

With thanks to Linnett Kong, Angela Miller, and Eleanor Ruma-Blofson for their support and encouragement.

Acknowledgments

Grateful acknowledgment is made for permission to reprint from the following copyrighted material. Any inadvertent omissions will be corrected in future printings on notification to the publisher.

"The Appeal of the Death Trip" by Robert J. Lifton. Copyright © 1979 by The New York Times Company. Reprinted by permission.

Dromenon Journal. From an interview with Elaine de Beauport. Vol. 1, no. 5–6, Feb. 1979 "Arts and Minds."

Call Me Ishtar by Rhoda Lerman. Copyright © 1973 by Rhoda Lerman. Reprinted by permission of Holt, Rinehart, and Winston, Publishers.

The Centering Book by Gay Hendricks and Russel Wills, pp. 10–13. Copyright © 1975 by Prentice-Hall. Reprinted by permission of Prentice-Hall, Inc., Englewood Cliffs, New Jersey.

"Centuries of Meditations" by Thomas Traherne. From *Seventeenth Century Verse and Prose 1660–1700,* vol. 2. Edited by H. C. White, R. Quintana, H. Wallerstein, and A. Chambers. Copyright © 1971 by Macmillan Publishing Co., Inc.

The Child's Conception of the World by Jean Piaget. Reprinted by permission of Humanities Press, Atlantic Highlands, N.J.

Cutting Through Spiritual Materialism by Chögyam Trungpa. Copyright © by Chögyam Trungpa. Reprinted by special arrangement with Shambhala Publications, Inc., 1123 Spruce St., Boulder, Colorado 80302.

"Discovering Your Radiant and Creative Self: A Transpersonal Arts Approach to Expressing One's Potential" by Paula Klimek and Jack Canfield. Reprinted by permission of the Institute for Wholistic Education, Box 575, Amherst, Mass. 01002.

"Earthrise: The Dawning of a New Spiritual Awareness" by Eugene Kennedy. Copyright © 1979 by The New York Times Co. Reprinted by permission.

East West Journal. From an interview with Jacob Needleman. Reprinted by permission.

"The Education of the Buddhist Child" by Rev. Roshi Jiyu-Kennett, O.B.C., Abbess. From *The Journal of Shasta Abbey*, 5, no. 12, December 1974 (formerly *The Journal of the Zen Mission Society*).

How to Discipline with Love: (From Crib to College) by Dr. Fitzhugh Dodson. Copyright © 1977, 1978 by Dr. Fitzhugh Dodson. Reprinted by arrangement with the New American Library, Inc. New York, New York.

If You Marry Outside Your Faith, pages 135–136. Revised Edition by James A. Pike. Copyright © 1954, 1962 by Harper & Row Publishers, Inc. Reprinted by permission of Harper & Row Publishers, Inc.

Abridged from *Island* by Aldous Huxley. Copyright © 1962 by Aldous Huxley. Reprinted by permission of Harper & Row Publishers, Inc.

"Little Gidding" in *Four Quartets* by T. S. Eliot. Copyright © 1943 by T. S. Eliot; copyright © 1971 by Esme Valerie Eliot. Reprinted by permission of Harcourt Brace Jovanovich, Inc.

Magical Child by Joseph Chilton Pearce. Copyright © 1977 by Joseph Chilton Pearce. Reprinted by permission of E. P Dutton.

Man's Search for Meaning by Viktor E. Frankl. Copyright © 1959, 1962 by Viktor E. Frankl. Reprinted by permission of Beacon Press.

The Masks of God by Joseph Campbell. Copyright © 1968 by Joseph Campbell. Reprinted by permission of Viking Penguin, Inc.

Meditation for Children by Deborah Rozman. Copyright © 1976 by Deborah Rozman. Reprinted by permission of Celestial Arts, Millbrae, CA.

"Meditation With Young Children" by Maureen Murdock. Copyright © 1978 Transpersonal Institute. Reprinted by permission from *The Journal of Transpersonal Psychology*, vol. 10 no. 1, 1978, pp. 29–44.

Table 2 from *Mental Health in the Metropolis: The Midtown Manhattan Study Book Two* by Leo Srole, Thomas S. Langner, Stanley T. Michael, Price Kirkpatrick, Marvin K. Opler, and Thomas A. C. Rennie. Copyright © 1962 by Leo Srole. Enlarged and revised edition, *Book Two,* copyright © 1977 by Leo Srole. Reprinted by permission of Harper & Row Publishers, Inc.

The Mermaid and the Minotaur by Dorothy Dinnerstein. Copyright © 1976 by Dorothy Dinnerstein. Reprinted by permission of Harper & Row Publishers, Inc.

Mysticism: Spiritual Quest or Psychic Disorder? Copyright © 1976 by the Group for the Advancement of Psychiatry. Reprinted by permission of the Commmittee on Psychiatry and Religion for the Group for the Advancement of Psychiatry.

The Only Dance There Is by Ram Dass. Copyright © 1970, 1971, 1973 by Transpersonal Institute. Reprinted by permission of Doubleday & Co., Inc.

The Phenomenon of Man by Pierre Teilhard de Chardin. Copyright © 1955 by Edition du Seuil. English translation copyright © 1959 by William Collins Sons & Co., Ltd., and Harper & Row Publishers, Inc. Reprinted by permission of Harper & Row Publishers, Inc.

Play of Consciousness by Baba Muktananda. Copyright © 1974 SYDA Foundation. All rights reserved.

Psychosynthesis by Roberto Assagioli. Copyright © 1965 by Psychosynthesis Research Foundation. Reprinted by permission of the Sterling Lord Agency.

Readiness for Religion by Ronald Goldman. Copyright © 1956 by Ronald Goldman. Used by permission of the Seabury Press. *Religious Thinking from Childhood to Adolescence* by Ronald Goldman. Copyright © 1964 by Ronald Goldman. Used by permission of the Seabury Press.

The Value Survey by Milton Rokeach. Copyright © 1967 by Milton Rokeach. Reproduced with permission of Halgren Tests, 873 Persimmon Avenue, Sunnyvale, CA 94087.

"Women and Spirituality" by Ann Squire. Quoted from the May/June 1978 issue of the journal *Religious Education,* by permission of the publisher, The Religious Education Association, 409 Prospect St., New Haven, CT 06510. Membership subscription available for $20.00 per year.

Yoga and Psychotherapy: The Evolution of Consciousness, by Swami Rama, Rudolph Ballentine, M.D., and Swami Ajaya (Allan Weinstock, Ph.D.). Himalayan Institute, RD 1 Box 88, Honesdale, PA 18431.

Your Child and Religion by Johanna L. Klink. Copyright © 1972 SCM Press Ltd. American edition published by John Knox Press. Used by permission.

Contents

PART THREE:
WHAT THE RESEARCH SHOWS AND HOW TO USE IT

PART FOUR:
ADOLESCENCE AND AFTER

PART ONE:

Spiritual Experience—
Our Personal Reality

CHAPTER 1

A Parent's Search

Parents wonder: what can we give our children? Love, a home, a little bit of culture. But supposing you want to give your children not just your love, and worldly goods, but something that can give meaning to their lives, whatever may befall them?
Johanna Klink
Your Child and Religion

The only thing you have to offer another human being, ever, is your own state of being.
Ram Dass
The Only Dance There Is

No one questions that the most important thing we have to offer our children is our own state of being: how wisely loving we are to them, to ourselves, and to others. The question is whether there are teachings that can make us wiser.

This book grew out of my own search for answers to this question and others. When our children were two and four, I wanted to find a helpful book that did not assume that the readers were trying to make their children more "religious," that is, better Protestants, Catholics, or Jews. I also wanted to know about the spiritual *experience* of parents and children, independent of belief systems and religious labels. What were other parents actually saying to and doing with their children?

When I couldn't find any book for the parent who is a "seeker," perhaps partly identified with one tradition, perhaps married to someone from another tradition, yet looking for wisdom in more than one place—I decided to write it.

In the past, tradition dictated what a parent was to do, and religious educators handled the rest. Outside the framework of organized, institutional religion, questions arise such as:

- How do other parents nurture a spiritual life?
- Do children need "religion" to build moral character?
- What about discipline, values, and ethics? Should I send my child to Sunday school? And what if I don't?
- Do children have mystical experiences? What is their spiritual life like?
- How can I understand what goes on in kids' heads? What are *their* ideas about the nature of reality?
- What is the best way to answer children's questions about God and death?
- How are educators helping children use "multi-modal knowing" and altered states of consciousness?
- What new directions are being taken even by traditional religious educators?
- How do parents think meditation and prayer changes things? What do children really think about prayer? Should I teach my child to pray?
- Is there a connection between religion and psychological well-being?
- Are "mixed marriages" unstable? How can parents from different traditions best share them with their children?
- How does patriarchal religious teaching affect my children and my relationship with them?

- What happens to spiritual development at adolescence? And after? What can we offer teenagers so they won't be attracted to cults?
- How do other families make daily life a spiritual activity?
- How do people find "meaning in life" without organized religion?

When I first started my research, I looked for answers from experts: developmental psychologists, sociologists, religious educators. I found much interesting research, which I have included. It was useful to find out what the experts know, and reassuring to find out how much they don't know. Most of all, I discovered that I and almost everyone else found the experience of other families even more valuable than the advice of "experts."

I decided to interview parents, beginning with questions about their own childhood experiences. Many parents wrote me that simply answering the questions helped them clarify their own thinking. One mother called the interview "thought-evolving." A psychotherapy patient of mine once told me that some books could do for her what our sessions did: trigger insight into who she was and what she really wanted. As you read through these pages, in addition to "advice," I hope you will also find something more valuable: an opening of new worlds that you will enjoy exploring with your children.

Is this book for you? Yes, if no single minister, priest, rabbi, or guru is telling you what to believe and what to teach your children. Sociologists declare that Americans have always been more religious as a group than people of other nations. What is new is the growing number of people with religious feelings or experiences who are unchurched.

A 1978 poll by the Princeton Religion Research Center and the Gallup Organization found that *41 percent* of the adult American population—61 million people—were unchurched. The Center defined "unchurched" as anyone who doesn't go to a place of worship except perhaps on high holidays. Of course, some of these are true believers who simply find it inconvenient to attend services. However, there was the astonishing finding that not only 60 percent of the unchurched, but also 50 percent of the churched, agreed with the statement "Most churches and synagogues have lost the real spiritual part of religion." Close to that number also agreed that "Most churches and synagogues today are too concerned with organizational as opposed to theological or spiritual issues."

In 1975, only 5 percent of the unchurched were explicitly antireligious. A 1976 Gallup poll estimated that 6 million Americans meditate, 5 million practice Yoga, 2 million are studying Eastern religions, and more than 10 million believe in psychic healing. People are seeking, and finding, practices that will lead to direct experience of unseen realities. The 1978 poll found that 7 to 10 percent of both churched and unchurched practiced a specific technique of meditation.

Andrew Greeley, in 1975, found that 35 percent of a representative U.S. sample answered yes to the question "Have you ever felt as though you were close to a powerful spiritual force that seemed to lift you out of yourself?"—his definition of a mystical experience. Similarly, the 1978 Gallup poll found that 43 percent of the churched group, and *24 percent of the unchurched,* had had "a particularly powerful religious insight or awakening."

Times have changed. More and more of us consider ourselves "spiritual" without following strictly the dogma or ritual of any one group. When those of us without labels or in interfaith marriages become parents, we must find our own ways of guiding our children. They will be exposed to myth, ritual, and religious teaching whether we are the teachers or not. Parents who feel confused or uncertain often relinquish the job to the culture as educator—to school or television. This book is for parents who want to be more conscious about that choice.

PARENT WORKBOOK

In order to get a better understanding of your own thoughts and feelings about the spiritual development of children, take a few minutes to answer the following questions before reading on to see what other parents had to say.

The responses of many other parents will be given later. What you find in the rest of the book will be more meaningful after you have sifted through your own mind, discovering both what you feel good about and where you feel stuck.

If you feel hesitant about doing the work involved (and it *is* work to put these subtle memories, thoughts, and feelings into words), consider why we often become more interested in spiritual concerns *after* we have children. Although we know our lives are imperfect, we can't help wanting "the best" for our kids. The paradox is that from our wish for our children to become the best possible people, we ourselves can grow.

The first group of questions has to do with your own experience as a child:

1. What was your parents' religion, in name (i.e., Jewish, Catholic, Lutheran, etc.) *and* in true attitude (i.e., what they *really* believed and practiced)?

Mother's religion

In name: Her parents' religion?

True attitude:

Father's religion

In name: His parents' religion?

True attitude:

2. What was your experience of organized religion as a child? (Include what your religious training was and what part of it you enjoyed.)

3. Did you believe as a child that prayer changes things? What prayers do you especially remember?

4. During your lifetime, including childhood, have you ever had the feeling that you were in close contact with something holy or sacred? When? Have you ever had what you would call a mystical experience? How old were you? What was it like? Has it had a lasting influence on your life?

The next group of questions has to do with your experience as an adult.

5. At what points in your life have you changed your attitude toward religion? Why?

6. How meaningful do you find life now, on a scale from 1 to 3, if 1 is very meaningful, and 3 not at all meaningful? What gives your life meaning?

7. What "religion" do you consider yourself now?

Do you take part in the activities of any organized religious group?   If yes, how often, and what about it is most important to you?

8. Do you meditate or pray?   If yes, explain *what* you do, and how often:

Do you now believe that prayer or meditation changes things?   How?

9. What part of your childhood contact with organized religion is meaningful to you now?

What part do you now think was destructive?

10. What spiritual teaching from your parents is meaningful to you now? Words or example? Who else was a source of inspiration?

11. If you have brothers or sisters, what religion are they now?

12. How would you define "spiritual" —not the dictionary definition, but what *you* mean when you use the word?

Now . . . as a parent:

13. Your children:

Age	**Sex**	**Name**

<u>Other parent's background</u>

His/her mother's religion in name:

    True attitude:

His/her father's religion in name:

    True attitude:

Other parent's religious belief in name:

    True attitude:

Are both of you living together?

14. If you don't belong to an organized religious group, do you worry sometimes that your children might be missing something? If so, what? What solutions have you found?

15. What do you think is the relation between your children's spiritual development and your own?

16. What have the children asked about God, Heaven, and death? What have you told them? Have you told them anything you don't believe?

17. How do you make specific activities a part of your child's spiritual development? (Another way of asking this is: How would you go about practicing a spiritual daily life?)

18. In this general area that you have been discussing, what would you like to know that you don't know? What kind of help would be useful to you? Are you interested in what other parents are doing?

19. What suggestions do you have for other parents?

WHAT DO WE MEAN BY "SPIRITUAL"?

I first presented the questionnaire in the Parent Workbook to friends of mine, then friends of friends, and then placed a classified ad in a small national magazine. It said: "Author wants to interview 'unchurched' parents who are willing to share thoughts, feelings, and questions about their children's spiritual development." I began to put together the results when I had as many responses as I could handle: about eighty from all over the country. A little under half of the respondents were, or had been, in interfaith marriages.

The respondents to the questionnaire fell into four main groups by their answer to the question "What religion do you consider yourself now?" The largest group consisted of seekers who found it hard to fit themselves into a given category: I call this group simply "spiritual." Some of these said their religion was "nothing with a name" or "no labels" or "has no name—it is my own constantly changing system" or "nothing formal, but I consider myself religious without following any doctrine or organization." Others defined themselves as "a child of God and a brother to all humanity and Christian in consciousness" or "a universal Christian—that is, I believe in the God within and try to love all people and recognize their God within." Yet others included "Jewish identity" along with their other practices. The last subcategory of this first group were those who had affiliated with teachings that welcome seekers from all religious backgrounds: devotees of Meher Baba, followers of Bhagwan Shree Rajneesh, students of the Gurdjieff Foundation, and others.

The next largest group was the "humanist," which means a positive commitment to faith in humankind. Humanists have no creed, dogma, or ritual, but work out their own attitude toward the unknown. They emphasize the dignity of life, just and loving relationships, and a better life for all people.

The last two groups clearly identified themselves either as Protestant, Catholic, or Jewish (I called them "religious") or as having no interest in religion *or* spiritual life.

I purposely left the definition of "spiritual" for the end of the questionnaire. *After* people had used the word, they could look back to see, "Now what did I mean by that?" This is a working definition rather than an abstract one.

People normally use the word in many different ways. At a convention of the Religious Education Association, I was horrified when one speaker said, "Everybody knows what we mean by 'spiritual' and didn't bother to define what *he* meant. In fact, the religious educators have as many meanings as we do. The exact meaning of "religious" is equally difficult to pinpoint, and as a result many researchers decide to limit "religious" to "having to do with religious institutions," which is exactly what I am *not* talking about.

My definition of "spiritual" derives from my own experiences, from psychology, and from physics. It is based on the fact that we are all, adult and child, unique personalities, living our life histories in time and space, and yet also part of a larger whole that stretches into infinity in all directions, and for which time-space concepts simply do not apply.

I present a few models or diagrams used to express the idea in chapter 7. I don't believe that any of them is more "true" than the others.

This relationship of the individual self to the infinite self cannot be adequately expressed in the linear sequence of language; we can only do our best to approach it through symbol, myth, or poetry. I once felt, while meditating, that "I" was a position, a point of view, on a four-dimensional infinite web. How could I draw that?

I have been collecting the variety of phrases that people use to express the "larger whole" of which we are a part. Here are some:

God	The Divine Ground
The Goddess*	The Numinous Element
Ultimate Reality	The All-pervading Energy
The General Field of Awareness	The Creative Life Force
The Ground of Being	Brahman
The Source	The Pure Light of the Void
The One	The Collective Unconscious

---

* See the chapter entitled "Girls and the Goddess."

The Creator

The Self

Universal Mind

The Center of Value

The Infinite

The Great Spirit

The Tao

Field Consciousness

World-Spirit

The Absolute

The All

The Spirit of the Universe

Mind-at-Large

The Oversoul

I hope I didn't omit yours.

You will not find discussions of theology in this book. Although I am aware that there are theological differences between a personal God and "Mind-at-Large," these differences were far outshadowed by the oneness of thought and feeling of the people who answered the questionnaire.

Most of these people have experienced that the Infinite is also within us, not totally separate and "supernatural." Christianity includes both a transcendent God and the mystical aspect of Christ, who can "live" in us.

As we shall see, recent findings in psychology and physics are beginning to show *how* the infinite is also "natural," although most of the time not in our conscious awareness.

OUR INFINITE CHILDREN

What does the interrelatedness of the individual and the "all" have to do with the day-to-day business of raising children? That is what we will be looking at in this book. Western psychology throughout years of competitive individualism has been more interested in the development of "autonomy"—our struggle to become independent, learn skills, leave home—and presents the autonomous "ego" as the ultimate in human development. Yet, although from the time egg and sperm meet we are constantly becoming more unique, more "ourselves," at the same time we are always embedded in a larger nurturing field, beginning with the womb, but not limited to it. The growth of a human being always and simultaneously involves both differentiation and unity.

The more we can experience our "ego" as part of this field, this unity, the less frightened, lonely, and insecure we will be, as children or adults. And the more we can experience our interconnectedness, the less willing we will be to destroy each other and our world.

Throughout the history of civilization, human societies have swung between two ideals. Since the Renaissance, our Western ideal has been an individual ego heroically mastering the world, as opposed to the Eastern ideal of the submergence of individual egos into a cosmic or social order. Our ecological crisis, some say, results from our overemphasis on "conquering Nature," unbalanced by any acknowledgment of our oneness with Nature. The amount of sheer physical suffering—famine and poverty—in many Eastern countries, some say, is also the result of imbalance: an overemphasis on spiritual ideals, discouraging individual initiative to improve life in the material world. As Western parents, we want our children to have the best of both: autonomy and a spiritual life.

Western scientific psychology is beginning to approach Eastern mystical thought by demonstrating that ordinary reality *is,* in a sense, an illusion. Starting from birth, we are always *constructing* reality from our perceptions, which we select from the mass of information that reaches our sensory systems. For example, we are *always* receiving energy in the form of the electromagnetic band: cosmic waves, x-rays, radiowaves, visible light, radiant heat. The information from all the television programs being broadcast in our neighborhood is around us every minute, although we do not become conscious of it until we turn on the TV set. Molecules in the atmosphere are transmitting the information of sound, air pressure, smell. We are always in the gravitational field. Our bodies are producing more stimuli: organ sensations, muscle activity (proprioception), thoughts and feelings.

Some of this information, like the TV broadcasts, we cannot know *directly* through our sense organs, so we build machines to receive it for us. In other cases our senses do pick up the signals but do not report them to our conscious awareness. In the words of Aldous Huxley, "Mind at Large has to be funneled through the reducing valve of the brain and nervous system."

Robert Ornstein says: "Our personal consciousness . . . cannot fully represent the external world or even our internal world, but must consist of an extremely small fraction of the entire 'reality.' . . . If we can realize that our ordinary consciousness is something we must of necessity construct or *create* in order to survive in the world, then we can understand that this consciousness is only *one* possible consciousness."

Another exciting discovery about the way our minds may process information comes from research on holography. A hologram is a three-dimensional image that can be projected from film exposed to the interference pattern of two laser beams. It has the astounding property that any portion contains essentially the same information as the whole. You can cut the film in half, and in half again, almost ad infinitum, and still be able to project the original image, albeit a bit fuzzier, from each small piece.

The holographic model has been used to explain how the brain may store memories and process perceptions. It has also been used by physicists such as David Bohm to describe "the implicate order," a higher-dimensional reality in which time, space, matter, and consciousness are all "enfolded." Fritjof Capra, in *The Tao of Physics,* describes the universe as a dynamic web of interrelated events in which "consciousness" is not separate from "matter" or "energy."

This is a tremendous change for Western science, which like its philosophy has always opposed "mind" and "matter," "spiritual" and "material," and has been looking for the ultimate physical building block. Eastern traditions have always considered consciousness an integral part of the universe, since human beings, like all other life forms, are parts of an inseparable organic whole. New Western scientific theories replace the "building block" with a "holomovement" or implicate order.

If the universe is a holographic *pattern,* then as part of that pattern, we ourselves contain the whole. Mind-at-Large is *in us* as well as *out there,* although we have to alter our ordinary consciousness to allow ourselves to know that.

Capra illustrates how, as we approach infinitely large astronomic distances, or infinitely small subatomic regions (and remember, that is what our bodies are made of), "We can only explain the observed phenomena by theories which describe a non-ordinary reality . . . the four dimensional world of space-time, of which we can have no direct sensory experience. At this level dualities are transcended. Particles [remember our bodies!] are merely local condensations of the quantum field, which is present everywhere in space . . . the reality underlying all forms."

Our senses and nervous system abstract or "unfold" from this implicate order the properties of time, space, causality, and separateness as we know them in our three-dimensional world. Young children have to *learn* how to do this (see chapter 7). We have become so used to these abstractions that we take them as fundamental "reality." We are already "enfolded" in the implicate order; spiritual growth is largely a process of becoming more aware (or staying aware) of what on a deep level we already "know."

Altered states of consciousness open us to these other realities. The next chapter focuses on the reality known by people—including children—who have mystical experiences. Chapters 3 and 6 show that there are many practices that allow people—on a regular basis—to change their consciousness. If they do, they may gain access to knowledge without knowing how they know, and sources of strength and guidance that seem far beyond the power of their "little selves."

General Systems Theory is another scientific model that makes sense out of the apparent paradox that we are simultaneously a whole, an organism bounded by skin, and yet also an unbounded entity, a dependent part of ever larger systems.

In General Systems Theory, the world can be understood as a hierarchy of levels of systems, each of which has its own laws. The workings of each level cannot be understood simply by understanding the behavior of its component subsystems. Each whole is greater than the sum of its parts.

The social hierarchy:

    humanity
    nations
    tribes
    families

    . . .

    the organism (us)

The organismic hierarchy:
    organ systems (circulatory, nervous, digestive, etc.)
    organs (heart, brain, stomach, etc.)
    tissues (muscle, nerve, etc.)
    cells
    organelles
    molecules
    atoms
    subatomic "particle waves"
    the quantum field
    ???? the holomovement

The physics we learned in school—classical Newtonian mechanics—is a useful set of rules that describes the behavior of the "level of organization" we call everyday three-dimensional reality. We all "know" that time can be measured by clocks, that we are bounded by our skin, and that objects feel solid. But Newtonian physics is only a "special case" of the higher-dimensional quantum-relativistic field in which our ordinary reality is embedded.

Arthur Koestler writes:

Each member of this hierarchy, on whatever level, is a sub-whole or "holon" in its own right—a stable, integrated structure, equipped with self-regulatory devices and enjoying a considerable degree of autonomy, or self-government. Cells, muscles, nerves, organs, all have their intrinsic rhythms and patterns of activity, often manifested spontaneously. . . . They are subordinated as parts to the higher centers in the hierarchy, but at the same time function as quasi-autonomous wholes.

This applies also to families, which family therapists have shown to be systems. Family life has "patterns of activity" that cannot be explained by simply seeing the family as a collection of individuals.

When we apply General Systems Theory to our own psyches, we see that like all holons, we have two tendencies: a *self-assertive tendency* to preserve our individual autonomy, to strive for freedom and mastery, and an *integrative tendency* to transcend the boundaries of the self and to be part of a more embracing whole. Andras Angyal, a psychologist, felt that these were our two basic needs.

The "something greater" to which we long to surrender may be our family, a community, a religious creed or political cause, Nature, Art, or the All. Koestler points out the irony that our self-transcending act of identifying with a group often turns into self-assertion at the level of the group. The group then fights to defend its corporate identity. He says: "Man has always been prepared not only to kill, but also to die for good, bad, or completely hare-brained causes. What can be a more valid proof for the reality of the urge toward self-transcendence?"

He notes, as has Robert Jay Lifton, that when the urge toward self-transcendence is frustrated, when the culture does not provide outlets, some people join cults and surrender their identity in "fanatical devotion to some cause, regardless of its merits."

While you can find many good books by psychologists on the subject of helping your child become a well-functioning separate person, Western psychology has mostly ignored the integrative tendency.

Parents have not. Here are some of their definitions of "spiritual" from the questionnaire:

Fully connected—with nature, other people, things. Living a life in a fully conscientious, caring, aware way.

Recognizing that we're part of a life force that encompasses all.

A feeling, a connection to a higher power of being—something larger than any person, time, or place, with a feeling of being uplifted out of the ordinary level of daily life.

The word "spirit" comes from the Latin word for breath, the life principle, "soul," and by extension has come to mean what is not material, not of the body, not of this world. Since religion dealt with this realm, the word spiritual came also to mean of religion or the church: sacred, devotional. The plural, "spiritualities," even came to mean the rights and tithes belonging to the Church. This association of the word with the beliefs and practices of organized religion is not what the parents who answered the questionnaire had in mind.

Beryl Soparkar, philosopher and mother of fourteen, said, *"Popular usage suggests that a spiritual person is more concerned with right living based on values other than materialistic. To make a child 'spiritual', or to teach him 'spirituality', I think popularly means to teach him moral or aesthetic values, usually through religious teachings or moral proverbs and the like. I think this popular usage of the word is inadequate. . . . I believe that a person generally considered 'spiritual' shows a certain inner peace, a serenity, a calm; such a person acts as if he sees decisions, problems, disappointments as transient, or at least as only part of the whole picture. Here's a tentative definition: Spirituality involves (a) an attunement of one's innermost feelings, with (b) a benevolent value set, and (c) a consciousness of man's smallness and interrelatedness in the mysterious, pervasive, and powerful whole."*

What moved me as I read through parents' definitions was the feeling that they were searching for words to describe real experiences. They were not simply repeating what they had read. Some use the word God, and some don't, to express their sense of unity and connectedness:

I think everything in the universe is spiritual because it's a part of God in some way. Everything from the mineral kingdom to the animal kingdom has some state of consciousness that we can learn to relate to.

The mysterious, the "awe-ful," anything that transcends the individual's consciousness. Experiencing wonder.

Our daughter Eve at age six defined *spirit* as "the part of you that loves somebody." Many parents mentioned that love comes with the sense of unity:

[Spirituality means] Relating to the nonordinary, nonrational. Implies wholeness and union. Experienced as love, wonder, awe, fear, comfort, and mystical feelings.

If you are spiritual you are of God—you are full of love. You recognize the God within everyone and try to stay in harmony with the whole universe.

Spiritual: power to relate deeply to others, to know them as they are and to respond to that in love. My spiritual life is development of this power. "Its "object" is not only God but all reality—tomato plants, children, my car, myself, everything.

Some parents were confused about the difference between "spiritual" and "psychic," which will be discussed in the next chapter. One mother even thought I was asking about "spiritualism"— belief in spirits. More often, the confusion took the form of what someone called a "miscellaneous file: intuition, psychic, unexplainable, the matrix of mind and body, the soul-soma of love and power to do and be, life energy, that high consciousness/collective unconscious that binds us beyond the physical plane."

I hope in this book to sort out the "miscellaneous file." The development of intuition and awareness of the mind-body matrix is discussed in part two, "Education of the Inner Life." Theories of personality development that take into account "higher consciousness," values, and morals are discussed in part three.

My own definition of *spiritual* has to do with the context in which we live our lives, our awareness of expanding into infinite systems—organismic, social, and cosmic—and the loving feelings that come from that awareness. Where the hierarchies move off into infinity, we can imagine something that includes all "lower" levels, cannot be sensed, and cannot be understood by knowing what goes on at other levels. I will not give it a name.

CHAPTER 2

Mystical and Peak Experience

Those pure and virgin apprehensions I had from the womb, and that divine light wherewith I was born are the best unto this day, wherein I can see the Universe. By the gift of God they attended me into the world, and by His special favour I remember them till now. Verily they seem the greatest gifts His wisdom could bestow, for without them all other gifts had been dead and vain. They are unattainable by book, and therefore I will teach them by experience. Pray for them earnestly: for they will make you angelical, and wholly celestial. Certainly Adam in Paradise had not more sweet and curious apprehensions of the world, than I when I was a child. . . .

The dust and stones of the street were as precious as gold: the gates were at first the end of the world. The green trees when I saw them first through one of the gates transported and ravished me, their sweetness and unusual beauty made my heart to leap, and almost mad with ecstasy, they were such strange and wonderful things. . . . Eternity was manifest in the Light of the Day, and something infinite behind everything appeared. . . . The streets were mine, the temple was mine, the people were mine, their clothes and gold and silver were mine, as much as their sparkling eyes, fair skins, and ruddy faces. The skies were mine, and so were the sun and moon and stars, and all the World was mine, and I the only spectator and enjoyer of it. . . . With much ado I was corrupted, and made to learn the dirty devices of this world, which now I unlearn, and become, as it were, a little child again that I may enter into the Kingdom of God.

> Thomas Traherne
> Centuries of Meditations, 1670

The current disposition of some young people to turn to mysticism represents an effort by various groupings of them in a state of marginal mental health to defend against the stresses of a society which has disappointed them by offering them insufficient external challenge. Of those who choose the mystical way of life, it is hard to say which ones are moving toward conflict resolution and which toward psychic breakdown. In any case they are all to some extent engaged in an attack on their parents' standards as representatives of the established social order.

> Mysticism: Spiritual Quest or
> Psychic Disorder?, *Group for*
> *the Advancement of Psychiatry, 1976*

At the beginning of every organized religion is someone's direct experience of spiritual realities. Institutions are founded, with their theology, rites, and texts, to help people participate indirectly in the "revelations."

It used to be thought that only rare people, saints or mystics, had such experiences; but as sociologist Andrew Greeley has shown, over a third of a national sample of Americans answered yes to the question "Have you ever felt as though you were very close to a powerful, spiritual force that seemed to lift you out of yourself?"

Twice this number—two-thirds—of the parents answering my questionnaire described mystical experiences, and even more—88 percent—had had either a "mystical experience" or a feeling of being in the presence of something holy or sacred. Clearly, this is not a rare phenomenon, and it often begins in childhood. Some parents remembered:

I had these incredible mystical experiences as an Altar Boy singing from ages 4–5 until 13–14. I remember most vividly when I was 10. I figured everybody was having it—it was only later when I shared it that I found out it was O.K. to listen to talks about Jesus, but not to be talked to by Jesus.

Several times—at ages 3, 4, 5—I would feel such a oneness with everything around me that it was awesome and wonder-filled. I talked to God out loud.

I was at camp, age 8 or 9, watching the sunset near a rock outside my bunk. I can still see the circle of barbed wire lying on the rock, each point silhouetted. Suddenly something went boingg *—words fail me here—everything was exquisitely beautiful and I was very happy. For a while, everything was perfect, and I knew all about it. I returned to that rock many times that summer. Even now a certain quality of light at sunset can trigger something reminiscent of that feeling.*

Another woman recalled a "moment out of time" from age ten:

I woke up and found myself sitting up in bed, in the middle of the night. It was snowing—everything was peaceful. I remember feeling extraordinarily clean and peaceful. A few years earlier I would go out at night when it was snowing—would dig a little hole and look up at the stars and feel that way. . . . There's always a yearning to find that same moment. I didn't connect this with what I was being taught in Catholic school.

The childhood memories were mostly of an ecstatic response to nature, or a sense of a presence. The problem with asking adults to remember is that the event must be filtered through an adult brain which creates and distorts. We all have memories that our parents insist never could have happened. Nevertheless, I found that people who did recall childhood mystical experiences valued them highly.

Later, they may have repudiated the religion of their childhood, but never these experiences.

Students of religious experience distinguish between "acute" moments of illumination and "recurrent" feelings of being in the presence of something holy or sacred. Sometimes they blend into each other. Greeley describes the mystical or ecstatic interlude as one in which "the person consciously experiences his intimacy with the cosmos." In my questionnaire, I deliberately did not define "mystical" in order to see what would emerge from people's responses. Their accounts matched those of scholars in the psychology of religion, who say that the core of the experience includes:

1. A deeply felt mood of joy, blessedness, and peace.

2. A sense of unity felt either deeply within the self or through the external world.

3. A sense that one has been in touch with immediate and objective reality—"the way things are"—a direct, intuitive knowledge or understanding of the world of which we are a part.

4. Ineffability: no adequate report of its content can be given in words.

5. Loss of awareness of time and space.

6. A sense of the sacred and holy.

7. Transiency—the state rarely lasts more than a few minutes, although there may be a long "afterglow."

8. What William James calls "passivity": one cannot force the experience to happen. It comes of itself.

In Greeley's study, the most common "triggers" of mystical experiences were music, prayer, the beauties of nature, moments of quiet reflection, and church services. Parents take note that 34 percent of his respondents reported that their trigger was "watching little children" and 18 percent reported "sexual lovemaking."

People from all cultures, religions, and historical periods have had such experiences, but the symbols they use to describe them vary with their belief systems. Here are some more examples from parents:

When I was 4 to 6 years old we lived near a small bird sanctuary where I was allowed to go alone and I found a spot there—rampant with violets in the spring—that was truly sacred and still haunts me with memories of extraordinary peacefulness and beauty. After that, each place we lived (we moved a lot) there was always at least one place—a tree, a stream, a hilltop—that felt special and became a refuge. As recently as last year I was hiking along and came into a grove of beech trees—and felt a flood of tears. . . . In a slightly different category—2 times, both within the last few years (age 43) —I have been outdoors—once on the hill behind our farm, the other time on top of a mountain—and had an experience in which it felt as if I had abruptly shifted to a whole new state of being— how to explain?—a simultaneous sense of incredible beauty and clarity and a "knowing" of the unity of all things—self included. Joy, bliss, delight, and deep peace.

Looking back and understanding enlightening experiences a little more, I had one when I was 7 during an Easter service, as well as one when I was 13 on a school bus, and one at the age of 21 when I was home. All three experiences gave me an awareness of much more than myself, a feeling of understanding and knowing, as well as peace. I also felt a great need to express what I had experienced to others. Each experience gave me the answers to the spiritual questions which I was asking at the time, although as a child these questions were not formally asked, but were simply a need to know.

As we read these reports, we begin to wonder whether our children are having similar experiences—even if we don't. Generally, children take them for granted, assume everyone is having them, and do not talk about them.

As a country child I had many experiences of identity with nature. I recall many times standing with bated breath watching a spider spin a wheel/web; sunsets so enthralling that one lost all sense of time and space; wading icy streams and playing with crayfish; hours spent enraptured with "tumble bugs" or an ant colony. . . . I recall hours and hours spent lying at night on the grass gazing at the stars—trying to comprehend the distance and the organization and the power and the light—and somehow feeling an integral part of it all. I term these "mystical experiences" in view of the fact that they were qualitative rather than quantitative (no sense of time —i.e., timeless or "eternal" as opposed to something to be measured or analyzed—even though I find myself trying to analyze— what a paradox!). At any rate, there was a conviction of great power beyond myself—but of which I could be aware. . . . Lasting influence on my life? It is my life.

Sometimes in church, during family prayer (when there was an important reason for family prayer) and sometimes in my own prayers. I don't know. Mountain climbing between the ages of 13 and 17, I sometimes felt that I was a part of the universe and that its rhythms and mine were one, that all the things we did daily were not very important compared to what I felt on the mountains. I deliberately try to get to the northwest corner of Wyoming once a year to recapture that feeling.

Whenever I went into a church, always had (and of course still have) an incredible feeling of something inexplicable. When at boarding school we were forced to go to church and had to walk there (2 miles each way) no matter what the weather, so during this period I lost this feeling as there was a lot of fooling around going on in church. We also had to go to prayers every night, and if we were naughty our mistress would make us read out of the Bible as punishment! The naughtier we were, the more verses we would have to read! So it has taken a lot of working out for me to realize "spirituality" and what it is. Acid [LSD] was a turning point in my life in that it focused the all pervading energy for me to see and helped to put things into perspective.

RESEARCH ON
CHILDREN'S RELIGIOUS EXPERIENCES

There has been very little research on children's spontaneous religious experiences (as opposed to an enormous amount on their religious *understanding*, which I report on in part three). Children who have these experiences are not self-conscious about them, do not talk about them unless asked, and almost no scientists *have* asked. In this book, since I am focusing on personal (as different from institutional) religious experience, I will not discuss "conversion" experiences, except to say that children as young as eight do have "crisis conversions" at revival meetings. Conversion experiences have more to do with social and group influences than the private feelings we are exploring here.

The one relevant study on children reported in *Research on Religious Development* (edited by Merton Strommen in 1970) was done by Greta Klingberg in Sweden in 1945. She wanted to find out if children between seven and twelve (i.e., in Freud's latency period, Piaget's concrete operations period—see part three) were as realistic and comparatively unemotional (compared with early childhood and adolescence) as the theories predict. She wanted to find out if religious experiences of a relatively profound nature could take place during those years. Her subjects, however, were from 9 to 13.

She asked 630 children to write essays, "Once When I Thought About God." She was looking not so much for "mystical" experiences as for any "deep religious feeling . . . security, serenity and trust; consciousness of sin and longing for purity, the experience of being answered in prayer, and of receiving forgiveness, of thankfulness and joy, of revelation and certainty." She found all of them, although expressed rather matter-of-factly. A girl of ten wrote: "Another time I was up on a hill near my house. I went there and was looking at the flowers and then I thought, 'So beautiful! Has God really done this? And I felt so happy.' "

While admitting that the children she studied had been exposed to a lot of religious instruction, Klingberg points out that the religion of adults is also a "result" of environmental influence, but no one denies that a genuine religious life is to be found in adults: "If the word genuine is to be used in this connection, it must be in the sense that *the personality is engaged in the experience.* This can clearly be true of religious experience, even when it is based on attitudes which have originally been learned. Conversely, a demonstration of genuine religious experiences in childhood does not indicate that the child's religion has developed independently of the religious milieu." Klingberg concludes that "no maturational mechanisms deprive children of this age of a rich inner life."

In 1963, Elkind and Elkind hypothesized that if they asked fifteen-year-olds about a "sense of a presence of God," they might find this less rare than the intense, sudden mystical experience. In fact, they found that of their 144 junior high school subjects (who were asked to write essays answering the questions "When do you feel closest to God?" and "Have you ever had a particular experience when you felt especially close to God?"), *most* could describe immediate personal experiences of God in detail. Triggers for "recurrent" experiences (the first question) were church or synagogue, "times when I am alone," anxiety, fear or worry, and prayer. Triggers for the "acute" experiences (the second question) were thankfulness for escaping death or injury, meditation, grief, First Communion or bar mitzvah, and a few spontaneous "revelations." The sample was half Protestant, one-fourth Roman Catholic, and one-fourth Jewish.

As with adults, both acute mystical experiences and the sense of being in the presence of something holy or sacred are much more common in children than most people think—although not universal.

Havighurst and Keating, summarizing research on "The Religion of Youth," note that "direct personal experience of the presence of God is claimed by some children and adolescents and not by others. This is a central, basic phenomenon which must be reckoned with by anyone interested in religious development."

One mother noticed this "central, basic phenomenon" in her own family. She comments:

I think a lot of children's life is mystical experience. I used to go for long walks in the woods by myself—lying on the grass and watching the stars—even fireworks—I totally lost myself. Children's lives are so much wonder . . . but it may not be so for all children. My son once said, "There's some kind of thing that happens to you, to me, to David [his brother], but doesn't happen to Amy [his sister]. I don't understand it."

What of the part of the population who do not have these

experiences? Greeley himself admits that he is one, for all his interest in the subject. For him, the essence of the religious life is not the pursuit of religious experience, but the loving service of others.

I gave the questionnaire to a separate group of traditional churchgoing parents, whom I call the "believers." Only 18 percent admitted to a "mystical experience," although 29 percent said that they had felt the presence of something holy or sacred, usually during a retreat, at Mass, or prayer. It seems that they have these experiences less frequently than the "seekers," and when they do, they describe it in traditional religious terms, such as feeling the "presence of God," or being "touched by the Holy Ghost."

Everyone expects teenagers to go through emotional storms, some of which may be religious crises (see chapter 14). However, more of my respondents said they had their *first* mystical experience in childhood or young adulthood (twenty to thirty) than in the teenage years:

My interest in Zen started in college, but I never did anything about it. At about 26 I was reading Alan Watts, when the barrier between myself and everything else dissolved. It was a great feeling—like being at home.

A man age forty-five reported:

We've been taught to think that if you can't fit an experience into a logical, rational, sequential framework, it's suspect. . . . I had just come out of the Army at 20. I was in an empty lot—it was a lovely summer night—when I felt myself transported—an opening up of space for me—my feet were still on the ground—it just happened. I'm still trying to duplicate it . . . it was a sudden surge of rhapsody—nothing to do with values.

I don't know if it changed me. . . . What I do know is that I became aware of another level in me . . . it focused me . . . it had to affect relationships, what I want out of life. The memory of it gives me great pleasure—a little small blessing—but I feel there is a danger of self-congratulation, the feeling of being chosen.

Another parent wrote:

I had two very heavy spiritual experiences while on LSD at ages 26 and 28. I was having a conversation with something that wasn't visible, tangible, material. . . . Lasting influence? Definitely . . . it's the window of the house that I'm living in.

A forty-four-year-old man of Jewish background described an experience he had under the influence of LSD at age twenty-five that changed his life:

I was watching a cow eat an apple that I had given her. While eating, she shit. Suddenly I saw the apple turn into some form of energy and the energy went through her body and out in turds, into the ground. Then the energy came out of the ground into the cow's mouth. It seemed like a continuous circle through the cow, into the ground, and then back back into cow. I knew I was seeing the life cycle, and a great joy and peace went through me. I felt as if I had seen "God," and a part of my energy was linked to every blade of grass, star, space, life . . . everything was sort of connected.

He felt his childhood contact with religion (he was in an orphanage, and forced to march to synagogue) was hateful, and now calls himself a "humanist" or "ecologist."

Notice that people included their experiences with LSD and other psychedelic drugs alongside those that were spontaneous. For them, the fact that an experience was drug-induced is worth mentioning, but in no way invalidates it.

Mystical experiences have had a bad name in a rationalist society. Freudians consider them pathological, a state of passivity and withdrawal, at best a regression to infantile union with the mother. Abraham Maslow was one of the first Western psychologists to demonstrate that perception of the universe as a unified whole, and our place in it, is a help to personal growth. He called such perceptions "peak experiences" instead of "ecstatic," or "mystical" or "transcendent" to emphasize his belief that they were *natural* phenomena deserving of study by psychology.

Although in the East these experiences have been considered accessible to anyone who wanted to strive for them, Western psychology before Maslow mostly considered them an aberrant form of behavior. Studies such as Greeley's show that statistically speaking, at least, this simply is not true—unless you want to call one-third of the population abnormal. Andrew Greeley found no evidence to confirm the image of the mystic as someone who is escaping from reality or on the road to schizophrenia. In his study people who had mystical experiences scored higher than nonmystics on tests of psychological well-being.

It is also true that both Maslow and Greeley point out the danger of seeking ecstasy as an end in itself (see chapter 14) and the danger to the personality of an overload of intense emotional experience. Only two of the parents answering my questionnaire reported feeling negative about their spiritual experiences:

I went through a time (age 10–14) when I prayed and felt there was a power that heard me, and I felt very special. I felt as a teenager that I was in touch with spiritual people who had lived throughout the ages and that I was one of them waiting for my mission to be revealed. Also, in my late teens, I had drug experiences of feeling close to other people, having a sense we all knew what was happening. Also being alone outdoors away from everything having to do with humans. These experiences have not had a lasting influence. I have deliberately closed that part of me. The answer I was waiting for—what relation this feeling had to why I was alive—wasn't forthcoming.

Two times, when I had taken LSD, I experienced a sense of unity with the totality of all consciousness, some kind of total connectedness with all other persons, with inanimate objects, and with some essence I called "God" at the time. . . . The memory of these feelings helps me feel more connected to other people who experience spiritual and mystical events. Hence, I would say the lasting effect is to feel less alone in some way. This is not happening at a very conscious level and I rarely think about these experiences. In addition, the experiences frightened me and I avoid them.

The capacity for mystical ecstasy seems to be present in varying degrees among us—much like a talent for science, music, or poetry. Greeley points out that "there is some poignancy in the fact that people who have such capacities, which could mean extraordinary happiness to themselves and others, ignore or repress or minimize them because our society has told them for so long that they do not exist or are a form of mental derangement."

As parents, our job is not necessarily to *develop* these capacities in our children, but simply to recognize and trust them. Children with personal "mystical" experience may have less need for what Abraham Maslow calls "the paraphernalia of organized religion—buildings and specialized personnel, rituals, and dogmas." They may develop myths and symbols of profound personal meaning out of their private revelations. The religion of a child who has not had direct personal religious experience will more likely be based on what s/he is taught to believe, on parental example, and on the experience of love and empathy.

PSYCHIC EXPERIENCES— RELATED BUT DIFFERENT

Like mystical experiences, psychic experiences are much more common than is usually believed. I will distinguish between them operationally, as did Andrew Greeley when he asked a national sample of Americans about both kinds of "paranormal" experiences. "Psychic" or "Psi" refers to specific abilities. Greeley asked about *extrasensory perception* (ESP) which he defined as a communication with someone else without the use of ordinary media of perception, and *clairvoyance*, seeing something that is happening at a great distance. There are others.

When Greeley asked about ESP ("Have you ever felt as though you were in touch with someone when they were far away?") over half his sample (58%) said yes! In addition, one-quarter of the American population has had a clairvoyant experience! ("Have you ever seen events that happened at a great distance as they were happening?")

Research on psychic experience in children shows that it peaks at the age of four and tends to disappear after age seven. A friend of mine tells how once when his daughter was three and in the playground with her mother, he unexpectedly left his office and went home for a snack. His daughter (in the park) said gleefully, "Daddy's home! He's eating an apple!" (he was). Her mother said, "That's impossible, dear. You know he's at work." It is easy to overlook these moments.

Jan Ehrenwald, a psychiatrist, regards the symbiotic stage of child development (roughly two to seven months) as the cradle of ESP. At that age extrasensory perception is a means of preverbal communication gradually lost in the course of separating from the mother and becoming an individual.

In order to account for the flawless interaction and the delicately balanced regulatory functions operating within the mother-child unit, child psychiatrists and analysts have talked about empathy, intuition, or remnants of animal instincts lost to man. Others suggest that "one unconscious" is able to communicate directly with "another unconscious." The child's mind cannot stay open to a barrage of stimuli crowding in from outside. As we grow, we screen our perceptions to prevent ourselves from sensory overload—and become more "immune" to psychic experiences.

Although most researchers think that children's psychic abilities must wane in the course of development, Joseph Chilton Pearce believes that if we could develop them along with the rest of our faculties, we would not be so frightened by them as adults. To those who are unprepared, a psychic experience may be disorienting, like vision flooding back into the eyes of a blind person whose sight has suddenly been restored.

Silva Mind Control, *est,* and many other trainings demonstrate that anyone can recover psychic ability using certain processes and under certain conditions. Psychic ability is nothing special. As with other abilities, some will have more than others. Some children will be truly gifted. It can be a dangerous gift.

I have chosen not to include techniques of encouraging the psychic development of children, because it can be destructive to them. Rudolph Otto coined the word "numinous" to stand for the holy without its moral factor, the *mysterium tremendum* the aweful, overpowering energy. The numinous element can easily overwhelm and destroy an unprepared "ego." In that realm lies the demonic as well as the angelic, the fury of God speaking to Job out of the whirlwind as well as the white light.

Many people are interested in "other realities" because of the powers that are traditionally associated with access to what W. G. Roll, a parapsychologist, calls Field Consciousness: telepathy, clairvoyance, psychokinesis, mediumship. Sages warn against selfishly pursuing such "powers." Psychic development is concerned with learning how to gain control over these forces, so that we can use them for our own purposes. The repeated warning is that almost no one can use them safely. People who hope that "psychic" powers will make them more powerful personalities are in grave danger of exploding those personalities.

The danger exists even if we adopt Roll's scientific view that occult practices derived from the magical practices of tribal societies, medieval Europe, spiritualist seances, and religious rituals are "the emergence of a technology without the support of a basic science. . . . Inventions as basic to modern life as the compass, the smelting of metals, and irrigation systems were made well before the scientific age." You can still get burned smelting metal if you don't know what you're doing.

All children long to have superpowers to compensate for being small and relatively powerless. As adults we can find other ways to be heroic.

As destructive as the parents who use the child's talent to gratify this longing to be special are the ones who react with fear or ridicule. Samuel Young in *Psychic Children* quotes interviews:

> *"When young I felt desperate and confused because nobody believed me."*

> *"My family, friends, and teachers thought I was strange, too introverted, and highly imaginative. I would say that up until five years ago the experiences upset and confused me. Now that I understand them, they are of help in many things."*

> *"I used to pray to be 'normal.'"*

Some of the "believers" who answered my questionnaire reported psychic experiences, and many felt their prayers were answered. Here, those who came from a religious tradition that acknowledges "miracles" were able not to be frightened:

I felt I was close to God when my sister was in the hospital a few years ago. I went to a novena while she was in the hospital. Her leg had become paralyzed. On the last night of the novena I heard a voice say, "Your sister will be walking tonight." When I went to the hospital that night she could move her toes. She walked the next day.

What we can do for children is accept without fear whatever psychic ability they do show. Treat it as any other talent—to be appreciated but not pushed, and above all, not to become the central focus of parent-child interaction.

THE TABOO ON THE NONRATIONAL

For those of us who were growing up when Science reigned supreme, there was a taboo on speaking about one's personal acquaintance with altered states of consciousness or "other realities." One parent writes:

In my family, if something wasn't rational, it didn't exist. At the same time I had intuitive sensings and even direct experiences that were not rational, so they remained very private, not something that was safe to share. It was indicative of being weak, female, stupid—it was not O.K. I had more embarrassment around that than about sex.

She's right. The taboo can best be understood by noting the similarity between our attitudes toward "irrational" experiences and toward sexual impulses. We fear their intrusion into our daily civilized life. This is the world of the id, the underworld, hidden from the "light," populated by demons. At the same time it is fascinating.

Just as forms of pregenital sexuality (pleasure associated with the mouth or skin, rather than intercourse itself) used to be considered perverse in an adult, but is now considered part of "normal" foreplay, so the "primary process" mystical or psychic experiences of the child were considered pathological in an adult (even if the rational intellect was in no way impaired). Both are repressed by an adult who must cut off the "inner child" in order to feel mature.

The challenge is to learn to control these eruptions. We can channel the energy so that it is allowed some gratification without overwhelming our daily life in which we have other things to do besides have sex or visions. This psychic work of channeling energy is hindered rather than helped by families in which the subject cannot be discussed.

Children are quick to sense that certain subjects make their parents anxious. Even when parents don't say, "No, no!" we quickly learn not to talk about those feelings. The next step can be not to think about them, and the *next* step is to lie to oneself consciously and pretend that one did not have certain experiences (of lust or ecstasy). If we repress them, we can never integrate them into our sense of who we are. The split-off psychic content becomes immeasurably more terrifying, as it now exerts a constant threat of erupting into consciousness, disturbing the status quo, and perhaps destroying it.

Andrew Weil, in *The Natural Mind,* points out that all children like to alter their consciousness. Most often they do this by spinning (like the whirling dervishes, a Sufi order). They may even hold their breath, or sniff glue, or take drugs. Weil believes that the repression of this urge creates negative habits in adulthood, such as dependence on drugs for consciousness change.

To parents who wonder how to share their own religious or spiritual experiences with their children, I would ask, "What's stopping you?" It helps to become aware of the power of the taboo or its remnants. Two years ago I met regularly with a group of psychiatrists, psychotherapists, psychologists, and biologists, supposedly to study "Consciousness." What happened was that one by one we "came out of the closet" and revealed to this group of esteemed colleagues our private spiritual experiences. It was like coming home. We saw how we had created for ourselves our own loneliness, the desert area separating our scientific "rational" lives and our real experience. I have heard similar stories of groups listening to one person talk about out-of-body experiences (such as a group listening to a tape of Elizabeth Kübler-Ross describing people who clinically died and were revived) and then one after another saying, "You know, something like that happened to me once."

We tend to keep silent about these things, not only because we are afraid others will think us crazy—we ourselves wonder if we are crazy. We have internalized society's judgment. Since society is changing, this sharing is becoming much easier. Some parents say they have no difficulty talking about their spiritual lives with their children, as we will see in chapter 8. When the parent feels comfortable living with more than one construction of reality—accepts it as something natural—then the child will too.

PART TWO:

Education of Inner Life

CHAPTER 3

Without Religion:
Teaching Children New Ways
of Knowing

The children are asked to write a full analytical description of the [parts of the gardenia], illustrated by an accurate drawing. When that's done there's a short rest period, at the close of which [the story of the Buddha's flower sermon, in which he picked up a flower and silently held it up for everyone to see] is read to them. . . . So we tell the boys and girls to stop thinking and just look. . . . Liberate yourselves from everything you know and look with complete innocence at this infinitely improbable thing before you. . . . Look at it alertly but passively, receptively, without labeling or judging or comparing. . . .

Every course the children take . . . everything from dissected frogs to the spiral nebulae, it all gets looked at receptively as well as conceptually, as a fact of aesthetic or spiritual experience as well as in terms of science or history or economics. Training in receptivity is the complement and antidote to training in analysis and symbol manipulation. Both kinds of training are absolutely indispensable. If you neglect either of them you'll never grow into a fully human being. . . .

Aldous Huxley
Island

A revolution is happening in education. American "how-to" has done it again. Innumerable adults have discovered, in "human potential" workshops, how to expand their sensory awareness, rediscover their bodies, use their creative imaginations, experience their feelings, and contact their center, or higher self. What the workshop leaders have created is a "technology": exercises that lead to a direct *experience* of these goals, which cannot be reached by lectures about them. Parents and educators have begun to think that if these dimensions of awareness can be *taught,* and it is never too late to learn, perhaps it is also never too early. Why not start in childhood?

At the same time, brain research has provided a model which suggests that we *always* use nonverbal modes of knowing along with the verbal. The left hemisphere of the cerebral cortex (in about 98 percent of right-handers and two-thirds of left-handers) seems to specialize in what are called the rational, verbal, linear, and analytic functions: language and logic. Using these functions, we split a whole into its parts, the better to understand the parts. The right hemisphere seems to specialize in grasping the pattern or form of the *whole:* kinesthetic, spatial, or "intuitive" processes, which often work through images. People whose hemispheres are disconnected can see a picture of a key presented to the left visual field, which sends messages to the right side of the brain (which controls the left side of the body). Yet when asked, "What is it?" they will say, "I don't know," and they don't—in words. But their left hand can select the key from an assortment of objects.

This model not only suggests that most teaching in schools is lopsided, educating mainly one-half of the brain, but it also shows what the new "techniques" have in common: access to and use of a large part of our nervous system that often is unconscious.

Our society has so overvalued and overemphasized the realm

of the "left brain"—logical intellect—that most of us have relatively underdeveloped access to the powers of our "right brain"—pattern-grasping, nonverbal mode of knowing. One of the patterns that people often get when they turn off left-brain "chatter" is their connection with the source of all life and energy.

Transpersonal educators believe we can learn to experience the divine within ourselves. In practice, this usually means teaching children how to alter their consciousness in order to be able to relax and "center" at will, and to contact inner wisdom. Developing a meditative, nonjudgmental awareness eventually can transform the way we hold all the contents of consciousness: thoughts, feelings, and body sensations. Ira Progoff has defined religion as "the social place we go to work on our inner life." Transpersonal educators have found secular ways of teaching children to work on their inner lives.

Jean Houston, a humanistic and transpersonal educator, has helped many individuals discover abilities in themselves that they thought were impossible. She calls her workshops New Ways of Being. Houston maintains that most education, with its exclusive emphasis on rational, linear knowing, has been a failure because not enough of the human being is educated. "If you have a tree, and you pull out all its roots but one, it doesn't do very well. . . . We do not train children to use their own consciousness. Instead, we give them subjects to learn." She has used her "multi-modal knowing" approach successfully with "problem learners," teaching them to "think with the whole body." There is no conflict with the goal of teaching basic skills, simply the observation that in most classrooms those with innate left-brain abilities do well, and that too often remedial teaching of the others means *more* of the verbal teaching that didn't work in the first place. She says:

> *Our brains are as different from each other as are our fingerprints, with enormous variations in styles and talents of perception and learning. Some people are naturally kinesthetic thinkers, others think in images, others in sounds. Classical education tends to inhibit these and frequently causes these nonverbal thinkers to feel inferior and begin a process of failure that will last all their lives.*

Techniques for stimulating right-brain functions include the use of internal imagery, fantasy, involvement of all the senses, and awareness through movement. Some of these methods could be summed up as the role of art, which is more than "arts in education." That phrase still suggests the split between "the arts"— dance, drama, music, poetry, sculpture—and "education," meaning doing your work in science or reading.

Elaine de Beauport at the Mead School for children three to twelve used painting, weaving, music, and body movement to pattern the learning of language and math. She says:

If all our teaching is done in verbal or number symbols— that is, you never give me materials with which to work; what you give me instead is the alphabet and you teach me numbers and the sequential procedures—then I have to learn what you teach me and, through testing, give it all back in the mode that you taught me. This is terrific if my procedural strength happens to be sequential—and if I'm willing to accept your symbols instead of creating my own. I sit down and shut up and receive your symbols peacefully and we've got a good thing going. The problem is that this is all that's going in schools. If, on the other hand, I should have interrelational, associational, spatial capacities with strength in my right hemisphere, the fact that you want me only to do a procedure that I don't think is interesting really bugs me. If at eight I can create a painting of a clown but you want me to write "the clown is here," your mental task is not as exciting as my mental activity. It is moronic compared to my mental activity. Plus, you not only want me to use a procedure that is not my strength, you don't even want to see the symbols I create. I can make many complex sounds with my voice which are symbolic, as is my form on a skateboard, and when I paint, that is symbolic too. But you don't want to honor the symbols that emerge from my stronger side. You won't let me use my brain.

Jean Houston and Robert Masters also point out that *time* might be a real weakness of those with right-hemisphere strengths. Time is sequential. Right-hemisphere children are more attuned to a "timeless" world of pattern of form. They suggest that time "lapses" should be understood, not punished as unwillingness or disobedience, and should not be a factor in grading.

These educators do not think it is necessary to delay the teaching of reading. In fact, Robin Beebe reports in the New Ways of Being journal, *Dromenon,* on a public school class of problem readers who improved one year for every six months they spent in a program using art experiences.

How can parents use these new approaches? First, we can try to make the people teaching our children aware of them, if they aren't already. We can also do some consciousness raising about the way *we* separate "art" and "education," and the different values we assign to them.

I became aware of my own assumptions recently when I asked our daughter Eve why she added an extra curlicue to her lowercase *g*. She had started to read and write about eight months before. She said, "It looks prettier that way." I immediately wanted to tell her that she was doing it *wrong,* that art is art and writing is writing! At six and a half, she had not yet made that separation, and I still wanted her to, in spite of having read Jean Houston. Fortunately, I kept my mouth shut, giving my inner voice a chance to say, "Wait a minute! Eve just invented calligraphy! She will learn to write a plain *g* when the situation calls for it." And she did. She was lucky to have a teacher who told her, "Eve, that's beautiful. Let me show you another way to do it that will help you write faster."

The real brain is more complex than the left-brain/right-brain model suggests. No single model does justice to the way it processes information. We can use the left-brain/right-brain data to remind us that we do not have to choose between rational and intuitive modes of knowing. It makes sense to develop *both.*

HOW TO CHOOSE OUR
STATE OF CONSCIOUSNESS

The first step in work with consciousness itself is training the attention. Too often, children are chided for not being able to concentrate, but no one thinks to show them *how*. It is like telling someone to "relax and stop worrying." Beginning meditators are struck by how difficult it is to keep attention focused on one object, whether that is the breath, a mantra, or a flower. They also discover that with regular practice it becomes easier to concentrate without being distracted, as we learn not to "pay attention" to the thoughts that come and go. (Deborah Rozman, in *Meditation for Children*, suggests six concentration exercises.)

After concentration comes the ability to relax and let go of the left-brain chatter of thoughts. This is a state of *passive* alertness, of being, not doing, foreign to our Western emphasis on performance and production. In it we *observe* what happens, rather than always *making* something happen. When what we observe are images, we enter the world of creative imagination. When we observe our body sensations without interfering, we expand our awareness of internal states.

Listening to the body gives easy access to new states of consciousness, because we are choosing to attend to the messages that are usually part of the (mostly unconscious) background noise. Once we make them the figure instead of the ground, our entire construction of reality changes, and we usually enter a state of deep relaxation. Sometimes these techniques of focusing awareness on the body are used for relaxing as an end in itself. Whenever we are anxious, it is useful to be able to quiet the mind. Deborah Rozman says, "Children are more tense than we realize." It is a great advantage to be able to feel calm and relaxed in any situation—taking tests, for example.

"Centering" techniques offer more than relaxation, something that is hard to describe in words. It has to do with contacting a core of inner strength in ourselves that is always there, whether or not we are *doing* anything. It is the place from which we move. Gay Hendricks and Russel Wills in *The Centering Book* mention how some children have described this feeling: "Being right on"; "Being balanced"; "Feeling solid."

Exercises to reach this place are familiar from Hatha Yoga: awareness of breathing, and consciously relaxing all the muscles in the body (sometimes after tensing each one first). Here is the exercise called Feeling the Center from *The Centering Book:*

This activity is best done on the floor, the children either sitting cross-legged or lying on their backs. If the sitting position is used, remind the group members to sit squarely on their sitting bones, with spines straight and hands relaxed in laps. If the lying position is used, be sure everyone is lying straight— legs relaxed and loose, back and head in straight alignment.
INSTRUCTIONS:
Most of the time we use only a small part of our lungs when we breathe. If we can learn to fill our bodies with breath by breathing more deeply and smoothly, we can increase the energy that flows through our bodies. Let's begin by letting our bodies relax . . . becoming very comfortable and closing our eyes.

And now, becoming aware of your feet and moving them around a little to become aware of how they feel, send them a message to relax. Let all of the tension go out of them and feel them rest comfortably on the floor.

Now relax your legs. Let go of them and let them sink into the floor, feeling relaxed and heavy.

Let the feeling of relaxation enter your chest and your stomach. Feel the middle of your body become soothed and relaxed. Breathe deeply and smoothly, letting all of the tension go out of your body.

Now let your neck and face relax. Feel the tension draining out of your face as you feel the soothing feeling of relaxation enter your face and your neck.

Relax your arms and your hands, feeling them resting comfortably, completely supported. Breathe deeply, sending the feeling of relaxation to your arms and hands. . . . (Pause thirty seconds)

Inhale slowly through your nose. Let your stomach fill up with breath, then fill your chest. Breathe out smoothly, emptying your chest first, then your stomach. Try to let the breath come and go smoothly and peacefully. Let it flow in and out of your body, filling your body with energy. Feel yourself breathing deeply, and smoothly, the energy flowing in and out of you. Listen to your breath flowing in and out of you."

Pause (ten breaths)

The center of your body is where it balances. For many people that balance point is just below the navel. As you breathe in, imagine that your breath is pouring into your body through the center of your body. Let yourself feel the energy rushing into your body through the center, just below the navel. Feel your breath flow into your body, up through your chest, filling your head. Hold the breath inside you for a moment, then let it flow out, carrying with it any tension you feel. Breathe through your center, filling your body with energy, then let the breath flow out of you, relaxing your body completely.

Pause (ten breaths)

Let yourself feel the center of your body, so that you can come back to it when you want to relax and feel balanced. Anytime you have something in your head that you don't like, breathe it out and then replace it with pure, clean energy when you breathe in.

Now feel the alertness coming into your body. Feel your feet and hands begin to stir. Feel your muscles begin to move. Open your eyes, feeling rested and full of energy.

The martial arts of Aikido and T'ai Chi are also centering practices. They develop awareness of the life energy—called *ki* in Japanese and *ch'i* in Chinese—in order to allow it to flow unobstructed through the body. These exercises are more than techniques of self-defense; they release tension and enable the body to move harmoniously from a center of perfect balance.

Other ways to stimulate multi-modal knowing include the use of storytelling, myth, and music. (See the "Resources" section at the back of this book.)

Training in relaxation, quieting the mind, focusing attention, and "letting be" can be an end in itself or a preparation for the development of other powers of mind, which can be achieved by the use of visualization, "guided fantasy," or "inner imagery." Learning to exercise the creative imagination helps us to develop intuition, and contact inner wisdom.

In *Awakening Intuition*, Frances Vaughan offers exercises for adults to develop their intuitive faculties. She defines intuition as "knowing without knowing how you know. . . . Intuition allows one to draw on that vast storehouse of unconscious knowledge that includes not only everything that one has experienced or learned, either consciously or subliminally, but also the infinite reservoir of the collective or universal unconscious, in which individual separateness and ego boundaries are transcended."

She agrees with Deborah Rozman that the practice of meditation is one of the most direct ways of developing intuition. In *Meditation for Children,* Rozman writes, "Through meditating we learn to 'tune in' so we can be wise in everything we do. This guidance is available to everyone because it is part of each person's nature, just as the mind, feelings, and senses are part of each person. Like a hidden gold mine, it is untapped in most people, but those who know how to contact it have a great wealth that is always there for them to use."

Some teachers have begun using meditation (usually called "centering" or "quiet time") with children in their classrooms, with results that sound unbelievable. They describe the children becoming more creative, more attentive, more self-reliant and self-controlled, more accepting of themselves and others, more cohesive as a group. I would have found these testimonials hard to believe if I had not seen a videotape of Maureen Murdock's kindergarten class meditating. The children, initially bouncy and fidgety like most five-year-olds, happily settled into their "quiet time" circle and quickly went into a deep, though brief, guided meditation.

Maureen Murdock used meditations from Deborah Rozman's books. She explained to the children that "we are so busy all day long that there is little time to listen to ourselves, and that this is what we are going to do in our quiet time." She found that consistency was important—to start at the same time every day with the same prearranged signal (such as turning out the lights or sounding a chime or a triangle). If a child didn't want to join in, s/he was offered an alternate silent activity but was not allowed to disturb the others. Before long, everyone wanted to participate.

Murdock suggests that if you want to try these structured meditations with your own children at home, start with each one individually, not a group of siblings.

Three of her kindergarten children initiated "quiet time" at home with the entire family, leading their parents in the meditation they had done at school. Other teachers, observing the harmoniousness of Maureen's class, wanted to know what she was doing, and before long she was leading a meditation group for teachers and administrators.

Each meditation began with the same basic breath and relaxation exercise:

Find a comfortable spot. Sit up straight with your legs crossed, and with your hands palms up on your knees. Now close your eyes. Close your mouth and breathe in through your nose to the count of three . . . hold your breath to the count of three . . . out. (Repeat three times.) Now breathe the way you normally do, concentrating on your breathing, being as still and quiet as you possibly can. In . . . and . . . out. . . . Now we are going to squeeze the muscles in our body. Now squeeze the muscles in your toes and feet, squeeze, squeeze . . . hold it . . . and let go. (This is repeated for legs and thighs, bottoms, stomach, chest, shoulders, arms and hands, making a fist, neck and face, nose and mouth.) Now your whole body is relaxed and quiet, you have let out all of your energy. Just sit quietly and go deep inside yourself.

THE CIRCLE AND DOT MEDITATION

Still with your eyes closed, concentrate on the center between your eyebrows inside your head. Now in that center put a dot . . . and around the dot put a circle. You are the dot and the circle is the world around you. Notice what color your dot is . . . notice what color your circle is. Now put love in your dot with you. Fill your dot with love. The more you love, the bigger your dot gets . . . bigger . . . bigger . . . and bigger until it is one with the circle. Now look and see what color the circle is. Has it changed? . . . Is it the same?

For the first two months, she kept the meditation between three and six minutes. By the end of the school year, the children were meditating fifteen to twenty minutes. When the children opened their eyes, she asked them if anyone wanted to share with the group what picture they had in their minds during the quiet time, or how they felt. Here are some of their experiences:

Kirsten: "My dot was light pink and the circle was red and blue. The dot got bigger and bigger and changed to a lighter color until it was a large ball of white light. Like a balloon."

Christina: "My dot was black and my circle green and they grew as big as this room."

Philip: "My dot was red and my circle light blue and when it got bigger, it turned around. Moving slower and slower."

Jennifer: "My dot was yellow and my circle blue and when it got bigger, it turned into all the colors of the rainbow."

Watching Maureen's videotape showed me once again how limited I am by my own stereotypes of what is possible for children. Five-year-olds meditating? In the East, of course, this would not be unusual. Rev. Roshi Jiyu-Kennett,* a Soto Zen Buddhist abbess, describes her experience:

I am often asked, "How do you teach meditation to children and what is the best age to start at?" In the East the average child is taught to meditate as soon as it is possible for it to sit upright; i.e. around one or two years old. No doctrine is put into the child's head. The mother and father, and the rest of the family, will sit quietly in front of the family altar; the child, without being restrained, will either sit for a few moments or roll around on the floor with the parents taking no notice. The parents thus express their knowledge of the child's latent understanding and do not treat it like less than themselves. In a very short time the child wants to sit down like the parents, as do, interestingly enough, the dog and cat. I have sat down to meditate and my cat has come up, looked at the wall and then sat down to look at it with me. Thus, if the parents meditate, the child will meditate too. I have seen children at the age of two and a half doing formal meditation in the laymen's meditation hall in Sojiji—and doing a wonderful job. I have photographs of them. These children do a meditation so pure and exquisite

---

* "Roshi" is a title given to a certified Zen master.

it is unbelievable to watch; but they would not be able to discuss the Buddha Nature with you. . . . Their explanations are not as the world understands explanations. And yet every part of their bodies will express the "all is one" and the "all is different"— they will express the Buddha Nature for they have learned to meditate with their whole being untrammeled by duality. They are indeed <u>whole</u> creatures and can teach us much.

Deborah Rozman emphasizes "grounding" the energies contacted in meditation in activity—games, drawing, science, or writing. Like breathing in and breathing out, we need both receptivity and activity, working on ourselves and working in the world.

Although Deborah Rozman maintains that parents can lead children through these exercises as well as teachers, there is some difference of opinion about that. Steve Kull, a California researcher, points out that entering a meditative mood alone with the mother may be threatening. Children may (appropriately) resist the regressive pull to reentering a state that they recently left, the preverbal, symbiotic phase of the mother-child relationship.

When I tried to do the Circle and Dot Meditation with our daughter Amelia (whom we nicknamed Mia) when she was four and a half, she gave me a real surprise. I lit a candle. She didn't want to close her eyes. I said, "O.K., let's just look at the candle." She said, "Do you want to see what we do with a candle in Mia-world?" I said, "Sure," and she proceeded to take me through a series of nonverbal "exercises," movements, and sounds. So much for being the "teacher."

WORKING WITH DREAMS AND GUIDED FANTASY

If you feel uneasy about meditating with children, or if they resist it, you still have access to one of the best, spontaneous ways of working with imagery to develop intuition and psychological integration: dreams. The dream presents us with realms of psychic experience not available to logical thought. Deep emotional changes can be made by working with dreams and with guided fantasies in a dreamlike waking state.

Before the recent research on states of consciousness, people were thought to have only three "normal" states: waking, sleeping, and dreaming. Now we know that simply by closing the eyes and entering the image world, we can be in another state in which we can "continue" the dream. Jung called this "dreaming the myth onward."

The easiest way to begin giving children access to the magic door of dreams is simply to share them. That means sharing yours when you feel like it, when you have a dream that is interesting, funny, or scary, and listening to theirs. We made an illustrated storybook out of a particularly wild, hallucinatory dream Amelia had one night when she was delirious with a fever.

Hendricks and Wills's *Centering Book* suggests many techniques to continue or complete a dream. Working with a scary dream means, first, acknowledging its psychic reality, and then, if you want to go further, mastering its conflict or learning from its message. This does *not* mean interpretation. It may be enough to ask the child to imagine another ending. You can encourage a child to complete a "falling" dream by seeing where s/he is falling *to* and, when s/he gets there, to bring back something beautiful or useful —a song, a picture, or a new invention. Dreams of falling can change into beautiful dreams of flying. Another technique for scary dreams is to suggest to the child that in the next dream, or in a dreamlike state, s/he approach the frightening figure, unmask it, and ask, "How may I help you?" Techniques from Gestalt therapy which work beautifully with adults can also be used with children. This means assuming the role of the various dream images, giving them a voice, and letting them speak for themselves.

For adults who are interested in working with their own dreams, I strongly recommend Ann Faraday's book *The Dream Game,* which synthesizes Freudian, Jungian, Gestalt, and many other approaches to understanding dreams. She says, "A dream can give literal information about things and people in our external world; it can tell us how we *feel* about them, and it can reveal the workings of our own inner world with all its conflicts and healing power sources. . . . The willingness to confront and embrace the things you fear in yourself is the essential clue to integration . . . in the inner world it is fatal to run away from something frightening, for victory lies in going directly into it."

Continuing and completing a dream may lead to the resolution of personality conflict. It can also go one step further, and be a guide to the future, indicating directions in our lives of which our conscious minds have only the dimmest awareness.

One evening, while writing this book, which still didn't have a title, I was rereading *The Dream Game* and came to the section on "dream power." I decided to ask dream power that night to please help me with the title. Dream power obliged with three titles: "Deliver the Message," "Unseen Realities," and "The Infinite Child."

I also had two dreams, which I wrote down later. In the first, "Judy A. (a chubby, pleasant, conventional girl I knew in high school) is on roller skates and biking across country with her husband. She lives in a cute apartment near the East River. I say, 'But you were never athletic as a child!' She smiles, and I see a blue animal with pink spots that is part horse, part giraffe. I think, 'That is my answer—that anything is possible and the irrational exists.' "

In this dream, Judy A. is both the good-hearted Manhattan matron I know she has become, and is also transformed into my Zen master. Dream power reminds me that we cannot know what we will become or what our children will become. We can only do our best, becoming who we are. We do not have to become someone different, or be more "religious." The dream is poking fun at me, yet reassuring me that unseen realities are accessible to anyone —even Judy A., even me.

The second dream speaks for itself: "In a fancy French restaurant. I go out for a smoke. Someone says, 'We don't want just another thesis on "I Had an Ecstatic Experience." ' "

The use of imagery and guided fantasy blends into the use of the creative imagination for healing. As Deborah Rozman says, "When we begin to consciously become aware of the fact that we are continuously using the imagination to create our reality, we can begin to wilfully create images of beauty, of harmony, and of success by imagining them." Also related to the power of ideas is the use of affirmations, or positive thinking, to reach desired goals. None of this is new. William James discussed the phenomenon of "mind-cure" in *The Varieties of Religious Experience,* published in 1902.

He says, "The spiritual in man appears in the mind-cure philosophy as partly conscious, but chiefly subconscious; and through the subconscious part of it we are already one with the Divine without any miracle of grace, or abrupt creation of a new inner man . . . its founders have added systematic exercise in passive relaxation, concentration, and meditation, and have even invoked something like hypnotic practice." He compares the practice of the mind-curers to the practice of "recollection" in Catholic discipline, or the practice of the Presence of God.

James continues:

The mind-curers have given the widest scope to this sort of experience. They have demonstrated that a form of regeneration by relaxing, by letting go, psychologically indistinguishable from the Lutheran justification by faith and the Wesleyan acceptance of free grace, is within the reach of persons who have no conviction of sin and care nothing for the Lutheran theology. It is but giving your little private convulsive self a rest, and finding that a greater Self is there. The results, slow or sudden, or great or small, of the combined optimism and expectancy, the regenerative phenomena which ensue on the abandonment of effort, remain firm facts of human nature, no matter whether we adopt a theistic, a pantheistic-idealistic, or a medical-materialistic view of their ultimate causal explanation.

WORKING WITH FEELINGS

The aim of all these techniques is to learn that we do have control over our state of consciousness. With that comes responsibility for creating our own experience, out of the contents of consciousness, including our emotional life. Transpersonal educators as well as psychotherapists aim to help children learn how to work with their emotions and integrate them into the whole.

We *have* our feelings. They are probably generated by the old, mammalian part of our brain, the limbic system that anatomically surrounds even more ancient brain nuclei. Presumably our ability to observe our feelings comes from the neo-cortex, the evolutionarily most recent structure that folds above and around the limbic system. Self-consciousness is considered to be a function of this cortex.

The first lesson about feelings is that "we," or our cortex, do not control their coming. It makes no sense to hate ourselves for feeling angry or sad, as so many of my patients do. What we *can* control and teach is what we do with these feelings, in thought, word, or action, once they arise.

The most helpful attitude is to allow them fully into consciousness, to notice, "I'm happy," "I'm sad," "I'm frightened," without assuming we have to *act* on the feelings, or even to explain or justify them. They are simply there. Although we may want painful feelings to go away, that aversion to pain is simply another feeling to notice. The *est* training teaches how to "experience your experience." When we do this, the feeling-state can run its course and will shortly disappear, to be replaced by another one.

Watching the changing flow of feelings, thoughts, and sensations *without judging* is a basic awareness practice. *The Centering Book* introduces it with simple instructions for "thought watching." Even more important for children than meditations is our opportunity as parents to *model* this nonjudgmental awareness in our everyday conversations with them. Haim Ginott illustrates in *Between Parent and Child* that we can talk with our children when they're upset in such a way that we give them words for their feelings, which the children may not even be fully aware of. Children often express their feelings nonverbally: by sulking, moping, or fighting. Helping children express feelings in words not only helps them feel loved and understood and prevents many unnecessary parent-child conflicts, it also helps the disturbing feeling disappear.

Dr. Fitzhugh Dodson, in *How to Discipline with Love,* calls this "the feedback technique." He strongly recommends that children be allowed to express *all* feelings, including negative ones. The essence of the feedback technique is to listen carefully to what your child is saying, formulate in your mind what you think s/he is expressing, and then feed back *in your own words* the feelings s/he has expressed. You do not ask *why* s/he feels a certain way; you simply accept the fact that s/he does. This technique is derived from the work of Carl Rogers, and of course, it works with adults, too. No one wants to listen to rational explanations until they are convinced the other person understands and accepts how they feel.

Here is part of an example from Dodson. Jeff (age five) is talking about his brother Bryan (age three):

Jeff: Dad, Bryan is getting into my toys and messing everything up.

Dad: That must really bug you when Bryan gets into your stuff.

Jeff: That's putting it mildly! It really makes me mad! He's got no right to get into my toys. He's got his own toys to play with and he should leave my toys alone.

Dad: So it makes you just furious when he gets into your toys.

Jeff: It sure does. Sometimes I wish I didn't have a brother. I just hate him!

Dad: Sometimes you hate him so much you wish you didn't even have a brother.

Jeff: I sure do! I wish I could flush him down the toilet so he'd never come back!

They keep this up for a while, at the end of which the father offers to take constructive action to teach Bryan to keep out of Jeff's toys.

A whole class of psychiatric disorders comes from repressing or denying feelings, which makes them persist. We can help our children learn that both positive and negative feelings are present simultaneously much of the time. To feel integrated, instead of "good" or "bad," we need to learn to include them all. We know we have succeeded when the child is free to say, "I'm mad at you! I hate you!" and equally freely says, "I love you!"—often two minutes later!

WORKING WITH THE BODY

We still speak dualistically about "awareness of the body" as if "the mind" becomes aware of "the body." In fact, these practices and others lead us to an experience of how our body is always part of our total psychic content although often outside the center of awareness. Integration of the whole person can begin with "body" as well as "mind." Robert Masters calls his form of body work, based on the exercises of Moshe Feldenkrais, "psychophysical re-education."

Traumatic emotions, habitual "postures" of defending against unpleasant feelings, can all be held in the *structure* of the body itself, limiting the ability of "the mind" to go beyond. This was noted by the psychoanalyst Wilhelm Reich, who called the resultant postures "character armor" and worked to free "the body" in psychotherapy.

Reich noticed that depressed people may be permanently collapsed in the chest, from the weight of the burdens of the world on their hunched shoulders. This structure prevents even happy life experiences from giving them a "lift." Some "macho" men are so fixed in the aggressive position of chest and ribs out, shoulders back, that they cannot breathe freely. Their rigidity prevents them from feeling tenderness, even when they want to.

In the spiritual disciplines known collectively as Ashtanga Yoga,* an important preliminary is the practice of *asana*, or Yoga postures, which make the body more flexible. We must loosen our structure before new forms of consciousness become possible. In the twentieth century, Dr. Ida P. Rolf, who called her work Structural Integration (now known as Rolfing®), discovered that in a series of ten sessions of manipulating a person's deep connective tissue, she could bring head, shoulders, pelvis, and ankles more

---

* Ashtanga Yoga consists of the eight steps of classical Raja Yoga: moral restraints (such as nonkilling), moral observances (such as austerity), *asana*, control of the *prana* (life energy), withdrawal of the senses from the objects of perception, concentration, meditation (*dhyana*), and communion with God (*samadhi*).

into alignment. When these elements are aligned, "gravity is the therapist," supporting us instead of pulling us down, allowing us to use the potential inherent in our structure.

All of us are somewhat out of alignment because of congenital problems, shortened scar tissue, or compensations from old injuries that we may not even remember, as well as from defensive postures. Dr. Rolf's major discovery (which modern medicine so far ignores because medical schools teach that it is "impossible") is that the adult physical body can change dramatically. There is good theoretical reason why this is possible. Even bone tissue is constantly regenerating itself, changing position in response to the stresses on it, and it is the connective tissue (muscles, ligaments, tendons, fascia, and ground substance) that supports the bones of the skeleton.

What does this have to do with spirituality? Nothing, necessarily, just as psychotherapy does not necessarily lead to enlightenment. What we do know is that rigidity of any sort, mental or physical, locks us into one fixed way of responding to reality, one fixed way of being in the world.

OTHER WAYS OF KNOWING

Traditionally, only religions offered the disciplines—prayer, meditation on Scripture, or participation in ecstatic rituals—that taught how to change our consciousness. Religion was the school in which people were taught to get beyond the greed and anger of personal desire, to feel their participation in something greater. Now there are secular disciplines, nonreligious "trainings," to reach those goals.

In chapter 9, I describe how the *est* Young Person's Training teaches many of the skills described in this chapter, and uses them to help children gain awareness that they are responsible for their own lives. Actualizations, the Institute for the New Age, the Sufi Seed schools—all have workshops for children. New spiritual groups are arising all the time.

At best, the transpersonal educators are righting the imbalance of the traditional curriculum which ignored the inner world and only taught one way of knowing. They do not necessarily make us better people. Robin Beebe points out that "intuitive" simply means the simultaneous mode of knowing drawn from the unconscious or preconscious. *What* is known does not have to be "spiritual." You can know intuitively how to manipulate people! She warns that we can overdose on the spiritual aspect; we also need intellectual, physical, and social communication skills. The challenge is to keep all our capacities developing rather than isolating *one*. Integration is the goal, before transcendence.

At worst, for adults (and possibly for children), the workshops and exercises become silly games or new forms of self-absorption if pursued as ends in themselves, without grounding in our everyday lives and values. I think this happens less often than critics of the "me" generation claim. The desire to serve often arises in the process of inner development. In Abraham Maslow's hierarchy of needs, the desire for self-transcendence arises *after* we have achieved self-actualization.

As in character development, it is who we are, not what we say, that counts. This also holds true for access to altered states, creative imagination, and intuition. The games we play and the techniques we use as parents are less important than our own awareness. When Chögyam Trungpa, Rinpoche, set up a preschool for his Buddhist community in Boulder, Colorado, there were no Buddhist "teachings." The spirit of Buddhism was conveyed by the psychological state of the people who worked with the children.

At times, games can be useful—as a way of sharing our explorations. When we go on a hike with children, though we may teach them the names of the flowers, the real thrill is being in the meadows and under the sky together. If we meditate, the children will want to try it. If we accept feelings, so will the kids. If we tell them stories, sooner or later they will be telling stories to us.

CHAPTER 4

"Should I
Send My Child
to Sunday School?"

A mother writes:

My husband and I are both twenty-nine. We have three children: Amy, eight, Moira, six, and Brian, two. Both my husband and I were "churched": he, Dutch Reformed, me, Lutheran. When we left the church, it was because we found too many Sunday Christians, too many judges and hypocrites. I guess that sounds harsh but we felt beautiful inside and couldn't stand to be judged "bad" because I wore blue jeans to church and my husband was letting his hair grow long. . . .

Other mothers and I have had many a discussion about our children's spiritual needs and ours, too, for that matter. But nothing has ever been resolved.

I dislike the patriarchal image of God the Father and prefer to tell my children that we are part of a life force, that much holy spirit springs from our mother earth. . . .

I often wonder, though, if our children are really picking up on those qualities usually termed Christian which we hope they are learning by example—compassion, loving one's neighbor, reverence for the earth, cooperation. I think they are, but I do wonder if we should "formally" get the kids together and talk about it like we did in Sunday school.

This chapter is about answers to that question. I began by asking adults what they remembered from their Sunday school or other religious training. I asked first, "What was your experience of organized religion as a child? What was your religious training? What part of it did you enjoy then?" The next question was "What part of your childhood contact with organized religion is meaningful to you now? What part do you now think was destructive?" Take some time now to answer these questions for yourself, if you haven't already.

Eighty-nine percent of the parents who answered the questionnaire had spent at least one year in Sunday school or religion classes. Of these, only 18 percent considered the experience totally destructive; 13 percent found it wholly meaningful; another 17 percent considered it a "necessary stepping stone" to where they were now; and almost half (44 percent) were ambivalent. Eight percent were totally neutral.

A 1978 Gallup poll called "The Unchurched American" (mentioned in chapter 1) found that a majority—74 percent—of the unchurched still want their children to have some religious education (as compared with 95 percent of those in the "churched" category). They also found that one of the greatest differences between the churched and unchurched was that the former were more likely to have had religious training in the home.

The question "What did you enjoy about your early religious training?" does not mean that religion is about "liking" or "enjoying," or that what a person remembers consciously is what was most important. I simply chose to ask what people *do* remember, and begin with that.

Can you guess the one Sunday school activity that over 50 percent found both enjoyable at the time and meaningful in a lasting way?

It was the music and the singing. As one parent said, "Singing in the choir was my first experience of fraternal love—being one with others, not as lonely. It was a secure feeling."

This theme was reechoed in many questionnaires. Our culture has a poverty of nonreligious contexts in which people can sing together. If we don't go to church or synagogue, we are left with the national anthem at ball games. People also remembered their aesthetic responses to ritual and "the mystery and beauty of churches."

The rest of the childhood memories of attempts to "teach" religion fit well with research findings discussed in chapter 7: that before age eleven *abstract* religious teaching is meaningless to children.

Sunday school was mostly playtime for me—we drew. When I was a little older, I wanted a Bible with my name on it, so I worked hard. Mostly I wasn't inspired—inspiration came from singing in the choir. There was a lot of power in those songs—that was the real communion. The rest of it was some man talking about stuff—most of it didn't make sense and what I did understand I knew wasn't true. [The respondent was Protestant as a child, is now "no label."]

Sunday school at a young age was a fun, creative time, social time. I didn't learn much about what a Christian believes other than the Ten Commandments and Jesus. Stories were always interesting for me—I loved to imagine living barefoot and riding donkeys. Mostly I enjoyed the social part of church. I didn't like the church ceremony when you do a lot of scheduled rituals to worship: stand up and sit down, say this and then that. It never gave me any high feelings. Sometimes singing did, though. [Protestant as a child, now "all one."]

I sang in the choir and liked the songs. Often the unctuousness of the rabbis destroyed religious feeling. [Jewish both as a child and now.]

I attended Sunday school and summer Bible school as a child —Presbyterian and Congregational. I was fearful of people, so it was mostly something endured, rather than enjoyed. I gave up on

God at four years when we planted lima beans to demonstrate His great powers. . . . I hated lima beans! (I also hated the nap I had to take at Bible school, and the teacher who enforced it!) Happy aspects included Sunday school clothes, the walk with my brothers to and from the church, the singing. . . . [Protestant as a child, now "gone beyond."]

The *quantity* of religious teaching was in no way related to its future value:

We attended an Episcopal school, my sister and I, and spent our Sunday mornings in church, singing in the choir. I always enjoyed the singing and the rhythm of the litany/prayers. There were well-educated and sometimes loving nuns at St. Hilda's, but for the most part I hated the regimentation and endless study of Latin and the Bible. The curriculum included twelve years of "religious knowledge," five years of Latin with history, music, art, and English courses. We wore uniforms and attended chapel daily with Mass on Thursdays and Sundays. What is now meaningful? Nothing that I can recall. [Religion now: "no name."]

The one unambiguous finding was that people remember with fondness activities they did *with* their parents, and resent times they were *forced* to go to church, synagogue, or Sunday school:

What part meaningful? Very little of it, at least on a conscious level. . . . I really have a leftover feeling that I was coerced into going to church, and I resented it; my father didn't really care if I went, but it was very important to my mother for reasons that she did not communicate to me. [Presbyterian as a child, now "no name."]

Forced to go to Sunday school. Only part I liked was social hour after church, but would not have attended either on my own. . . . Meaning? None. Destructive? I may have been able to use the Sunday mornings spent in church for a better purpose. [Now agnostic.]

I gave the questionnaire to a control group of people who still belong to the organized religion of their parents. These "believers," although they value their religious tradition, also insist they would *not* force it on their children. A twenty-five-year-old college student with four children was brought up Baptist and is now Methodist. She says:

As a child I went to church or Sunday school because I was made to. It was almost like a punishment or a means of getting me out of the house. I believe I could have appreciated it more if someone at home could have helped in my teachings. I feel the only real form of religious training I had was to learn to pray.

A twenty-three-year-old mother of a ten-month-old son who was the oldest of seven children, all of whom are Catholic, demonstrates in her own life the ideal model of this group:

I was raised in a good Catholic family. I went to a Catholic grammar school and high school. I had the old form of religious training up to age seven, question and answer. I was taught starting in seventh grade the new way, including the new views. . . . I considered the organized religion of my childhood the basis of my religious beliefs now. I now can see many faults, but the basic beliefs are still true. The destructive part might have been the fear that nuns instilled in us of punishment for doing bad. I would have liked them to emphasize the good in God.

My parents, although I am aware of some of their faults, were ideal models. I wish I as a parent could set such an example for my children. They are a true example for a wholesome life. [She and her husband bring their little boy to Mass sometimes.] It's a nice time we spend together including preparing to go, and after the Mass.

To other parents, she suggests, "Give your children a good solid background and then from there they can make decisions accordingly on their own, and I feel that they will feel good about themselves and develop into good, understanding adults." She adds, "To be able to act, not only preach, what is right is a hard thing to accomplish."

Children are notoriously quick to spot hypocrisy in its many forms, and the unchurched parents who answered my questionnaire reported acute examples:

I went to church and we were sent out after a few hymns to Sunday school. I never really knew what it was about actually. I was pretty bewildered about it all. When I was about to be con-

firmed (not my idea), I used to miss the class and hang out down-
town, but still I got confirmed! What is meaningful now? Familiarity
with the beauty of various churches . . . organ music and some of
the prayers. Destructive? Being forced to go to church while at
school—using Bible reading as a punishment! [Anglican as a child,
now "no official religion."]

I attended Catholic grammar and high schools. Early in life I
had to accept being a minority—i.e., we were poor in a wealthy
environment. The nuns favored the children from the "good"
homes. The discrimination that I grew up with helped me to be
more tolerant—and skeptical. When you are pushed down for so
long it is hard to stand up. Catholic training in general is one of
submissiveness and penance. [Now nonpracticing Catholic.]

My father was a Methodist minister who also beat his wife and
children. I saw a lot of hypocrisy in this! I was very positively influenced by my mother and her parents as to seeing God through
love, nature, goodness, etc. I enjoyed the singing at church and
summer revivals in big tents, with spirited singing and high emotional sermons and testimonials. [Now "no religion in particular."]

I had to go to [Jewish] Sunday school and get confirmed—it
was important to get "in" with a certain group of people. It was
horrible—very materialistic. What you wore to Sunday school was
what was important. We humiliated the teachers every Sunday because they didn't dress well. It was not spiritual but social—who sat
next to who. I enjoyed almost none of it. Everything about it was
mean. I was idealistic and yet went off every week to be
mean. . . ." [Now Jewish.]

NEW DIRECTIONS
IN RELIGIOUS EDUCATION
Among Protestants

Religious educators are not unaware of these issues. They agree
on the uselessness of "teaching" something you do not yourself

believe. Johanna Klink, a Dutch Protestant pastor, puts it succinctly: "False holiness is odious." She says, "You can send your children wherever you please, but what really matters happens at home. There the concern is for life rather than for religious rites: how to speak at table, how conflicts are resolved and strangers received. What matters is that children should notice that their parents still recognize a 'higher calling' and believe in something that is more than life itself. . . ."

Anna Mow, another Protestant, writes, "It is not only the special 'religious' moments in the family life that have spiritual significance, but *all good family experience is religious experience.* The religious values are communicated there: love, beauty, reverence, justice, courage, faith, joy, kindness, helpfulness, sharing, cooperation, obedience [and respect for each other]. . . . There is never any argument against *lived out* religion. Children who resent the religions of their childhood do it because they have a memory only of a *profession* of religion which was not a part of daily life."

The director of a Sunday school told me:

If I had my druthers I would write a curriculum for the home. Sunday school at best is supplemental. Maybe it would reinforce things parents are teaching and maybe it would help the children focus on things their parents are weak at or overlooking . . . but values and ethics are taught by the model of the parent in the home. . . . A lot of parents think that Sunday school will bail them out—'Let's send the kids to Sunday school so they'll get moral, get spiritual, get religious'—and I say that's not possible. The thing that's wrong with Sunday school is that it's there to satisfy adult needs. The child's need is to love and be loved, to experience, to gain perspective on life, to make friends and be friends . . . the adult need is to propagate the institution.

With the awareness that "what matters is what happens at home," Protestant (as well as Catholic and Jewish) educators are devising new ways to affect the family as a whole. All three offer a form of "marriage encounter" weekends to help couples to become more loving and to live their beliefs within their relationship.

Dr. Margaret M. Sawin, a Protestant educator, designed a "new model for religious education" called Family Clusters. A Family Cluster is a leader-led group of four or five complete family units "which contract to meet together periodically over an extended period of time for shared educational experiences. They provide mutual support, for each other, learn skills which enhance living within the family, and celebrate their beliefs and life together." Dr. Sawin defines a family as a group of any persons who live in relationship with one another, recognizing that these days a "family" can be one parent with children, a couple without children, adults who live together, a single person, a three-generation family, a "blended family" of adults and children from several marriages, as well as the traditional nuclear family of two adults with children.

In the two-hour weekly sessions of her Family Cluster groups, preschoolers, teenagers, parents, and grandparents share in play, singing, and socializing, as well as a meal preceded by grace, and an hour of a structured "experiential learning" exercise based on a theme chosen by the families.

At the First Baptist Church where the program began, it was so successful that one Family Cluster chose to continue for four years, another for five. It looked as though Dr. Sawin had found a way to provide the functions of the extended family at its best. Other places, however, have met resistance from family members unwilling to find and dedicate two hours a week to be together.

In her book *Family Enrichment with Family Clusters,* Dr. Sawin lists seven other Protestant family growth groups, and seven more human-potential family skills groups, as well as Catholic groups. "Family Weekend Experience" has been developed for a Worldwide Marriage Encounter.

In addition, many churches have developed kits for parents to use at home. (See "Resources.") Perhaps the most ambitious of the curricula for parents and teachers is "Attitude Education" from the Union College Character Research Project. It includes materials age-graded from nursery school through high school for each of six units: "Christian Social Potential" leading toward sensitivity to the needs of others; "Growth in Magnanimity"; "Vicarious Sacrifice" for development of Christian courage; "Vocational Adjustment" to encourage "a vocation based on a dominating purpose in the service of mankind"; "Adjustment to the Universe," teaching a faith in the friendliness of the universe; and finally, "Vision."

Part of what Dr. Sawin is trying to accomplish happened naturally years ago in the small-town church. John H. Westerhoff III, in *Will Our Children Have Faith?*, points out that

The typical church was a community neighborhood congregation where all ages knew each other and regularly interacted. Many hours were spent at the church, not only in worship, but in a variety of social activities. . . . The Sunday school was especially important in that it was a lay-directed organization where women could play a significant leadership role. Always concerned about community, celebration, the religious affections, and the biblical story, these Sunday schools included plays and musicals, parties and picnics, social service projects, and community activities.

His point is that as homogeneous communities and stable extended families have disappeared, people look to schooling and instruction as the panacea for our needs. The end point of this line of development has been a church school "with teachers, subject matter, curriculum resources, supplies, equipment, age-graded classes, classrooms, and, where possible, a professional church educator as administrator. . . . All this must change."

Westerhoff continues:

It appears that as Christian faith has diminished, the schooling-instructional paradigm has encouraged us to busy ourselves with teaching about Christian religion. As our personal commitment to Christ has lapsed, many church persons have turned for solace to teaching about what the Bible says, what happened in the history of the church, what we believe, and what is right and wrong. Sometimes, even when the school has succeeded, it has only produced educated atheists. . . .

The old Sunday school appears to have cared most about creating an environment where people could be Christian together and where persons could experience Christian faith and see it witnessed to in the lives of significant people.

Many churches of all denominations have realized the problem, and some have established a special hour for "family worship" before the main service, followed by classes for the parents simultaneous with those for the children. Randolph Crump Miller, in *Your Child's Religion*, observes:

> *Some parents think this is a tremendous demand on them, but other parents welcome this opportunity. Only a very few churches have said that if you do not register with your child, your child may not attend Sunday school. However, in such churches, there is 100% cooperation of parents and children attending the family worship together. . . . This is an extreme form of coercion on the part of the church, but it works. One church that tried this system had a limited enrollment because of its facilities, and had a waiting list for a number of years.*

The parents' class "asks two fundamental questions: (1) What is the meaning of the Christian Faith to me as a parent? (2) How can I be a mediator of the Gospel to my children where they are?" It is primarily a discussion group led by a husband-and-wife team, with a resource leader present. "Children and their parents often come from the family service full of questions about the experience they have just had . . . these questions are often the self-starters of the class session. . . . All of this becomes grist for the mill in discussions at home."

Some programs are dedicated to improving family communication by group meetings, others by bringing everybody to church, others by providing a structured curriculum to help parents who do not know what to say or how to say it. Still other religious educators think it is best to say very little.

"When parents ask me to tell them how to teach their young child religion, and I reply that the best thing they can do to this end is to give them as little religious instruction as possible until they are over seven years of age, I am usually met with an incredulous stare, or the parents think I am joking." R. S. Lee, in *Your Growing Child and Religion,* is not joking. His point is that we must pay attention to the developmental level of the child. Early misunderstandings create later trouble.

The Reverend James Diamond suggests that we save Sunday school until the children begin to ask ethical questions. Once, when conducting a workshop on religious education, he found that no parents could recall *ever* having been asked by a Sunday school teacher about their own experience of God. It is ironic that religious schools ignore children's spiritual experience as much as elementary schools do, while overemphasizing intellectual content.

In chapter 2 we saw that children do have mystical experiences, although this is rarely acknowledged. A woman brought up in the Dutch Reformed Church reports:

As a little girl, in my private life I had the feeling of being in close contact with something holy or sacred when I went to sleep at night and was lying in the dark. It wasn't confused with what I came to dislike about the church, or with seeing my friends at church.

Another parent, when asked what was destructive, said:

Stupid Sunday school lessons. It would have been wonderful just to talk, ask questions, and not answer someone else's.

The Reverend Diamond points out that when the directors of the Sunday school do not allow the children in the sanctuary, but keep them in the church basement, they are again refusing to acknowledge the children's ability to *experience* the presence of God. This attitude is part of what will eventually drive these children away from religion: leaving unsatisfied their spiritual "yearning of the heart" (which in early childhood is "beyond the ability of the head to understand").

This thought was echoed by a parent who remembered:

When I was in high school I had a feeling for God that I found at special times, but was rarely nourished by the church service (Congregational). I explored different religions looking for an enrichment of that special feeling I had felt a few times on my own. I went to Sunday school until one day when I was in high school the teacher said, "I think it's great so many of you still come to Sunday school. You're too old to come because your parents make you. So you must come because you really get something out of it." I thought about what he said, and never went to Sunday school again.

Ronald Goldman, a British Protestant educator whose research in the development of religious understanding will be reported in more detail in chapter 7, feels very strongly that

in our concern to build a spiritual foundation for our children we have often been over-anxious to provide a ready-made religion, a complete system of beliefs and ideas, which we impose on them. This is often done with great sincerity and from the best of motives, but in the long run it may impede a child's spiritual growth because passively acquired information is more quickly forgotten and ready-made religion is more easily jettisoned.

A cosmic security, an ultimate faith in the kindliness of the universe, is not transmitted by verbal assurances, but by adults who themselves trust life, whether or not this is verbalized into a belief in God. . . . The Bible is not a children's book . . . the present weakness of Christian education is . . . trying to teach too much (and too much which is inappropriate) at too early an age.

Harold Loukes, in *Friends and Their Children: A Study in Quaker Education*, says that the Friends

have regarded all experience as potentially religious, all life as sacramental. This has been the implication of the rejection of ritual, not that they withdraw from physical reality in search of the transcendent Other, but that they should be open to the word of God in common things. . . . Religious education can start with the world as it is, and by the widening and deepening of the understanding of it lead on to ultimate questions.

Two inspirational books that I can recommend highly to Christian parents are both written with great sensitivity to these issues and to the realities of raising children. Johanna Klink gathered questions from four- to five-year-old children "about God, about death, about why and what for." She found no difference between Roman Catholic and Protestant families in the children's questions. The purpose of her book, *Your Child and Religion*, is to help those in the Christian tradition "to gain a more profound understanding yourself, and in your attempt to explain these things to your children." She quotes from parents and teachers, and from autobiographies—including Jean-Paul Sartre's.

Anna Mow, in *Your Child from Birth to Rebirth,* writes: "A real religious understanding, besides a loving relationship and a content knowledge, requires an *illumination* which the teacher cannot give. The role of parents and teachers is to help in the preparation for this *experience which God gives.*"

Perhaps most enlightening for Christian parents is the example of Jesus himself, who did not teach children a catechism. Rather, when the children were brought to him, "he took them up in his arms, put his hands upon them, and blessed them." (Mark, 10:16) "And they brought unto him also infants, that he would touch them: but when his disciples saw it, they rebuked them. But Jesus called them unto him, and said, 'Suffer little children to come unto me, and forbid them not: for of such is the kingdom of God. Verily I say unto you, Whosoever shall not receive the kingdom of God as a little child shall in no ways enter therein.' (Luke 18:15-17)

Among Jews

Jewish parents are in a unique position of belonging simultaneously to a religion, an ethnic group, and a culture. To deprive children of their "Jewishness" is more than not teaching religion. It is keeping them in the dark about their family origins and the history of their people. In addition, since the history of the Jews for roughly two millennia has been that of an oppressed minority, ceasing to defend or identify with the minority is equated with an act of betrayal. As Abraham Franzblau says, "The problem of survival has always been the basic problem of religious education among the Jews."

Some refer to themselves as "Jewish atheists" or "culturally Jewish." One of my respondents was a "Jewish Buddhist." These people feel they can keep their sense of roots without the religion. Rabbi Hayim Donin feels otherwise:

> Jewish parents expect education to be relevant and support those philosophies that view education as an integral part of life itself. Yet, in Jewish education, many actually insist on irrelevance. How else can one categorize the inevitable demand by parents who have themselves drifted far from religious tradition to "teach my child to know he's a Jew, not to be religious."

What parents are essentially asking is for a Jewish education to transmit a "feeling" of peoplehood and an "appreciation" for Jewish values, while stopping short of inspiring the youngster to abide by those values, or stopping short of the religious practices with which that peoplehood has been historically identified. While such parents would like Jewish education to affect their child's emotions, they want it to be irrelevant to their behavior. The difficulty in granting that wish is that everything having to do with being Jewish is ultimately grounded in the Jewish religion. The religion and culture of the Jewish people have been so intertwined from its very inception as to make any attempt to separate them doomed to failure. . . .

If "Jewish" children are to be raised, a family may just have to accommodate itself to a fuller return to religious practices. Parents have to overcome the fear of "losing their children" to successful Jewish education, which among some parents is apparently as real as the fear of "losing a child" to a mixed marriage.

In America, a common direction of change in Jewish families was that the first generation of immigrants was Orthodox, the second generation was Conservative, the third was Reform, and the fourth assimilated. Part of the assimilation was, according to Irving Greenberg, "the assumption of moral progress, the persuasion of the universal truth, the sense of unprecedented tolerance, love, and brotherhood: all of these images absorbed in contemporary culture come to an end in the . . . unparalleled catastrophe of the holocaust," the murder of six million Jews in World War II. Greenberg believes that the end of the "modern" period was marked as well by "the incredible and unparalleled redemption—the Exodus of our times—the rebirth of the State of Israel."

While it is true that allegiance to the State of Israel has provided for many Jews a solution to how to be Jewish without being religious, for others it poses a new spiritual problem. For Jews throughout the centuries, self-transcendence was through identification with God's covenant with "the People of Israel," a mystical community that extended throughout time and space. As one parent puts it,

"When the Promised Land becomes a piece of property rather than a state of mind, you have bloody battles."

Jewish education has been changing over the last few years. *The Second Jewish Catalogue* gives an extensive account of recent developments and how to find nursery schools, day schools, afternoon schools, high schools, camps, retreats and weekends, and family education. There are a "Family *Mitzvah*" program; an adaptation of Margaret Sawin's Family Cluster called the *Mishpacha*; and the family *Havurot* developed by the Reconstructionist movement. This type of *Havurot* is composed of ten or fewer families that meet monthly to pursue programs of Jewish education for adults and children, to celebrate, and to provide a surrogate extended family.

Judith Targan, in *The Jewish Catalogue*, writes:

> By now it is clear to all Jewish educators that parents are the real teachers of their children. The school should supplement and reinforce what is lived at home, and family education should be considered the most viable supplement to the traditional Jewish classroom. . . . We use words like "identity," "survival," "knowledge," "loyalty," "observance" —without really defining and identifying what we mean. . . . If our goal is to create an "identified" Jew (whatever that may be), then perhaps nonclassroom activities (camps, retreats, youth groups) are best suited to this purpose. If we want to create an "educated" one, then the classroom becomes an important tool.

Another trend in contemporary Judaism has been a return to the mystical tradition. "The American Jewish milieu, a cradle of conceptualization and demythologizations of Jewish belief, has offered little opportunity for either temple-affiliated or non-temple-affiliated Jews to enhance their personal lives with the recognition of a personal God," writes Moshe Waldoks in *The Second Jewish Catalogue*.

This parent's experience was typical:

I went to a Jewish Sunday school from age eight to thirteen. I learned songs, holidays, history. From fourteen to eighteen, I taught the kindergarten class in the Sunday school and definitely enjoyed that. The synagogue, it seems, was a place where I developed confidence and was liked. I have little sense that I took the religion seriously, and I gave up all observance when I went to college. I married a Jew and observed some holidays for a sense of family. I do remember liking two rabbis as a teenager and young adult and I felt they were kind and wise people. The identification with Jewishness and the Sunday school stuff all seems pleasant and part of my identity. I can't think of anything destructive unless it was the absence of any concepts of mysticism or spirituality.

Among Catholics

American Catholic parents have emphasized to me that the church has changed, the nuns and priests have relaxed, and as a result much Catholic education is very different from the rote catechisms and obey-or-go-to-Hell theology that alienated many of the parents answering my questionnaire. The Catholic church has developed marriage encounters, "family-centered programs," and "family learning teams." Some parishes have adopted a system of religious instruction that insists on the participation of parents.

The "Decree on Christian Education of Vatican II" proclaimed:

Since parents have given children their life, they are bound by the most serious obligation to educate their offspring and therefore must be recognized as the primary and principal educators. This role in education is so important that only with difficulty can it be supplied where it is lacking. Parents are the ones who must create a family atmosphere animated by love and respect for God and man, in which the well-rounded personal and social education of children is fostered. Hence the family is the first school of the social virtues that every society needs. It is particularly in the Christian family, enriched by the grace and office of the sacrament of matrimony, that children should be taught from their early years to have a knowledge of God according to the faith received in baptism, to worship Him, and to love their neighbor.

Ernest Larsen and Patricia Galvin, in *Will Religion Make Sense to Your Child?*, prepared a handbook for Catholic family discussion groups that emphasizes the "new emphases in religious thinking":

Vatican II has greatly emphasized the role responsibility plays in the life of the laity today. A responsibility to . . . find out what the Church does have to say to the world today; what real meaning and relevance Christ does have in our own individual lives and in the lives of all men. What did He do that makes a difference to me as I live through this day? . . . We must define in our minds the role of religion (our relationship with God); the reason why God became man; what He asks of us. Only when this is understood in a way that becomes a deep part of our lived life (that is, not just things we believe, but deeply internalized motives that cause us to act in certain ways), do we become real teachers. We become communicators. This is because religion is not the kind of thing that can simply be taught—it must be genuinely communicated so that it touches our lives; moves us to action, decides our destiny. Only exposure to someone else who believes can instill living religion. We can only teach it if we live it.

Since Vatican II, there have been even more new developments within Catholicism: liberation theology, the Charismatic movement, and Catholic feminism.

To a Catholic parent who is wondering what it would be like to send children to a catechism class that enhanced, rather than suppressed, their spiritual experiences, I recommend a little paperback book translated from the French called *How to Teach Religion* by Marie Fargues. This is her description of children's religious experience:

Children today do very well without God. They accept life such as it is offered to them: "This is the way it is." . . . All the poetry, the dreams, the joy they need they find in abundance around them or in them. They transfigure, if need be, their daily reality, no matter how drab it may be. They have not yet touched the limits of anything. They are like a little bird born in a large cage that does not know that it is a prisoner. In place of the need of God, what we notice is the sense of God. This is it, the point of support for education in the faith. The little beginner . . . seeks himself and his enjoyment, more or less; but at the same time he is seeking God, more or less. God is then at work in his impulses of sensible fervor that contain as first fruits his impulses of spiritual love. . . . They will be clarified on one condition, namely, a very great and respectful discretion on the part of the educator on this plane of the spiritual life.

While respecting their religious experience, she believes we can add intellectual content:

It is vain, and moreover contrary to the nature of things, to give children, no matter what their age—six, eight, ten years— rational instruction and abstract explanations that lead to perfect theological formulas. It is just as unsatisfactory, and also unworthy of the human intellect even in its period of formation, to maintain religion on the easy plane where a child has no difficulty in moving, when we know that this religion wishes to grasp the whole man. In one case we end in a dry knowledge that has no power over life; in the other we end in ignorance.

She concludes:

The true teacher of the interior life is the Holy Spirit. But He does not act alone. How can we explain that so many baptized children show themselves to be so little Christian? It is not God, it is man who has failed them. Speaking of the primacy of the supernatural in this holy work, many well-intentioned persons falsify the catechetical problem. Our action is situated on the human plane. What God expects of us is not that we act in souls and transform them, it is that we till the soil.

DESTRUCTIVE RELIGIOUS EDUCATION

The religious educators are concerned that the teaching in Sunday school should not be meaningless. For some parents, the teachings were actually destructive. Both Protestants and Catholics had some bitter memories of the emphasis on sin, guilt, and prohibitions:

I got religious instruction daily in Catholic school, and enjoyed none of it—kneeling hurt. I argued starting in first grade. "Don't try to tell me infants who die are in limbo!" What was destructive was an intense feeling of being the rebellious naughty girl. You're not supposed to speak up or question—the fear of authority is destructive of freedom. . . . When I was fourteen, my parents said, "Why are you turning away from the thing you were raised to do?" (not believe) when I didn't want to go to church anymore. [Now "no religion."]

Training was traditional, religious education through confirmation at age fourteen . . . phony, coercive, hard to believe. . . . None is meaningful now. The emphasis on fear and guilt was destructive. [Lutheran as a child, now agnostic.]

We went to Sunday school (Presbyterian) for social reasons. What other people get from church is a sense of belonging, but I never felt I belonged. I became an atheist in college when my mother was dying. So did my brother. Looking back, none of it was meaningful, and what was destructive may not have been the teachings of the church, but how they were channeled through my mother. The ethic was "being unselfish," i.e., masochistic. The whole emphasis was on sin and forgiveness. Why can't religion be about joy, about how lucky we are to be here at all? [Now atheist.]

I enjoyed music and became a psalm leader, eventually a Sunday school teacher. . . . I went on to seminary and became clergy. . . . The music and ritual did teach me to appreciate aesthetics. . . . The Bible stories were a great treasure to have. . . . What was destructive was the emphasis on guilt. I later unloaded the guilt feelings and God. [United Church of Christ, now humanist.]

Jews as well found parts of the tradition destructive:

I was raised traditionally Jewish—five years of Hebrew school and Sunday school. Disliked it, but as first-born son it was expected of me and I was compliant. Found very little in the religion I could relate to, a vengeful God that presented a contradiction in terms, men living in hypocrisy and phony holiness. The religion made a virtue of being persecuted and suffering. [Now "draws from many disciplines."]

Some people mentioned the destructiveness of an exclusive

group identity which makes recognizing our common humanity even more difficult. On the other hand, some unchurched parents fear they are depriving their children of a clear sense of religious group identity (although in chapter 12 we will see that research has not shown this to be harmful). Being part of a true community, as we have heard, is a beautiful experience, but hard to find, even within a church.

Barbara Hargrove of the Yale Divinity School outlines four aspects of the "social function" of religion, which is exactly what unchurched parents have chosen to live without. Whether we like it or not, the United States is becoming more pluralistic, with more than one sacred myth and secular ones as well (such as the "land of opportunity" with Thanksgiving Day and Fourth of July rituals). Hargrove, of course, deplores this pluralism. Here is her "social function" of religion:

1. In every culture there is some sort of myth or sacred history which ties some kind of creation story into a sense of identity for the society and for individuals as members of that society.
2. This sacred story provides, in addition to such an understanding of origins, patterns of behavior by which the social life is ordered, patterns which are understood to be a mark of its members' social identity.
3. In every society there are certain rituals which offer both a time to learn the sacred history and a way of acting it out which involves individuals at other levels than the strictly intellectual.
4. This ritual involvement not only reinforces the religious identity and perception of the world that is characteristic of members of the society, it also provides expressive outlets for tensions created as the individual conforms to behavior patterns required by the culture. . . .

And here are some parents' critiques—their answers to the question "What part do you now think was destructive?":

Close-minded attitudes—each religion centered on preservation of its own doctrine and structure—exclusiveness and rules about not associating with other religions.

Attitudes of having answers rather than of the spiritual life as a

*quest-adventure. Stress on structure rather than religious experi-
ence of individuals. [Catholic as a child.]*

*I went to Congregational church some Sundays. Some Sunday
school, not much. It confused me and I didn't understand it very
well. Was in children's choir, which I liked. Regular church was
boring. Meaningful? Little, if any. Destructive? Stifling belief systems: People aren't divine, only God is. We need to be redeemed,
Jesus does it for us; we are separate and better than other religions,
etc. [Now "no organized religion."]*

*We were judgmental of other people—wary of other cultures
—shielded from theater and drama. We were supposed to be grateful that we were white, Protestant, American. [United Church of
Christ, now humanist.]*

Parents don't want their children to be set against people of
different beliefs. On the other hand, they don't want their children
to be confused. One mother wrote: "How do other parents who
practice no particular religion expose their children to churches, or
do they? Is it possible to do this without confusing a child? What
have been their experiences?"

Another mother of a six-year-old found a Sunday school where
"they sing songs and have talks—about Buddhism, Judaism, Christianity—and celebrate everything." This was her solution to her
problem: "I would like my child to have access to the cosmos, but
I don't want to do the work. I want her to feel familiar with religion.
I do feel there is something beyond and regret that I don't have
time to study it myself. I would like my daughter to get some awareness of how all peoples connect."

The priest who ran this Sunday school (under the auspices of a
large church) wanted the children to have an experience of and
commitment to "a universal common humanity." Although the
children and their parents loved the school, he was later dismissed
by the church for being too "secular."

He felt deeply that there was no problem with "confusion,"
since he defined religion in the simplest sense—as caring. He says:

*People confuse religion and piety—pious practices. Every-
day experiences at the school demonstrated spiritual values.*

People say, "Should we introduce values into the school?" but the values are already there: in how you treat the children, whether they get a sense of their inherent worth as a human being. Values emerge constantly—every time the children have a fight, for example. The children themselves want to be treated fairly and want justice to be done. We also tried to recognize the values that are already present in the communities; to help the children to affirm themselves and their own backgrounds (which were ethnically and economically as well as religiously mixed). We did have regular chapel services and Bible stories, to introduce them to traditions they reverence. There was no need for indoctrination.

SHOULD I SEND
MY CHILD
TO SUNDAY SCHOOL?

From people's stories you can find data to support some religious education, and data to support none. Even among those who reported "something destructive," over half also found something meaningful. And almost one-fifth of all the parents felt that even the pain involved in their religious education was a valued part of the process of becoming who they are now. Content with their present, they accept their past as perfect, no matter how bad it was at the time:

I was in Catholic school until first or second grade. It was traumatic—I was fearful of authority—half my class was throwing up. I was fairly religious in high school—then rejected organized religion for a couple of years in college. . . . It was all a necessary stepping stone. . . . I don't think I should have been raised differently. [Now "no name."]

I was in Sunday school, then I was a deacon (Dutch Reformed). A lot of what I felt as a little girl I would not call religious now. I wanted to be a good girl and please God. I was charged up by the ideals of good life; memorized verses of the Bible . . . part of it was ego—to do something good and get stars for it. . . . by high school, I developed a hatred of the church, which was hypocritical, prejudiced, and involved with money. This aspect of it caused me to reject the whole thing. . . . I also feel the extreme moralistic thing was destructive—I saw everything in black and white, and that made it hard for me to accept myself. . . . Sunday school and the church were good for nurturing something in me, keeping something developing. It was really rich. Even though the forms were shed, they helped me nourish this thing, which could take new forms later on. [Now doing the Gurdjieff Work.]

You can also take comfort in the stories of children who *sought* formal religious training, overcoming the reluctance of their parents. If you happen to have that kind of child, s/he may let you know it. S/he may go with friends or grandparents, or even get you involved!

At age seven, under influence of my grandmother, I attended her church a great deal. I enjoyed it, loved, respected, admired, revered my grandmother. Quiet woman, taught by presence. Going to church without Grandma was never the same. She allowed me to enter into her devotion, experience her faith. Later, I was active in youth groups and choir—a home away from home. Parents not involved. Considered me a bit weird for being "religious." [Now "all this and more."]

One time, when I was coming home from kindergarten, someone said, "Are you a Protestant or a Catholic?"

"I don't know."

"Then you must be a Protestant!"

I felt very out of it—so I chose a church and joined a Sunday school (ages six and seven), got myself baptized (without my parents). It was accomplishing my goal of finding out what this was about. My parents were embarrassed by my devout membership in this church. One year I was Mary in the pageant, and they had to come. They felt they had to find some organized religion we could all attend—and joined the Quaker meeting. [Now "nothing with a name."]

What does this all add up to? Should you send your child to Sunday school?

Yes, if your child wants to go, for a sense of tradition, to celebrate festivals, for the joy of singing and being with friends. Yes, if you want it, and you go, too. Encouragement for spirituality will come from the child's sense of wonder, from your example, and from other adults who are able to transmit their love—possibly a Sunday school teacher.

No, if your child hates Sunday school or if you think that the teachers are presenting dogma in a way that disconnects "religion" from the children's private spiritual experiences. No, if you think they are pushing too much doctrine too soon, because that is more likely to make your child reject your tradition after adolescence.

In the next chapter we will hear from parents who have decided against Sunday school, and are making daily life a spiritual activity.

CHAPTER 5

"—And What If I Don't?" Daily Life as a Spiritual Activity

I asked parents who don't belong to an organized religious group, "Do you worry sometimes that your children might be missing something, and if so, what? What solutions have you found?"

Some of the parents were satisfied:

Do we worry? No! Organized religion is a bummer and in my opinion is not the truth of how it really is—or even near, or even seeking the truth. Most of it is a dead fossil of someone else's direct experience. Our approach is to try ourselves to be in touch with "the truth" as well as possible and express it honestly as we are actually experiencing it, deal with situations as they come up, rather than set out to "teach" anything.

We want a feeling in the home that permeates on another level —to teach by love and example.

No, I don't feel my son is missing anything from lack of involvement with organized religion. I believe I have transmitted to him in words and by example that standards of ethics and life values can come from within one's self without the teachings of any particular religion.

Do I worry? Yes, I'm afraid [my son] might not be learning how to put square pegs in round holes! Actually, I feel so strongly that what we do and learn and know must come from inside each of us that I feel organized religion can offer very little of positive value. And because of the strength of my faith, I don't think my child will ever feel that being "out" of things is a bad way to be. If he misses the world as church, then I will feel he has missed something.
Others just as strongly missed a group:

I think that people who don't tie into an institution are missing a sense of community—the key to the religious life is sharing it. It's not enough to be fulfilled in yourself; that's a gross distortion of spirituality. Institutions tend to breed hypocrisy—I realize that—but it's still better to affiliate than to go it alone. It makes you stand up and be counted.

I do not worry because [in our daily living] I share with [my child, age four and a half] knowledge and tools for him to use which will show him that he is beautiful and magnificent, how to share, talk about feelings and be unafraid. Little thoughts here and there in answer to questions about death, about love, about God. . . . It's difficult to tell you examples of thoughts because they are interspersed with other daily thoughts such as, "Can I walk to Grandma's?" Once he wanted to go to Sunday school with friends, and he went. He was thrilled, had fun, and really loved the snack. My only wish for any "organized" spiritual involvement is to be in contact with more parents and people who feel as I do to share with.

I am just now beginning to sort the whole thing out for myself. I hope to be in touch with others who feel the way I do not only about religion but about schooling, too. I find that this is very difficult, especially here in Nova Scotia. There is an ashram in Bridgetown which I hope to go to next month and perhaps through that I can meet some others. There is nothing like being with others of like understanding to help in your own evolving. . . . I feel quite alone, but at the same time I shy away from organizations! I hope that some kind of small group will someday happen that we can become a part of, to work and live together.

Some were finding or creating their own groups:

I can give [my daughter] the individual stuff—the myths, etc. —but I miss the group stuff. The solution wouldn't be Sunday school, but getting together with other families to celebrate holidays. . . . I'm not a part of organized religion today because I'd rather pick my own family.

As a single parent I often think about sharing time and activities with other families whose values are close to mine. I imagine it is a wish for extended family because my family is so far removed geographically, and because their values, the ones important to them, are not important to me.

I feel [my daughter] is going to have more exposure to different personal doctrines and beliefs than I did. I know that she will meet many spiritual people throughout her life—their lights will guide her way. We gather with friends (an extended "tribal family")—we feel unity in our individual faiths.

The only thing that [my daughter] is missing from not belonging to an organized Christian group is the formation of narrow-minded attitudes. I meet on a weekly basis with a small group of like-minded people and she comes sometimes. We visit the other people occasionally, so she is brought into contact with other spiritual people and she and I discuss, when it comes up, the meanings of things— "God" is in everything.

Only one parent was concerned about lack of social acceptance, which many reported was the main reason *they* had gone to Sunday school when they were young. This may reflect a more tolerant society, or simply the fact that they now live in larger cities than the towns in which they grew up.

For the most part, parents were divided into two groups: those who try to conduct a "home Sunday school," and those who don't.

One mother said, "I find a part of me values ritual when the ritual is based on personal experience and understanding. I miss religious ritual in my life now—the need for that is probably one of the things that brings people to churches."

FAMILY RITUALS

In the following descriptions of family rituals, notice that everyone enjoys them. It is not something parents do "for the children," but rather a way of sharing their own search for living religion.

Sam Mackintosh, who comes from a Catholic background, says: "I don't look for the organized religions to offer all that I or the kids need. We 'supplement' with our own homemade rituals, mind games, and so on." In January 1979, he began publishing a monthly newsletter called *The GreenBlade,* for sharing ideas about family religious customs (see Parent Resources). He says, "My hope is that by learning of family customs and practices that have been tried with some success, others will be encouraged to try things too; and that all of our readers will share with each other those things which seem to 'work' with their families."

For over five years, Mackintosh and his wife have met weekly with a small group to play "mind games" (based on the book of that name by Robert Masters and Jean Houston). Then they began making up their own games.

Our kids (ages five and a half and seven and a half) attend each week and usually fall asleep during the "deepening" exercises (for altering our state of consciousness)—but not always . . . now they sometimes lead us in games they make up.

Many of our games are "religious" in content—meeting the characters in the St. George and the Dragon story—and we often use religious holidays as occasions for games. We have a Christmas game in three parts. After entering an altered state, we experience the annunciation story from Mary's point of view: what it would be like to have God conceived in your heart. We see the Christmas tree as the universe dazzling with the radiance of God's light, and lastly, still in an altered state, we give everybody a piece of spice cake to eat, saying something like "this is the new world that is being given to you."

Ritual and liturgy are playing "mind games" and doing it with the whole being.

He cites the example of the Passover seder, which includes smells and nice things to look at: "You eat a lot and all the while everything is touching things deep in your heart."

Mackintosh's advice to other parents is: "If it's not fun, don't do it. Home 'religious' customs shouldn't be something you do with a solemn face. Play around with rituals: 'holy' water, incense, candles, chanting."

When a reader wrote *The GreenBlade* that "these beautiful things, believe it or not, seem strange and foreign (even unacceptable) to some members of my family," he suggested:

1. Do things for your *own* sake, because you enjoy them, because they help make *your* life have more meaning.

2. Don't try to "use" a festive occasion to moralize or teach a lesson (that we should be more kind or loving or whatever). Let the celebration be . . . a real celebration.

3. Start when the kids are as young as possible. . . . They don't realize that everyone in the neighborhood isn't celebrating the assumption of the Virgin Mary into heaven. . . . Don't *expect* teenagers to go along with you. As adolescents, their life task is to become independent of you.

4. Involve the kids as much as possible. Sometimes make them the center of attraction.

5. Relate your customs to *food*. When you have a special ritual to do, do it just before or after a meal; or better, between the meal and a special dessert.

6. Invite other families to join you in celebrating a special day. Your kids won't think you're so weird if they see other people doing what you're doing.

7. Don't make your rituals too wordy; let the symbols speak for themselves. For example, if you invite another family to join you for dessert on the 15th of August and your dessert is a big bowl of sliced peaches with lots of ice cream to go on top, you might say not more than a 15-second prayer while everyone is eyeing the ice cream: "Lord, on this feast of summer fullness, we thank you for all the good things of summer—especially ice cream. Amen."

8. It's surprisingly easy to start a custom. If you make a special dessert on *your* saint's name day, you can be sure the kids will want one on *theirs, too.*

9. Be resigned to the fact that some people will think you are crazy no matter what you do, so go ahead and enjoy yourself.

10. Trust the kids to respond, even if they don't seem to be too involved and don't put their response into words. Myths, stories, rituals, symbols touch us at a very deep level, far beyond the rational thinking levels. All we can do is expose the children to good things and hope that these good things will speak to the kids' hearts. But we can't *force* people (even little people) to love Good Things.

A mother who was for many years a good Catholic says she misses the sense of a community of belief:

A belief structure that goes beyond our individual family. I haven't found a solution to this. What we do happens within the family mostly. I feel very good about this—trusting our beliefs as being closer to what is real than I think my son would get in any religious institution that I'm aware of.

Each Sunday, my husband Clyde, Jered [her six-year-old son], and I do about an hour of reading-reflection-sharings. (The time isn't important but it takes about that.) For example, last Sunday we chose the idea of water in our life as the theme. It had been an extremely dry two weeks here and our garden desperately needed water—we have a shallow well and can't do much sprinkling. On Saturday evening it had rained in a huge thunderstorm which broke the week of drought. So we all had feelings of experiencing the storm on many levels fresh in our minds. We read the Bible story of Moses striking the rock with a rod to bring out water at God's command and talked about that as the power of God responding to the people's need. Then we read a story of Jesus healing the man who had waited by the miraculous pool for years and talked a bit about God's power coming in surprising ways. I did a short paragraph from a book about water called The Eternal River *on the theme of the miracle of water. Then we took a stack of old magazines and each looked for water pictures that appealed to us in some way and each made a collage of them to share—talking about them after they were finished. Finally, we shared a goblet of wine —noticing the way water worked through grapes to create the drink which warms us and is a sign of sharing. I feel something about the miracle of water in nature and its workings came alive to us in that process. Because our Sunday readings focus on Bible stories usually, it also showed how God chose to work through nature. The aim of this weekly sharing is to nourish us all in some way. We work in activities (the picture cutting) and physical sharings, like the wine, which involve Jered. The Bible stories are read from a children's edition with pictures.*

Most of the rest of what we do is very informal. We hold hands before meals and share our thanks for what was good that day along with the meal. Awareness of nature, others, God, and spiritual power is something that we share as we go—when a question arises, when we're actually looking at something, when it seems natural.

WHAT OTHER PARENTS DO

These parents are applying the "mind games" discussed in chapter 3. More about meditation and prayer will be found in the next chapter. For many families these practices are an important part of a shared spiritual life.

One mother of an eight-and-a-half-year-old girl and a twelve-year-old boy says, "The children spend five or ten minutes each morning 'meditating.' They visualize themselves acting and reacting positively and with love first for that particular day—next, throughout their life. They send love and energy to grandparents and relatives and friends, especially focused on ones who are ill." Brought up Catholic, and married to a Catholic, this parent calls her religion now "universal—but that's an understatement." She does attend Roman Catholic services with the children to give them "a sense of order."

A mother of two sons ten and twelve years old says that her "spiritual daily life" consists of "living it. Talking about it when it seems appropriate. Kids learn more from example than talk. I do help the boys 'go inner'—call it fantasy trips or meditation."

For another family, spiritual daily life consists of "discussion of life and TV events; guided meditations on occasion." And for yet another, it is experienced "through answering questions honestly and openly, through reading spiritual literature aloud, through exposing our son to meditation and *satsang* [association with the wise] as well as allowing him access to any other religions and beliefs, via family, friends, etc."

We saw in chapter 3, and will again in chapter 7, the crucial importance of stimulating children's creative imagination. Rudolf Steiner called this "soul-milk." The mother of a four-year-old says:

I'm not very good at this yet. We are vegetarian and sometimes I try to explain why. Mainly what I do with [my daughter] now is try to allow her expression of her true self—through art, dance, exploring nature, and not imposing a great deal of restrictions. Sometimes I try to explain, but mostly I try to be a good example. I play down the materiality of Christmas with her and don't buy her a lot of presents, but others do and I don't stop that. She goes to group meditations with me if she wants to and sits quietly while we meditate, but knows she's not meditating. When I'm reading books to her or watching TV with her, I try to point out meaningless things that happen, or destructive, or kind and beautiful things.

Other parents emphasized the importance of awareness of nature. The mother of a five-and-a-half-year-old girl says:

I worry she is missing an identification with, or at least knowledge of, another level of consciousness, another kind of reality that our city existence really obscures. I think, in nature, it's easy to perceive this other awareness/level of knowing things. In today's urban society one almost needs an organization or at least someone to point out the possibility that something else exists, other than what we can immediately see, feel, and think about.

This mother, demonstrates the ambivalence many parents feel. Theoretically, in her advice to other parents, she expresses the thought that spiritual development will simply unfold:

Do only what you feel is best for yourselves and your child. If you feel religious, expose your child to it. If you don't, don't bother the child with it. Only tell the child what you honestly believe, and hopefully the child will develop a sense of his/her self and eventually a sense of others being like the self and therefore worthy of respect, understanding, and love. In time, from that sense of the inner being (of the self and others) will come an awareness of a higher level of existence which may be spiritual.

In her own life, she keeps thinking, "I should do something about formal moral, ethical, or religious instruction," and, in fact, is doing a kind of home Sunday school. "I read to my daughter— Bible stories, stories from the Talmud. We discuss the concept of God, the Ten Commandments, ethics, nature, being at one with it and with all of humanity. Occasionally, we celebrate a religious holiday, or the Sabbath, or watch a TV program on religion and discuss it."

Two more parents confess their own ambivalence:

In my day, we had Bible readings every single day in school. Today, when I hear a section of the Bible read, I know it by heart. I feel bad that my kids don't know these things. And yet I am embarrassed and feel it is dishonest of me to send them to a Sunday school where they would be taught such things. I want my kids to learn what I learned and to work through those things in the same way that I worked through them. But I know that this is impossible. They are themselves; and I have to be honest enough to be myself. I have to stand today for what I believe and where I am. I cannot pretend I am what my parents were, or what I was forty years ago.

When the children were young, I did worry. We made attempts at taking them to Sunday school—but, no doubt reflecting an ambivalence, they were not too excited about it. There's a corner of me that still feels guilty that only one of them got baptized. But more than guilt about that—there's a sense of sadness that there wasn't clarity in us to share with them—so it's evident that they are

in much the same confusion we were some twenty years ago.
("And the sins of the fathers . . .?") What we did do with conscious-
ness was to give them lots of exposure to the birth/growth/
decay/death cycle, and to promote their sense of wonder and awe
and playfulness and creativity. And to love them as wisely as we
could—with varying amounts of success. And to listen to their won-
derings and descriptions of experiences and questions and respond
as openly and honestly as possible.

Some families find their solution in the form of grandparents or
other relatives who can give children knowledge of a living tradition:

Tim has gone to church with grandparents. . . . He believes that
everybody has their own way of loving God and no one way is
better than any other.

I don't worry about organized religion. I think children may miss
holiday celebrations. Solution—they go with friends to church or
with grandmother to synagogue when they wish. We celebrate
some holidays.

I see the religious training as important in terms of exposing the
children to their culture. There are good stories and we share that
in reading and telling. [Our daughter's] Aunt Kate lives with us and
sometimes (three or four times a year) takes Amy to Mass with her.
She may want or need more exposure when older. I have given up
grace—but we hold hands and sometimes say a short blessing.

We are involved in Buddhism. The children learn about Christ-
mas, etc., at school and so I do what little I know about Hannukah
at home. Tara went to a Jewish Sunday school for a few months
when my father was visiting and loved it. She wants to go again but
I'm too lazy to drive her so it doesn't mean enough to me. I may do
so in the future.

For the previous generation of Jews, immigrant grandparents at
home counterbalanced the children's assimilation into the main-
stream culture. Contemporary Jewish parents are now often searching for Jewish roots for themselves as well as their children. A
mother writes: "I don't want to punish my children with my views
and my childhood. Just because I had a bad experience of religion,

I don't want my kids to have none. . . . We are learning Jewish customs together. It's a fun thing we can do together."

The issue of how children learn values and ethics is such an important one that I deal with it separately, in chapter 9. Briefly, both parents and educators emphasize the importance of open communication. Some parents' comments:

I don't feel my children are "missing" anything by not going to Sunday school. We give attention to the development of values through reading, conversations, experiences. . . .

I do try to point out mishaps as lessons rather than disasters and try to help them see that loving each other would solve their bickering easier than determining who was "wrong" or "right" (not too successfully).

Mainly, just try to share and communicate with your children those truths which their life's experience has shown them. You can always communicate with them according to their own levels of understanding and it's surprising how much they can grasp even at early ages. We have the opportunity as parents to not do the things that were done to us as children and to do those things we needed during our growth. Being what we believe, not saying one thing and doing another, will enable them to also be as they believe.

My friend Jane, after reading this part of the manuscript, suggested: "The emphasis on the importance of the home as an educational force in spiritual development might be enriched by discussing what we can learn/teach in homes where we do not go around practicing biblical virtues all the time, but rather squabble, bitch, etcetera."

I knew exactly what she meant. I remembered one day when I went for a tennis lesson shortly after reading *Whole Child, Whole Parent* by Polly Berrien Berends. Our daughter Amelia, then two-and-half, was with me. Every time I tried to hit the ball, she would run onto the tennis court. I wanted to squash her. I simply could not view the situation as one of "wholeness," as the book had recommended. Wholeness? I wanted one thing (to play tennis), and Amelia wanted another (to play with me).

I have only two suggestions, for myself and anyone else: to

accept and to take responsibility for what is, including our own negativity. Acceptance means observing without judging, without either indulging or suppressing the feeling. Amelia runs onto the tennis court; I notice my rage. Then I handle the situation as best I can (without squashing her). I also take responsibility for my part in creating the scene, and learn from that: i.e., next time, don't bring Amelia. My friend already accepts what she calls her "bitchiness" (in fact, she is not so terrible) and takes responsibility: at difficult times in her life she has sought help from a therapist who ran a parents' group.

The *est* training emphasizes that resistance creates persistence. Resisting negativity doesn't help. I know a woman who has been so actively nagging her young son to be less aggressive (Keep your voice down . . . Don't push . . . say "Good morning," and "I'm sorry") that she has one of the most aggressive kids I know—he's fighting back.

One parent answering the questionnaire wrote: "Being spiritual is *how* you do something—*how* you handle your negative states." Once we take responsibility for the fact that the negativity is *ours* (although it may be triggered by someone else's actions), we are in a position to handle it. This may be either appropriate action to change the situation, simply experiencing the feeling until it disappears if nothing can be said or done, or seeking love and guidance in meditation or prayer.

Repeated negative patterns, in which the same situation, the same anger, keeps coming up again and again, call for a deeper "meditation" on what's wrong here, and how we can change the pattern. One traditionally religious father wrote as a suggestion for other parents: "Get down to a serious commitment to yourself. You're not likely to do that in church, more likely by facing your evasions with highly competent professional help, preferably psychoanalysis."

A second group of parents say: *Don't* try to do a home Sunday school.

When it comes to raising a child spiritually, it's paradoxical—when you are least conscious, simply taking care of yourself, then things become whole. . . . Foster these things that are already there in the child. We talk about spiritual things as if it's something new —like "natural" foods. . . . Just be good people, trying to have a whole family.

Relax and let them experience themselves and you and be honest. We are all trying to spare our children the existential abyss which I know they'll have to go through—it's the only way.

I would not go about practicing a "spiritual daily life" as different from my daily life—period. How could one? I do believe quiet times are important for everyone and have tried very hard to provide the children with some privacy. This was very difficult with a large extroverted family of boys.

I worry they will miss ritual and appreciation of it. Community of others of similar beliefs and purposes. Familiarity with the biblical tradition. Others whose experiences will help validate their own. Solutions—I try to help the children see themselves as parts of a whole. Listen to them and trust I'll be led to guide as needed. Don't try to do a home Sunday school, but use all experiences as potential for growing awareness.

I think they miss out on some things I can't make up for, but I believe children chose their parents for what they need in this lifetime, and I assume that if my children needed a fundamentalist Baptist background or the ritual of the Episcopal church, they'd have been born into other families. What they can pick up from me is a sense of oneness of all life and a sense of God existing in all there is.

I believe my kids will someday be instrumental in spreading New Age consciousness, but that is not a trip I want to lay on them; they have to discover it for themselves.

In summary, whatever specific activities you choose to express your spirituality in the family, the most important theme seems to be that you are genuinely learning (or relearning) together, and expressing who you are.

One mother gave the following advice to other parents:

It is important to see religion as something to do with the chil-

dren—not to them, for them, or at them. It is helpful to get support in the search, since that is all that one is doing anyway. To pick out from the organized institutions what is useful; to feel that it is O.K. to be selective and not be excluded for that—I used to feel that one had to accept the whole thing or none of it.

A father writes:

Live in all interpersonal honesty and responsibility, insofar as you are able, at all times. Let them know they are loved and how difficult it is to love well.

And from the father of children ages one and three:

At the present time, I feel our older daughter already has spiritual understanding I may not have reached until I was much older than she is now. As a family, we often take time out to realize that all comes from God (planting, eating, traveling). She asks many questions which stimulate us all and I feel she already has as much real feeling of spiritual matters than I did after eight years of Catholic grade school. Relating to each other with love and understanding seems to be an incredible source of spiritual development and evolution.

CHAPTER 6

Meditation and Prayer: Changing Our Consciousness

Any meditation practice concerned with transcending ego is focused in the present moment. For this reason it is a very effective way to live. If you are completely aware of your present state of being and the situation around you, you cannot miss a thing. We may use various meditation techniques to facilitate this kind of awareness, but these techniques are simply a way of stepping out of ego. Technique is like a toy given to a child. When the child grows up, the toy is discarded. In the meantime technique is necessary in order to develop patience and to refrain from dreaming about the "spiritual experience."

Chögyam Trungpa, Rinpoche
Cutting Through Spiritual Materialism

Seventy-two percent of the parents answering the questionnaire either meditate or pray. Most forms of practice contain elements of both. In its form of listening and opening to grace or other communication, prayer begins to merge with the letting go of identification with the personal self taught in meditation practice.

When in 1978 the Gallup Organization asked a national sample of Americans whether they "ever pray to God," 98 percent of churchgoers said yes, and 74 percent pray once a day or more. Of the *unchurched,* 76 percent do pray, and 45 percent pray frequently.

What particularly impressed me was that no two respondents answering the questionnaire described the way they thought meditation and prayer changed their lives in exactly the same words. They were not simply repeating what they had read or been told; they were trying to communicate an experience. There *are* differences: Some refer to God, some don't. Though the concepts differ, like signposts on different roads they point in the same direction. Of the parents who now believe that meditation or prayer can change things, 36 percent did *not* believe that as a child. In this chapter, after examining the meaning of meditation and prayer to parents now, we will look at its meaning to children.

THE PARENTS' VIEW

One mother distinguished between meditation and prayer this way: "I meditate by being quiet within, settling all disturbing thoughts, setting aside. Tuning into awareness of everything around, the room or field, woods, and letting the light of that reality permeate my being. I also pray because I believe there is a universal compassionate source." She believes that prayer changes things by keeping one "in tune with the Creator. Strengthens one's spiritual soul and creates well-being and, of course, all kinds of miracles and blessings happen."

Claudio Naranjo, in *The Psychology of Meditation,* points out that the many techniques of meditation all lead to a way of being that may be called either self-emptying or centering. "It is the experience that in theistic formulations is expressed as conformity with

God's will and in alternative cognitive maps is expressed as a surrender to a Tao (Way) or Dharma (Law of the Universe)." Modern psychologists use the term Superconscious or Higher Self, referring to the expression of that Law within our own natures.

Parents reported:

I do Vipassana (mindfulness) meditation, * *and also at times meditate on or comtemplate those I love, the wonders and terrors of life, the quality of God. Prayer changes me. As my energies change in relationships, the relationships and others involved are changed (the we're-all-in-this-together phenomenon!).*

Now my meditation, though somewhat irregular, consists of sitting and trying to be "aware"—totally. Does it change things? Yes, because everything is vibrating energy and meditation and is an attempt to bring that vibration that we have control over into harmony with that of others, of the larger whole.

A woman who had been a Dominican nun from age twenty to thirty, and now has a six-year-old child, also combines meditation and prayer:

I have a process of centering my attitude with God or the deeper spiritual power in the universe—this is a matter of calling my attention back to that perspective many times a day. I give myself daily time for quiet meditation—mind silencing and centering. I do guided visualizations which are more a matter of personal growth than prayer. My husband and I share some Bible readings, reflections, and voiced prayer one evening a week. On Sundays, we have a family hour of readings and sharings.

I think prayer/meditation is an opening of the person (me) to spiritual reality and so creates an attitude that will take advantage of spiritual/real opportunities. Also, I believe in the power of God (higher power of Good) which can flow into me and around me when I have opened myself. That doesn't mean it won't rain on my picnic (it did rain) but that deeper exchanges which go beyond the importance of rain will happen as the spiritual power flows.

---

* A technique of Buddhist meditation in which the meditator simply observes thoughts and sensations as they come and go, rather than fixing the mind on a particular object of contemplation.

What of the 28 percent who do not meditate or pray? What is interesting is that over half mentioned the benefits that they thought these practices brought to others:

I believe that prayer and meditation is of great value to many people. The deeply felt convictions that I have, or attempt to realize, are not related to the organized concept of prayer as it is formulated.

Does prayer change things? No, if you mean physically move mountains, etc. But yes in the case of a person who is comforted by prayers and perceives changes being made by them.

The purpose of prayer is vague to me but I understand that many people are sure it changes things. I think if you want something badly enough, you'll get it. I think meditation is great for calming one and reassessing one's conditions and predicament. I don't take time to do it but have good memories of it when I was younger.

Several nonpracticers mentioned that meditation "can change an individual's perception, feelings."

All schools of meditation agree on the importance of retraining attention, to achieve a state of one-pointedness of mind. One of the two major ways of doing this is *concentration,* in which the mind focuses on a single mental object (which could be a sacred *sound* —a "mantra" or a Name of God—a mental *image,* such as a flower, or Jesus on the Cross, a *thought,* such as the idea of love, or a body *sensation,* such as the movement of the breath.) The other way is *mindfulness,* in which the mind observes its own flow of thoughts, feelings, and sensations, without interfering. Many methods combine these two.

The word "meditation" can stand either for the practices themselves—relaxation, centering, concentration, training of attention, etc.—or for the transcendent experience of unity to which they sometimes lead. In the religious traditions, Eastern and Western, the practices are considered simply preparation for reaching the higher states of consciousness: *dhyana,* * *samadhi,* † or communion

---

* *Dhyana:* prolonged absorption of the mind in the object of meditation.
† *Samadhi:* merging of the individual soul with the universal soul, or God.

with God. I will use the word "meditation" to refer to the practices, not to the goal. Many are grateful for the benefits of the practices themselves: self-acceptance and release of stress. People who do not "believe in God" are also nourished by this contact with their deepest self.

I meditate—deep relaxation, shutting off the left-brain tape recording, drifting—nightly before sleep, when agitated. . . . By turning off my life script I am open for energy around me. I am less tormented by my own tapes and can see other people for themselves, can hear conversations from a higher level (less ego of mine to hold me back). I feel more emotion, am able to give love freer and easier.

About five times a week, I begin meditation with acknowledgment of spirit and a request to be shown the next level of my development. I meditate for fifteen to twenty minutes, no set practice, sometimes watching breath, some mantra, some bare awareness, some visualization.

Does it change things? Yes. I believe my purpose is to fully manifest my spiritual essence. Meditation gives me the opportunity to remember that purpose and deepen the contact. I know it is my deepest self I pray to and I know my prayers are always answered in a way for my deepest good. It is when I lose this connection that I fall into negativity and lose my way. [As a child, this father did "not really" believe prayer changes things. "Praying that my grandmother wouldn't die. Praying that nothing bad would happen to my mother."]

In chapter 3, I gave an example of the meditations Deborah Rozman has used successfully with young children, as well as many of the nonreligious "centering" practices that have been adapted for secular schools. Rozman writes in *Meditation for Children*:

In meditation we learn to contact our inner wisdom by quieting our bodies, our feelings and our thoughts. It is only when we quiet these activities of our personality that go on most of the time and get them out of the way that our Real Self can surface. Then we become very clear, and in clarity the needed answers come. We may not know how these answers come or where they come from but we feel an inner sense of certainty about our Self. This is an extremely fulfilling experience and life takes on deeper meaning. We become more aware in whatever we do. Meditation . . . is very similar to "going into the silence" or to prayer which most religions teach.

One woman had a vivid memory of a time in childhood when the "needed answer" came:

I had been at my girlfriend's house and was headed home when I saw a group of older, meaner kids that I was really afraid of. I didn't know what to do and so I prayed and suddenly it flashed into my head that I could take the back way home, which I did. When I got home, I told my mother, whose reaction was "Wasn't that cute-silly of you to think that the answer came in response to prayer and not just because it was the obvious answer." The back way was the obvious answer, yet I was so scared I couldn't think of it. My mind was frozen. I remember standing there thinking, "Please God, help me, I'm afraid. I don't know what to do." And like a flash, the back way came into my mind.

Prolonged sitting meditation is not easy to do when young children are around. Here are three mothers with three different solutions:

I pray daily, quietly, throughout the day . . . asking guidance for myself and friends. I feel meditation is very important, but at this time I can't seem to incorporate it into my life. I am never alone! I know I will work it in there one of these days. . . . Does it change things? Yes, by making one more conscious and open for positive experiences to happen. By quieting the mind of distractions, one can move forward and make changes consciously.

I meditate. The frequency varies. I usually do it when the children have gone to sleep. I get myself "down" with mental sounds and stay there for about twenty minutes. Occasionally, also early in the morning before the children awaken.

A student of Bhagwan Shree Rajneesh says:

The meditations we do are cathartic or calming, and in today's crazy world the complex mind needs techniques of letting go of one's own craziness. I do the meditations whenever I feel I want or need it. On Sundays, I meditate with a group of people, and we usually do the "chaotic-dynamic" meditation . . . these are merely techniques that raise energy and eliminate tension so that a meditative state can occur. My daughter (age five) observes these group meditations. Nothing is forced on her. She is on her own path. [Does it change things?] The tensions and pressures of today are constantly pulling awareness to the periphery. These techniques are designed to bring awareness to the center.

For people who are interested in learning secular meditation, I recommend two books. *How to Meditate* by Lawrence LeShan, Ph.D., is a small paperback subtitled, "A Guide to Self-Discovery." Patricia Carrington, Ph.D., a psychologist, has written *Freedom in Meditation* and also has cassette tapes. The best introduction to Vipassana meditation is an inspiring book by Joseph Goldstein called *The Experience of Insight.*

PARENTHOOD AS A SPIRITUAL PATH

Different people, according to their temperament, gravitate toward one of the three major spiritual paths: the Way of Action, the Way of the Heart, or the Way of Knowledge. The meditative path of action involves total concentration on the task at hand, presence in the moment. This is the Way of artists and athletes, the practitioners of Aikido, T'ai Chi, Karate, Zen archery, or flower arrangement. It is also the Way of many parents of small children. Sweeping the house (or the monastery) can be a spiritual discipline. One parent says, "Meditation is awareness, and I try to do it all the time. Whatever you do, you do with awareness."

As Joseph Goldstein, a Western teacher of Buddhist Vipassana or Insight Meditation, says, "That's what our whole practice is: being totally in the moment . . . not seeking for solutions by wanting a certain state or having a certain kind of thought or conceptual understanding, but to be totally experiencing the process in the moment."

In the *Bhagavad Gita,** the Lord Krishna tells Arjuna:
I have already told you that, in this world, aspirants may find enlightenment by two different paths. For the contemplative is the path of knowledge; for the active is the path of selfless action. . . . you must perform every action sacramentally, and be free from all attachment to results. . . . Do your duty, always, but without attachment. . . . Desire for the fruits of work must never be your motive in working. Never give way to laziness, either. Perform every action with your heart fixed on the Lord.

A Christian expression of this Way is to invest every small work with infinite worth through an undivided attention to, and acceptance of, these actions as God's willing service.

By its nature, parenthood is a form of Karma Yoga—the path of devoted, selfless action. All of us are going to "lose" our children when they grow up and begin to lead their own lives. Parents who are overattached to the "fruits" of the endless duties of child care —who want their child to fulfill their own ambitions, to be rich or famous, or even to keep them from loneliness—are in trouble. Not only are they bound to be disappointed, but their desire to have the child be a certain way prevents them from giving the unconditional love that children need. In Werner Erhard's words, love is "giving people the space to be exactly who they are and who they are not."

The selfless service of Karma Yoga is also part of the Way of the Heart. In the *Bhagavad Gita,* this means serving all beings as manifestations of God. In Christian terms, this is loving and serving one's neighbor as oneself out of love for the One. In Judaism, the *Ethics of the Fathers* says the universe is based on three foundations: Torah or divine law, service, and deeds of lovingkindness.

Compassion can be the natural outcome of meditative experience, or a meditation in itself. Joseph Goldstein says:
There is a specific practice which the Buddha taught to make these states of mind a powerful force in our lives. It's called "metta bhavana" or cultivation of loving kindness. . . . It strengthens the ability to see without judging, and helps us

---

* A Hindu epic, part of the *Mahabharata,* a primary source of Indian philosophical thought. The *Bhagavad Gita* is in the form of a dialogue between the warrior Arjuna and his charioteer, the avatar Krishna (a divine incarnation).

avoid the very common tendency in spiritual practice to con-
demn who we are and seek in a grasping way to be someone
else. All along the way you see that the means and the end are
the same. To reach an end of peace and balanced awareness
and love we work on expressing these factors in each moment.

A beautiful book called *Whole Child, Whole Parent* by Polly
Berrien Berends (subtitled "A Spiritual and Practical Guide to the
First Four Years of Parenthood") is intended "to show the relevance of the great mystical teachings to the practical experience of
child-rearing and, at the same time, to bring to light the far-reaching
spiritual significance of even the meanest momentary details of our
experience as parents." She recommends specific products—toys,
books, equipment—and specific child-rearing techniques, always
based on the effort "to discover the underlying principle at issue.
Truth is either supremely practical or it isn't truth. It is only when
we see how truth is relevant, how it applies to or is revealed in our
most mundane experiences, that any kind of realization can be said
to have taken place. Sometimes it is our practical problems that
drive us toward truth—when all else fails." This book is one of my
favorite presents for new mothers.

PRAYER AS A
WAY OF THE HEART

The mystical Way of the Heart—Bhakti Yoga in the Hindu
tradition, but practiced by Christians and Jews as well—is constant
remembrance of God, unceasing meditation on His Name, with
love and devotion. In the Hindu tradition, Krishna is a manifestation
or incarnation of God the Unmanifest. In the *Bhagavad Gita,* Arjuna
asks Krishna: "Some worship you with steadfast love. Others worship God the unmanifest and changeless. Which kind of devotee
has the greater understanding of Yoga?" Krishna answers:

Those whose minds are fixed on Me in steadfast love, wor-
shipping Me with absolute faith. As for those others . . . they
also will certainly come to Me. But the devotees of the un-

*manifest have a harder task, because the unmanifest is very
difficult for embodied souls to realize . . .
If you cannot become absorbed in Me, then try to reach Me
by repeated concentration. If you lack the strength to concentrate, then devote yourself to works which will please Me. For,
by working for My sake only, you will achieve perfection.*

Betsy Caprio is a Catholic educator who brings insights and
experiential exercises from the human potential movement to junior
high school students in her book *Experiments in Prayer*. After quot-
ing the traditional catechism definition of prayer as "the raising of
the heart and mind to God," she adds her own: "Prayer is contact
with God, which may come through our attempts at communication
with him and/or his communication with us. In order to receive
God's communications, we must be receptive, aware, tuned in,
quieted"—that is, in a meditative mood.

She points out that

*prayer is a form of nonordinary consciousness when you're
praying in a way that takes you out of yourself. The Jesus
people know this. They talk about "getting high on God" or
"tripping out with the Lord." . . . We might ask whether so
many young Americans would now be fascinated by (and following) the religions of the East had they been introduced to
the rich contemplative heritage of Christianity during their own
religious educations. How many of these young people know
that the "cosmic consciousness" which makes Hinduism and
Buddhism (as well as drugs and the occult) so attractive is also
the result of Christian prayer?*

Many practices (such as much "prayer" in Christian churches,
or the telling of rosary beads) which began as a means of altering
awareness often become part of a ritual, the original purpose forgotten. The desert fathers meditated with an oral or silent repetition
of a single phrase from the Scriptures—not unlike the mantras of
Eastern tradition.

Strong within the Eastern Orthodox tradition is the Jesus
Prayer, or Prayer of the Heart, which follows Paul's injunction in 1
Thessalonians 5:17 to "pray without ceasing."

In *The Way of the Pilgrim,* the Pilgrim's teacher instructs: "Sit down alone and in silence. Lower your head, shut your eyes, breathe out gently and imagine yourself looking into your own heart. Carry your mind, i.e., your thoughts, from your head to your heart. As you breathe out, say 'Lord Jesus Christ, have mercy on me.' Say it moving your lips gently, or simply say it in your mind. Try to put all other thoughts aside. Be calm, be patient, and repeat the process very frequently." In time, the Pilgrim tells us, "it seemed as though my heart in its ordinary beating began to say the words of the Prayer within at each beat. . . . I simply listened carefully to what my heart was saying . . . doing this, I am filled with joy!"

Hasidism, the mystical sect of Judaism, has a similar Way of the Heart. Its founder, the Baal Shem-Tov (Master of the Good Name), said: "When I weld my spirit to God, I let my mouth say what it will, for then all my words are bound to their root in heaven." His disciple, the Great Maggid, once said, "I shall teach you the best way to say Torah. You must cease to be aware of yourselves. You must be nothing but an ear which hears what the universe of the word is constantly saying within you. The moment you start hearing what you yourself are saying, you must stop."

HOW PRAYER CHANGES LIVES

William James, describing the characteristics of the religious life, includes the belief that "prayer or inner communion with the spirit (of the 'higher universe')—be that spirit called 'God' or 'law'—is a process wherein work is really done, and spiritual energy flows in and produces effects, psychological or material, within the phenomenal world."

Some of the parents who responded to the questionnaire emphasized the psychological changes resulting from changes in thought or belief:

As a child, I thought prayers were a real waste of time and just plain stupid. Now I do Yoga every day in the relax position; I meditate on a warm spot in the sun with warm green water lapping along a soft white sandy beach. . . . I think it is the belief in the prayer and/or meditation that changes things—sort of the "leap of faith" idea. You must leap in order to have change.

I get in touch with my inner self, sometimes in waking, sometimes in dream states which I remember. I also do affirmations . . . affirmations change things (can be called prayer, perhaps) because beliefs create reality. To change the belief changes the reality. This is what I believe, anyway.

As a child I sometimes believed prayer changes things. Some prayers seemed answered, some didn't. Couldn't really trust. Now I see it changes me—and that changes my world and how I perceive it. Also—thought has power to create.

I believe that a miracle is no less a miracle if it happens through human instrumentation.

Two systems teaching a form of Christian meditation/prayer caused a powerful transformation in the lives of some parents. The more traditional is described in a book by William R. Parker and Elaine St. Johns called *Prayer Can Change Your Life.* Parker says:

In all my experience I have met no one individual who did not believe in a "power greater than myself." I have had them say, "I do not believe in God—I believe in 'nature' or 'Universal Law' or 'Creative Intelligence.' And that is all right, too. Carl Jung has said, "Whether you call the principle of existence 'God,' 'matter,' 'energy,' or anything else you like, you have created nothing; you have simply changed a symbol."

Parker's system rests on four points: prayer that is regular (with training in concentration and centering); positive (including affirmations of the God of Love within us as the healing and directing power of our lives); an act of surrender (we invite God's power to fill the void our surrender has created); and receptive ("we listen, wait for a sense of victory, a feeling of Presence, that tells us 'I am here. All is well.' ").

One parent invented her own similar system:

I don't meditate. I only pray when things look very, very bad or seem completely outside of my control. Most of the time I just talk to my "God," tell Him or Her what I'm doing, why I'm doing it, ask for advice or guidance. Sometimes when I can't seem to decide which is best I ask for a nudge in one direction or another. Sometimes when life is too easy, I ask for a challenge. Sometimes when it's too hard, I ask for a break. Sometimes I get mad and say, "Thanks a lot! That kind of help I can do without!" or simply "F—— You!" But fortunately he-she-it is very understanding and flows with me. I feel I am in ongoing conversation with my "God" (hard to give it that name but shall for simplicity's sake).

Parents also mentioned A Course in Miracles, a system which includes a "workbook" with a series of spiritual exercises, one for each day, which can be done anywhere and do not require much time. The aim is gradually to train the mind to a new mode of perception, thinking, and feeling which leads to a continuing experience of God's love, peace, joy, and forgiveness. A mother of three children who follows it says, "Its techniques are precise, systematic, and yet gentle and allow much freedom. I meditate every day. . . . When we use prayer or meditation, God helps us to experience love, share that love, and thereby feel joyful and alive. Here is heaven, right here, right now." This is how she answers the question: "How would you go about practicing a spiritual daily life?" "Through the application of love and forgiveness and the asking for spiritual guidance at all times. If I am not sure of what to do, I will stop, ask quietly for guidance, and give my child the answer I received. At the same time, I ask the child to do the same thing. It is wonderfully miraculous that most times our answers are the same." She is in the process of adapting the Course in Miracles for use with children. Another person doing that is Dr. Gerald Jampolsky, a physician who has created "miracles" with groups of children who have cancer. In some cases this takes the form of actual remission of the disease, but even in cases where the disease progresses, the radiance of these children in their transcendence of suffering and their acceptance of death has been an inspiration to adults as well.

CHILDREN'S PRAYERS

We have seen that, in most cases, people's present understanding of meditation and prayer bears little relationship to the requests they called "prayer" as children:

Never was prayer a form of meditation in the way I see it now. It was instead something to memorize, so that an entire chorus of soft voices would lift our symphonic consciousness. The "Lord's Prayer" stays in my head: "Give us this day our jelly bread," and "Deliver us some evil" as I originally misinterpreted it. . . . Now I sometimes meditate. When I need to find some strength, I deepen myself into a half-sleep trance based on Womancraft and ask my "guides" what I need to know.

I remember praying for good health in family, and the football team to win. Now I meditate or pray once in awhile. . . . I believe it changes things by connecting the conscious mind to the subconscious and the superconscious minds.

Another parent says that as a child he "was never sure":

I would thank God (I didn't want to ignore him if he did exist) but was afraid to ask for much. . . . [I now believe that meditation changes things] by changing the person. I meditate by simple, plain sitting, just being what is.

Johanna Klink points out:

In constantly repeated rites a child feels safe. He loses an inner balance when the regularity is interrupted. Evening prayers can be regarded as a protection against the darkness, the night, and loneliness, and can even be experienced as a magical necessity. . . . But prayers of thanksgiving are almost entirely swamped by the petitions. We are so used to this emphasis [on petitions] in prayer that we do not realize that we can arouse too many expectations in children which cannot be fulfilled, or at least not by God. No one who teaches a child to ask for things in prayer can expect the child to pray for the Kingdom of God on his own accord. He asks for a new scooter, a baby sister, and for the ice cream to come.

This matches the memories of parents answering the questionnaire:

I remember begging for something I wanted and promising to do anything to get it."

I did believe that prayer changed things, though the first time I really tested it seriously was when my mother was very ill and I prayed for her to get better soon. After being disappointed, I deliberately tested again—to find something I had lost. Being disappointed again, I was told that God did not appreciate being tested. I wondered how, if God were so exalted, omnipotent, the creator of all things, all-knowing, etc., mere people could understand him enough to tell me he didn't like being tested!

As a very young child I wanted prayer to be able to change things, but as it didn't, I soon grew disillusioned and stopped hoping.

Researchers have attempted to chart the "natural development" of children's understanding of prayer. I will cite one study at length, so that you can ask *your* children these questions, if you want another window onto their inner life.

The researchers, Diane Long, David Elkind, and Bernard Spilka, interviewed 160 elementary school children ages five to twelve. When I posed their questions to our children, Amelia, age four and a half, and Eve, age six and a half, I had some surprises. I had never taught Amelia or Eve any formal prayers. At the dining table we simply hold hands in silence. They have been in a synagogue, heard grownups say blessings, and, of course, they watch television. What I found is that in their own way, they do pray. Here are the questions, followed by Amelia's and Eve's responses:

1. *Do you pray? Do all boys and girls in the world pray?*

A: Yes, because God wants us to pray for his religions and we pray in synagogues.

Yes, but some don't like to pray and they don't go to synagogues to pray. Some Christians don't and some Jews don't.

E: Yes.

Yes.

2. *Do dogs and cats pray?*
A: No, because they aren't like people. Only trained dogs and cats do because their masters train them.
E: Yes, but in a different kind of way. They have their own way that's a secret.
3. *What is a prayer?*
A: I don't know.
E: It's like a letter that you send in the mail but the mail is in the air and you send it up to God or a goddess or something.
4. *Can you pray for more than one thing?*
A: Yes, because the religion isn't just one thing, it's a lot of things all in one; it's houses, trees, bushes, it's the whole wide world, even clouds and sky and sun.
E. Yes.
5. *What must you do if your prayer is answered?*
A: I don't know.
E: Just send another prayer if you want.
6. *What if your prayer is not answered?*
A: I don't know.
E: You can try again sending another prayer or you don't have to say any prayer.

To find out about the content of children's prayers and the feelings and fantasies associated with them, the researchers asked the children to complete these sentences:

7. *I usually pray when . . .*
A: When I'm sleeping and when I'm holding hands at the dining room table and I pray to God for him to bring jellybeans down on my head. . . .
E: When I'm at the table holding hands.
8. *Sometimes I pray for . . .*
A: My Mommy or Poppy for seagulls and everything . . . for God and sun and sky and everything. . . .
E: Sometimes I pray for my Mommy and my Poppy and the kitten and myself and my friends so I can go to their houses.
9. *When I pray I feel . . .*
A: Like jellybeans are coming down with candy and a party hat.

E: (Refused to answer.)

10. *When I see someone praying I . . .*

A: Start to pray.

E: Watch it so that if it's a different way to pray I'll know it.

11. *Where do prayers come from and where do prayers go?*

A: Prayers come from God and they are way up in the sky.

E: Prayers come from God 'cause if you send a prayer God might answer it and send it back to you. [I asked, "Has God ever sent it back to you?"] Sort of.

The researchers concluded that they had found three main developmental stages:

Age 5–7   Little comprehension of the term "prayer."

Age 7–9   Knew what prayer meant but it was a routine form, an external activity associated with fixed times: bedtime, church, meals, rather than personal and internal. Unclear about whether dogs and cats could pray.

Age 9–12   Prayer emerged as a private conversation with God involving things not talked about with other people —the older children prayed when they were worried, upset, lonely, or troubled. Altruistic desires appear.

Long, Elkind, and Spilka belong to the group of cognitive researchers I will discuss in chapter 7. Their main interest is in the growth of abstract reasoning. I think that when applied to prayer, this focus on the head, excluding the heart, can lead to false conclusions. Although they point out quite correctly that children's thinking and concepts (such as their "concept" of prayer) become more abstract as they mature, they dismiss the poetic earlier responses as "essentially meaningless." Their conclusion that the younger children have "little real comprehension" applies only if you think of prayer as synonymous with logical thought, and not as an experience.

A few months after I asked Eve and Amelia these questions, they started Sunday school. I was sitting in the classroom when the teacher asked, "Can anyone here tell me what a prayer is?" There was dead silence. Astonished, I asked a friend of mine who is a teacher why the kids said nothing, when I knew they were full of thoughts on the subject. "That's easy," she said. "The kids know that the teacher is looking for the right answer and isn't interested in what *they* think."

You may be wondering, "Should I teach my children to pray?" The chances are that if you don't, they will invent it for themselves, as Amelia did. One twelve-year-old who answered the questionnaire wrote, "When I was eleven, there was a coat rack in the storage room of my school that I thought was sacred. I used to pray to it, because I had no god or religion and I had been seeing 'Mork and Mindy.' " Teaching *petitionary* prayer, however—asking for jellybeans or sunny days or even good health—leads to disillusionment.

On the other hand, do not underestimate children's capacity for real religious experience. They can learn, if they are not already doing it, to alter their consciousness, to ask for and receive guidance. They are open to other realities.

Anna Mow, a Protestant religious educator, tells a story about a mother visiting her nine-year-old boy at camp. They had had no religious experience together at home. The boy said to her, "Oh, mother, the most wonderful thing has happened to me here. I've learned to pray. Come on, I want to show you our prayer room. It's in a cave on the mountainside." He took her up the mountain path. When they reached the cave door, the flag was up and the boy explained, "We can't go in now, someone else is there. It's so quiet in there. I know now about God."

PART THREE:

What the Research Shows and How to Use It

CHAPTER 7

Stages of Children's Spiritual Development: The Rationalist and Transpersonal Theories

What is the work of works for man if not to establish, in and by each one of us, an absolutely original centre in which the universe reflects itself in a unique and inimitable way? And those centres are our very selves and personalities.

Teilhard de Chardin
The Phenomenon of Man

One parent wrote: "I would like to know what goes on in kids' heads." Another said, "It would be really helpful to have a clearer sense of psychological development in relation to the spiritual life."

Before I began this book, I had searched the child-development literature for a summary of what psychologists had to say that was relevant to spiritual development. When I couldn't find any, I decided to write it myself. This chapter is the summary that I was looking for.

What I did find were two main groups of theories. All have in common an outline of the stages of child development, but value these stages as differently as people who maintain we are born with original sin versus those who believe in original innocence. The "rationalist" group (Piaget and Freud among them) see us as born ignorant, growing in understanding only as the brain and body mature. The early stages have no value in themselves, but are necessary way stations to be left behind as we reach the goal of "maturity." There is only one acceptable adult construction of reality. For Freud, religion was a wish-fulfilling illusion; for Piaget and his followers, a set of abstract concepts to be grasped only by the adult mind.

The second group values the early stages, when children are in touch with the living, interconnected web of the cosmos. For this group, which I have called "transpersonal," each stage of childhood develops faculties that we later integrate to reach our full spiritual potential. Development of the personality—intellect, body, feelings, intuition, and will—the end point of Piaget's and Freud's schemes, is for transpersonal psychologists only a midpoint on the road to higher consciousness.

Both groups have something to offer as we attempt to understand "what goes on in kids' heads," the better to understand and nurture their spiritual life.

RATIONALIST THEORIES: HOW CAN I UNDERSTAND WHAT GOES ON IN KIDS' HEADS?

Jean Piaget is the Swiss researcher who pioneered the use of the semiclinical interview—that is, asking children questions in order to find out how their minds work. Although often called a psychologist, he refers to himself as a "genetic epistemologist." That is, he is interested in how we (adults, too) construct our views of the nature of reality. He is interested above all in the development of "intelligence," which he defines as the ability to cope with the changing world through continuous organization and reorganization of experience. Piaget and his followers are called "cognitive" psychologists because they study cognitive abilities: reasoning, perceiving, remembering, believing. For Piaget, cognitive development is the pinnacle of human development. He says nothing about love. He views emotional behavior as dependent on the ability to think, communicate, and understand.

In *The Construction of Reality in the Child*, Piaget examines the development of concepts of cause and effect, time and space, in the child from birth to two. He has called this the *sensorimotor* period, because in this stage the child knows by means of motor activity and the senses—by touching, seeing, and hearing.

Early in this stage a child behaves as if an object (or person) is gone if it is hidden from sight. By the end of the stage the children have learned that the object or person is still there but only hidden; they can keep the "idea" of mother in their mind even when she has left the room. All this learning is a continuous process of what Piaget calls "assimilation" of reality to preexisting mental structures, and "accommodation" or change in our mental structures as reality gives us new information, and as new mental capacities emerge. For example, if we think the world is flat, but we are able to sail around it without falling off, we may "accommodate" our concept of the earth to this new information. Or we may "assimilate" the new information and say that we simply didn't sail far enough.

Notice that while Piaget suggests that the goal of the developing child's thought should be to separate "objective" from "subjective" reality, he himself supplies the theory that confirms what many scientists now say: that we always construct our own "reality." "Reality" can never be fully objective because we assimilate the news from the observed world to preexisting structures in our mind, and often reject what doesn't fit (for example, psychic experiences).

In the *preoperational* stage, from ages two to six, children begin to use language and attempt to generalize. Their "logic," as we will see, is very different from an adult's. Piaget called it symbolic, intuitive, or prelogical thought. Freud called the earliest mode of thought "primary process," the language of the unconscious.

In the stage of *concrete operations,* from age six to eleven or twelve, children are able to perform mental operations, "an action performed in the mind," provided they are thinking about something that can be touched or seen—concrete situations, actions, and sensory data. They can sort these data into systematic classes, and are interested in "the rules of the game." This is the age of the elementary-school child.

The stage of *formal operations,* the end point of cognitive development, starts around age eleven. Now the child can use abstract concepts and "think about thinking," and adult reasoning begins.

To parents who are interested in learning more about how a young child thinks, and how they use play and imitation to learn about the world, I recommend *A Piaget Primer* by Dorothy G. Singer and Tracey A. Revenson. The book covers not only language, thought, judgment, and reasoning, but also Piaget's later work on space, time, and number.

Piaget showed that for children, the universe is simultaneously alive and manufactured. Their world-view has correspondences with that of the mystic (and the nuclear physicist). The child does not yet separate "spirit" from matter. Objects have consciousness; the world is alive. Thought, however, is material; names adhere to "things" and are part of them. The child's lack of dualism between inner and outer, self and universe, differs from the mystic's in its "egocentric" emphasis on the primary role of human beings in creating nature. Piaget calls this "artificialism." Seeds are made in factories; the sun was lighted by a match. Things do not simply exist; they were created for our use.

Here are some of Piaget's questions from *The Child's Conception of the World* which you may enjoy asking your children (age three to twelve). Their replies give a window into their reality, their ideas about life, thought, consciousness and the way the world is. The children mostly like answering these questions; they do not worry about "proof" since they believe theirs is the only possible point of view. Although Piaget disregarded what he called "romancing"—the spur-of-the-moment myth-making children do for sheer fun—these poetic responses can be as interesting as more deeply held "scientific" convictions.

Piaget's Questions

Do you know what it means to think of something? [*Most children say yes.*] *Then think of your house. . . . What is it that you think with? . . . Supposing it were possible to open a person's head without hurting them, could you see a thought or touch it with the finger? . . . Does thought have strength?*

You know what a dream is? You dream sometimes at night? Then tell me where dreams come from . . .

Point to a few objects and ask "What is the name of that . . . and of that?" Then ask "What is a name? . . . How did names begin? How did the sun get its name? . . . Where are the names? . . . Do things know their names? Does the sun know its name? . . . Do the clouds know they are called clouds or not? . . . Has the sun always had its name, or was it first without a name and did it only get its name afterward?"

The "stages" into which Piaget classified children's answers can be found in *The Child's Conception of the World.* He used these questions on thought, dreams, and names to determine at what age the child distinguishes thought from "air" and "voice," words and names from the things themselves, and situates dreams in the head. None of these distinctions are achieved in his study before the age of nine or ten, and many not before eleven or twelve.

Here are Piaget's questions to uncover "animism," the child's tendency to attribute consciousness or life to what we call "things":

If I were to prick you with a pin, would you feel it? . . . If I were to prick the table, would the table feel it? Stones . . . flowers . . . metal . . . water . . . sun . . . moon . . . clouds? [*Ask "why" after each answer to see if the child replies arbitrarily or in accordance with a system.*]

Do you know what it is to be alive? Are —— alive? (Name objects—stars, bicycles, tables, anything.)

I asked our children these questions on consciousness. When asked if the table could feel a pin prick, Amelia, age four and a half, said "The table doesn't have a mind, so it can't think like people can. The table does not have skin and bones and blood so it cannot feel like people can so it cannot be dead." (Can the sun feel it?) "No, the sun is God and God does not feel any pain." (Do clouds feel anything?) "Yes, they feel the sun warming them up." (What does it mean to be alive?) "When something moves, that means it's alive—water's alive and people and animals, but rocks aren't. Houses that move in a hurricane aren't alive because the wind pushes them."

Piaget says that before age six or seven, the child considers all things to be conscious. From seven to nine, things that move are conscious: sun and bicycle, yes; table, no. From nine to eleven or twelve, things that move of their own accord are conscious: the sun and winds, yes; bicycles, no. After eleven or twelve, consciousness is restricted to the animal world. Amelia fits his stages, but not the age grouping.

Amelia's sister, Eve, age six and a half, gave these answers: (If I were to prick you with a pin, would you feel it?) "Yes, I would feel it because we have nerves—plants don't have nerves." (Could the sun feel it?) "Yes and no. God made the sun, and God is part of the sun and he can feel anything, even the air." (Does God have nerves?) "Yes." (What is a living thing?) "A living thing is something God creates that moves." (Is a bicycle alive?) "Sort of, because a bicycle drives you around and when you turn the wheel it lets you do it—it's dead when it's broken."

"Participation" is Piaget's word for the relation "which primitive thought believes to exist" between two beings or phenomena which, though disconnected in space, and without "intelligible causal connection," are still felt to have a direct influence on each other. This "primitive thought" reminds us of the quantum energy field of the physicist, with its "nonlocal" connections, the "general field of awareness" of the psychic researcher, or Jung's "synchronicity." All children attempt to use "participation" magically, to modify ordinary reality.

You can ask your children, "How did the sun begin? The moon? Clouds . . . rivers . . . mountains . . . stones?" if they haven't asked you first. Children are very interested in the origins of things. Up until the age of seven, according to Piaget, they give credit for origins to human agency (or divine, which Piaget sees as the same thing in the child's mind—a big person in the sky). His name for this is "artificialism." From age seven to ten, he found they said the origin is half natural, half artificial. After eleven, human activity has nothing to do with it.

Some critics objected that the child's conceptions of the origins of things might be biased by what s/he learned from religious training. Piaget denies this. He insists that the tendency to participations, animism, and artificialism come first. The first spontaneous questions a child asks are often "Who made the . . . ?" in which the whole idea of *somebody making* demonstrates artificialism.

Piaget says, "The child's real religion, at any rate during the first years, is quite definitely anything but the over-elaborated religion with which he is plied. . . ." Even where we can trace the influences of religious teaching, we see that it is distorted by the child, assimilated to the child's ideas.

A delightful example of this—as well as of typical changeable responses of an eight-and-a-half-year-old to questions on life, names, participation, and artificialism—comes from one of Piaget's little subjects, GAVA (the first four letters of the subjects last name), who said the sun is alive because "it keeps coming back." Notice how the questioner repeats questions in different forms to test whether GAVA's answer represents a deeply felt conviction, or a "romancing" reply:

Q: Does the sun know when the weather is fine?

G: Yes, because it can see it.

Q: Has it eyes?

G: Of course! When it gets up it looks to see if it is bad weather and if it is it goes off somewhere else where it's fine. |animism|

Q: Does it know that it's called the sun?

G: Yes, it knows that we like it. It is very nice of it to make us warm. |participation|

Q: Does it know its name?

G: I don't know. But sometimes it must hear us talking and then it will hear names and then it will know.

Q: When your Daddy was little was there a sun then?

G: Yes, because the sun was born before people so that people would be able to live.

Q: How did it start?

G: It was made in Heaven. It was a person who died and then went to Heaven. In Sunday school he is called God. [artificialism]

Q: Where did this person come from?

G: From inside the earth.

Q: Where from?

G: I don't know how he was made.

Q: How did that make the sun?

G: The person was very red and that made the light. Even in the morning, before the sun is out it is light all the same. . . .

Q: What is the sun made of?

G: It's a big red ball.

Q: Made of what?

G: Of cloud. I don't know.

Q: Did it start a long time ago?

G: Since there have been people.

Q: Not before?

G: No, because there wouldn't have been anything to light.

Q: Did it start at the same time as people or after?

G: It started as soon as there were little children.

Q: Why?

G: So that children should have the fresh air.

Q: If you were to speak to the sun, would it hear?

G: Yes, when you say your prayers.

Q: Do you say your prayers to it?

G: Yes.

Q: Who told you to do that?

G: At Sunday school I was always told to say my prayers to it.

According to Francis Buckley, in *Children and God,* contemporary Catholic theologians study the findings of developmental psychologists such as Piaget and Gesell to help them decide when a child is capable of committing sin. They have concluded that a child can probably commit *venial* sin around age 7 (the age of reason by church law) but that it is certain that most children cannot commit *mortal* sins before 10 years of age.

A child may receive communion before s/he is capable of committing sin, and before perfect knowledge of matters of faith. What matters is the "discernment" to distinguish the Eucharistic bread from ordinary and bodily bread, and to approach the altar with devotion. This was considered possible around the seventh year.

The accompanying table diagrams Piaget's stages and five other stage-developmental theories we will examine. Notice the total agreement on the *ages* within each stage, although the interests of each author differs wildly! Stages blend into one another: the age given for the change from one to the next is always approximate.

RONALD GOLDMAN
AND CHILDREN'S IDEAS
ABOUT GOD

Religious educators were quick to adopt Piaget's theories and research methods in order to study the process by which children acquire their religious beliefs, their understanding of Bible stories, their idea of God, and so on. They are concerned with redesigning Sunday school curricula to fit the stages of cognitive development.

In chapter 6, "Meditation and Prayer: Changing Our Consciousness," we saw the questions Long, Elkind and Spilka asked children about prayer. Ronald Goldman, an educator from the Church of England, showed children a picture of a child kneeling down beside a bed, and asked them: "What is the picture or idea of God the child in the picture has when he is praying?" Here are some typical answers:

A six-year-old: "He wears a long dress, long hair, and sometimes he don't have no shoes on him."

A ten-year-old: "He'd have little children sitting on his knee. He'd be a kind man with a beard like Jesus did, and clothes like Jesus."

At about eleven, there is a move from human to superhuman emphasis: "A man with a beard, an old kind gentleman, dressed in a gown. He'd be standing in the clouds, with lots of glory around." Beginning at about twelve, God is seen as a shadow, a cloud, a flame, a dove, or a bright piercing light.

CHILDREN'S DEVELOPMENTAL STAGES (TO ADOLESCENCE)*

Age	Piaget (Cognitive)	Goldman (Religious Understanding)	Harms (Symbols of God)	Catholic Church	Freud (Psychosexual)	Steiner (Spiritual)	Pearce ("The Biological Plan")
0	sensorimotor				oral (0–1½)	development of the physical self (the spirit incarnates)	0–7: body-earth knowing: 0–1: structure knowledge of mother
2	preoperational	prereligious	fairy-tale image		anal (1½–3)		1–3 or 4: structure knowledge of world (earth) with mother as matrix
					phallic or Oedipal (3–6)		
6							3–7: slow birth of individuality
7	concrete operations	sub-religious	realistic	(7+) Venial sin possible Age of Reason	latency (6–11)	the "change of teeth" predominance of the soul (art and imagination: the aesthetic, feeling self) (7–14)	social self level: structuring a knowledge of personal power through physical interaction with the world: earth as matrix
11							
12	formal operations	personal religious thought	individualistic	(10+) Mortal sin possible	genital (reworking of Oedipal themes leading to mature sexuality)	Predominance of the spirit (abstract thought)	primary process level: developing pure "mind-brain interactions" (abstract thinking) with Self (mind-brain and body) as matrix

*For adult development, see part four: Adolescence and After.

Goldman also told children the story of Moses and the burning bush, and then asked, "Supposing Moses had got over his fear and looked at God. What do you think he would have seen?" A girl, twelve years and eight months old, answered: "Moses could have seen a man like himself. It says in the Bible, God made man in his own image. Or a fierce animal. God can take the shape of anything he wants. Or it could be a dove, the sign of the holy spirit, to show the holy spirit is gentle."

"Older and more able" pupils tended to reject a visualized concept. God becomes an "idea of love."

In *Readiness for Religion*, Ronald Goldman offers his practical suggestions, based on cognitive research, to counter "the ineffectiveness of Christian religious teaching in schools." He calls the period from age two to seven *pre-religious* (comparable to Piaget's preoperational period), noting that children of this age have an "obvious interest in religion . . . all part of the fascinating world of adult behavior, conversation, and ideas which they cannot understand."

At this stage, the child accepts almost everything s/he is told or exposed to, everything is a source of wonder, and concepts are "inaccurate." Goldman recommends staying away from any formal education during this time, but rather using Sunday school to "enrich general experience and artistic expression" and to answer the children's spontaneous questions.

From seven to eleven (Piaget's period of concrete operations), children are *subreligious*—concrete in their thinking still, but interested in learning facts about Bible lands and Bible society. One can begin to introduce "religious themes," but only at thirteen are concepts now within the grasp of (the adolescent's) intellect and experience. Goldman says: "We need to have lived long enough to have experienced the real problems of the human condition before we see the point of what religion offers." Now, finally, they can understand the Gospels, and he suggests problem-centered discussions of what Christians believe (i.e., a moral dilemma, followed by "What would a Christian do? What would the consequences be?").

He is concerned that if introduced to the messages of the Gospels too early, children can only respond in a literal-minded way, so that when they reach adolescence, they reject the entire gospel as "childish," remembering their childish interpretations. Children also tend to regard the Bible as a "supernatural book, dealing with holy people in a holy land, clad in special holy clothes, all in a special holy period of time. This remoteness of Bible-society also encourages adolescents to dismiss Biblical teaching as irrelevant."

One of the parents answering my questionnaire illustrates the effect of bad religious teaching:

The tenets of the Congregational Church I found were absolute and it was unthinkable to question. You didn't talk about Congregationalism with anybody. God and communion and red velvet and knowing just how much to bow your head at prayer time were things you simply obeyed and followed others about; you didn't question. . . . I felt the awe of the church, but I didn't know what this God was, or why bleeding Jesus was something to worship rather than be ashamed of and avoided. I was confused by the insincerity of the adults. I found inconsistencies in what Congregationalists claimed to believe, and I didn't know how to reconcile them. In addition, I didn't quite know what everything was about anyhow. What and where were Galilee, Jerusalem, Bethlehem, Nazareth, Judea? What did Moses in the bulrushes have to do with bleeding Jesus? It was all a big mess of confusion to me.

Ronald Goldman admits that there is more to religion than a body of knowledge to be absorbed. He says, "One may learn the Bible and not be religious, since religion is a way of life to be lived, not a series of facts to be learned." Unfortunately, both cognitive researchers and Sunday school teachers often forget that.

Ernest Harms:
Children's Symbols of God

In chapter 3 we saw how in the 1970s educators have objected to the one-sidedness of research and teaching that emphasizes only rational, verbal, "left-brain" modes of knowing. Ernest Harms realized this in 1944. He wrote: "By the use of a verbal question method, the rational and verbal part of the religious experience was studied, [but] . . . the most important part of the contents of religious experience falls outside of that sphere of consciousness which the average individual is able to verbalize." This is true for adults, and even more so for children, who play with toys, imagine, and express themselves in fairy tales before they use rational language.

Harms, who was interested in the development of religious *experience* in children, not simply their religious *understanding* of belief systems, found the following solution. He asked thousands of children to imagine how God would look to them, if they were to picture Him in their mind, or to imagine the appearance of the highest being they thought to exist. After about two or three minutes, the children were asked to picture on paper what had come to mind. Adolescents, who frequently object to "imagining" or drawing an image of God, were given the choice of drawing the meaning of religion as such and of the highest ideal expressed in religion.

Whether or not you "believe in God," you may be surprised to find out what your child's "God-concept" is, using either Goldman's verbal questions or Harms's request for drawings. In Western society, no child can live very long without developing some concept of God. Even if the parents are atheists or agnostic, the children get what V. Peter Pitts calls "an impression of the 'fact' of God" from peers, neighbors, teachers, television, movies, books, and paintings.

Studying his collection of drawings, Harms, too, found stages of development. From age three to six (Piaget's preoperational), the children expressed their version of the deity as a *fairy-tale image,* but with a kind of awe for the high and exalted. They drew God as a king, or as a daddy of all children, someone living in a golden house above the clouds.

The children from seven to eleven (Piaget's concrete operations period) were termed *realistic.* They used conventional symbols derived from the teachings of institutional religion, such as the crucifix, the Star of David, or a priest. When the God-father, angels, or saints were drawn, they were depicted as human figures helping people on earth. Harms writes, "At this period, the child—more than at any other period—seems to be willing to adapt himself to institutionalized religion and its teachings."

The drawings of 4,000 adolescents and postadolescents (Piaget's formal operations stage) fell into three groups, all individualistic. One group used conventional symbols; another made creative, original, abstract or symbolic drawings, such as light breaking through a dark sky. Harms called these expressions of deep emotional experience. The third group was the most astounding. These young people drew religious motifs which they had never seen. They made paintings resembling mandalas and symbols from early Egyptian cults, Persian mythology, Celtic sun cults, and medieval alchemy. Some of these teenagers came from the poorest districts of a New York suburb. Where did these images come from?

Harms, who was a follower of C.G. Jung, did not find this unusual, since Jung had observed in his patients dreams and fantasies of "an impersonal character, which cannot be reduced to experiences in the individual's past . . . they correspond to certain *collective* (and not personal) structural elements of the human psyche in general, and, like the morphological elements of the human body, are *inherited* . . . I have called this the *collective unconscious.* . . . the archetype . . . represents or personifies certain instinctive data of the dark, primitive psyche, the real but invisible *roots of consciousness* . . . This original form of *religio* ("linking back") is the essence, the working basis, of all religious life even today, and always will be, whatever future form this life may take."

Like Jung, Harms believed that our life task is "to perceive the voice of [our] innate religion," which will be different for each individual. He felt strongly that *this* should be the task of religious education in the "individualistic" adolescent and post-adolescent years.

Sigmund Freud:
Psychosexual Development

The cognitive stage theories choose to examine a child's intellectual development. Complementary to them are theories of emotional growth which also lead toward the goal of the "mature ego" of postadolescence. Sigmund Freud outlined a biologically determined progression of "psychosexual" stages of emotional development. These do not have fixed ages, but rather blend into each other.

In Freudian theory, at birth we are *oral*, our psychic energy centered on sensations and fantasies involving the feeding process: feeling hungry and greedy; the pleasures of eating, sucking, and biting; feeling full and satisfied; falling asleep; fantasizing being eaten. When sphincter control develops, around eighteen months, we enter the *anal* stage. This is the age of toilet-training, power struggles, and ambivalence. At three to six, according to Freud, the *phallic* or *Oedipal* phase begins, with conflicts around desire for exclusive possession of the parent, and fear of punishment for those desires. From seven to eleven (Piaget's concrete operations), comes a period of emotional quiet, the *latency* age. The awakened sexuality of puberty brings a reworking of Oedipal conflicts, leading to the final stage: mature, *genital* sexuality.

Freudian theory can be invaluable for understanding a child's emotional life. Some seemingly inexplicable problems of early childhood (such as fears of spiders or wolves from three to six) make sense in the light of Freud's analysis. But to Freud, all "religious" experience is ultimately reducible to other instincts or drives. He viewed the original symbiosis with the mother as that unity which we must escape forever if we are to become autonomous, mature adults. Any return to it is regression, a form of psychopathology or sickness. Although neo-Freudians added the idea of "regression in the service of the ego" as a way of condoning the use of prelogical or intuitive thought for creativity, mystical experience is still viewed simply as a way of resolving conflicts by returning to infancy.

Much of the so-called psychology of religion has been an attempt to explain religion in this manner. Several researchers have postulated that children turn to "God" when they discover that their own parents are not all-powerful and all-knowing (a moral and intellectual crisis at the age of six). Religion, to Freud, is the adult's projection on the cosmic plane of emotions, fears, and longing that were originally attached to father and mother: "He creates for himself the gods, of whom he is afraid, whom he seeks to propitiate and to whom he nevertheless entrusts the task of protecting him."

Rationalists who say that since in childhood the boundaries between self and reality are "blurred," all subsequent mystical experiences are "regression" to childhood, forget that *in fact* the cosmos permeates us every second of our lives, not only when we are children. Andrew Greeley points out that "in the mystical interlude, the adult 'remembers' his union with the cosmos once again and experiences it as occurring in the here and now." The rationalist psychologists "have fallen victim to the same fallacy as those technologues who thought that to build an industrial society while ignoring the environmental and ecological processes was a form of human progress. Both groups assume that man is sharply distinct from the rest of reality—and then lament man's alienation. In fact, man is inextricably enmeshed in the universe. It is the beginning of wisdom to understand this fact; it is the beginning of mysticism to enjoy it."

TRANSPERSONAL THEORIES: SPIRITUAL GROWTH BEFORE AND AFTER THE MATURE EGO

Rudolf Steiner

Departing dramatically from the rationalists are the transpersonal theorists who place value on early modes of knowing. Rudolf Steiner formulated a philosophy of education based partly on his spiritual theories, which he called Anthroposophy, and partly on careful observation of children. He described child development as proceeding in a series of metamorphoses, psychological as well as physical.

From birth to the emergence of the permanent teeth (around age seven) he says the *spirit incarnates,* as seen in the body's swift growth and the will to motion. The child must learn to manage this physical body in space and time. Steiner has specific recommendations to parents and teachers about what the child needs at each stage. During the first phase, that of physical development:

What you say to him, what you teach him, does not yet make any impression, except in so far as he imitates what you say in his own speech. But it is what you are that matters; if you are good this goodness will appear in your gestures, and if you are evil or bad-tempered this will also appear in your gestures—in short, everything that you do yourself passes over into the child and pursues its way with him. The child is wholly sense-organ, and reacts to all the impressions aroused in him by the people around him.

In his theory, age seven—the *change of teeth*—represents a crucial turning point (which has also been noted by Piaget, Freud, and the Roman Catholic church). Free will begins, as does a new form of curiosity about the world, the ways of society. Steiner called this second phase, from seven to fourteen, the predominance of soul or feeling, manifest in the child's new capacity for aesthetic experience. He felt it was very important at this age to present facts in a way that stimulates the imagination, to call the child's whole being into play by directing the child artistically. He called this the "milk of the soul."

He also noted that during this period, at the age of nine, the child faces an inner crisis when outer reality begins to separate from subjective experience. At this age children feel alone and begin to doubt themselves and the adults around them. Some children become depressed to find themselves alone.

The third great transformation of puberty releases the power of abstract thought, which Steiner called the *predominance of the spirit*. Ideally, at the end of this third phase, body, soul, and spirit have come into balance.

Steiner's ideas about education have been successfully put into practice in a series of schools. As Steiner once wrote: "If you are specially desirous of having formulated axioms, then take this as the first principle of a real art of education: you must be able to observe life in all its manifestations."

By concentrating on unfolding rather than training, by respecting the stages of development and stressing the dangers of too early cognitive teaching, Steiner's ideas from the 1920s sound like contemporary educational thought. Although he can be rigid about what may and may not be taught at each age (current thinking is that development is more fluid and elastic), he fits into the current "right-brain" research when he emphasizes the soul-milk of "fantasy and imagination . . . the higher truths in fairy-tales and myths."

In his schools, like Ronald Goldman, Steiner recommended not teaching the Gospels until the ninth or tenth year. The younger children were taught gratitude in the contemplation of everything in nature, and celebrated the festivals of the year. "Through this naturalistic religion during the early years, the children are gradually led to an understanding of the Christ mystery, when they reach the higher classes."

Joseph Chilton Pearce

Joseph Chilton Pearce, writing fifty years after Steiner, comes to somewhat similar conclusions from a different perspective. In his book *Magical Child,* he attempts to correlate "mind-brain functions" with neurological development and information processing. The first stage, roughly from birth to seven, is consciousness on the level of *"body-earth knowing"*—"consciousness of one's body in physical rapport and interaction with the living earth" for which the mother's body is the "matrix." At this stage, he tells parents that

> the rule for communications of instruction, demands for compliance, or response to queries is: unless |the child| can touch, taste, feel, smell, hear what they refer to, no communication takes place. . . .
>
> Nature programs the child to do two things from ages one to seven: structure a knowledge of the world exactly as it is, on the one hand, and play with that world in ways that it is not, on the other. . . . Structuring a knowledge of the world takes at least six years because the world is filled with many things and its processes and principles are strict. . . . the world is a very practical place, and nature provides the child with a very practical intelligence: his/her ability to interact through the five senses and body movements. Nothing more is needed.

From three or four to seven comes "the long birth of individuality," and at age seven, the *social self level:* "Age seven has historically been called the age of decision because the objective self system becomes functional at this time." This social self level means "consciousness of one's self as individual, as unique, and as separate from the world." The third level, which Pearce calls "primary process" (not the same as Freud's term) is "consciousness of one's total hologram effect, of the life system in its total thinking sense, what Carl Jung called a *collective unconscious*, James and Huxley called *Mind-at-large*, Deikman of Langley Porter calls the *General Field of Awareness*, and what the ancient Chinese may have meant by the *tao*, the flow."

In Pearce's system, we are not meant to outgrow the earlier stages, but to add new abilities:

> Ordinary adult awareness should almost surely be a neat balance among these three functional systems because they are right here in our heads. We should be aware on a body-earth level, a social self level, and a primary process level. . . . Each stage of development should enhance the previous stage. Growth is designed to incorporate more and more, not continually lose the unfolding levels of consciousness. . . . Yet we largely lose our child awareness and apparently never develop awareness of the primary process. . . . we seem stuck in one segment of the operation, that intermediate developmental stage of social consciousness. . . .
>
> Classically, we have referred to our ordinary, rather isolated awareness as real or normal consciousness. We have called any awareness of the other two functions altered states of consciousness and have been conditioned to believe them pathological aberrations. There are people, who manage, through rigorous and lengthy disciplines, to become consciously aware of the primary process, that general field of awareness apparently embracing all thought everywhere. . . . Although these altered states (mystical experiences) are largely denied validity by the academic community, they are so rewarding that people devote years of their life or risk their bodies and brains through drugs to attempt to experience them.

Derived from this theory is a set of instructions for parents who want to help their children keep consciousness of body-earth knowing and reach primary process. He emphasizes the importance of a ground of security in early bonding with the mother, whose body he calls the matrix for all later learning:

> Around age seven, a dramatic shift of brain growth and logic will occur. The child's matrix will (or should) shift from the mother to the earth. S/he will then have the living earth as the place of power, the safe space, and the source of possibility. The child will be bonded to that earth. . . . For most of us this bonding to the world, or matrix shift, is blocked by anxiety in much the same way that bonding to the mother is crippled or warped |by physical separation at birth, in cribs, playpens, and day-care centers |.

Pearce's book is valuable for its poetic attempts to systematize knowledge of consciousness and brain function. It is also annoying in his insistence that he knows "nature's biological plan." Although he is constantly talking about what parents "should" do, I found that part of the book too general to be useful. He himself admits that he was not able to prevent his son, who showed amazing musical creativity at age four (composing songs at the piano, sight-reading music at five, playing Bach at six), from losing all this by the time he was eight. Pearce blames this on the fact that the boy had learned how to read books. He recommends that we not teach children to read until they are eleven. But how can we (or even "should" we) keep our children illiterate in a society where everyone else is reading?

Models of Spiritual Development

The many ways of imagining the connection between the child's unity with the world and the mystic's can be divided into linear and nonlinear models. The first simply continue the line of development past the "mature ego" or "formal operations" stage.

Herbert Koplowitz, a cognitive psychologist who has departed dramatically from Piaget by suggesting that there is a stage of "unitary operational thought" *after* formal operations, says: "Children *seem* mystical because they're not caught up in the rational—sometimes not even in the concrete. But the mystic can choose to be rational—if only as a game—which the child cannot."

For an adult who has reached Unitary Operational Thought, Koplowitz says:

> *Reality is thought of as being continuous, and the boundaries which separate one object from another are thought of as being drawn by the knower. . . . one is conscious of constructing objects and takes responsibility for that construction rather than treating objects as discoveries. . . . Opposites, which had been thought of as being separate and distinct from each other, come to be seen as interdependent and as poles of each other. Causality, which had been thought of as linear, is seen in Unitary Operations as pervading the universe, connecting all events with each other.*

Koplowitz observes that Piaget, in his own way, is as "egocentric" as the children he observes, if we define egocentrism as "treating an aspect of one's knowledge as though it were an aspect of reality." Egocentrism is a standard human behavior, and does not stop at childhood.

Linearity rules our "left-brain" language and thought. Nonlinear patterns are hard to write about, easier to draw (see illustrations). These models consider the development of the personal self in its *continuing* relationship to the original unity, or Self.

There are models in nature for orderly growth and expansion (the rings in a tree trunk) and also for dramatic transformation (caterpillar into butterfly). Humans do both. Rudolf Steiner spoke of metamorphosis every seven years—at birth, age seven, and age fourteen—with new abilities emerging at each stage, abstract thought like butterfly wings. But this model ignores the fact that we do not quite shed earlier experience like cocoons.

We continue to carry our earlier experience reverberating somewhere in our neural network, locked somewhere in our body structure. Under hypnosis, in psychotherapy, while undergoing Rolfing, or in other altered states, the earlier experience can reemerge and we can feel what it was like to be three, to be afraid of Daddy, to have fallen off a bicycle. We are rarely totally transformed.

Steve Kull, a California researcher, points out that the total field of experience is an ongoing ground on which our differentiation rests. He has found that there is *always* communication between that level (God, Mind-at-Large, Higher Self) and ours, not always conscious. Adults sometimes remember the moment when they lost the sense of connection with that ground—often around the age of seven. Later in life, sometimes this connection can be regained.

Eleanor Ruma-Blofson, Ph.D., puts it this way: "The child has to give up something to get something else. S/he does lose spontaneity and magic temporarily to get realistic and literal. In adolescence and young adulthood there is the possibility of getting it all together, the poetry *plus* the rational."

The model of a circle with expanding boundaries helps resolve the common confusion that in order to reach "higher" spiritual states, you must first "lose your ego." Psychologists tell parents that their job is to build a healthy ego. How do you build an ego and at the same time prepare for its disappearance? As one mother said, "We want our children to be able to put bread on the table and a roof over their head, and yet . . . keep their sense of connection with the rest of the universe." We don't want our children to spend their entire lives in a deep trance, never making a contribution.

The solution to this paradox is to separate the different meanings of the word "ego." Freud coined it to refer to the executive function of the mind that meets the demands of external reality, mediating the conflict between the instinctive impulses from the id and the commands of conscience, or superego. More recently, "ego psychologists" have expanded the concept of ego to include conflict-free functions such as memory, perception, and language, in addition to defenses against id impulses and anxiety. Clearly, we do need this conflict-free ego in order to survive in the world, and from this point of view, to "lose" it would be to go crazy—unable to think clearly, talk sensibly, or perceive reliably. Psychiatrists consider a person healthy who has good "ego strength." Another favorite phrase is "ego boundaries." Someone with poor ego boundaries presumably experiences the constant terror of disappearing. We don't want our children to get frightened, as a patient of mine once did, every time she looked in the mirror.

In the psychological system of Vedanta (the chief philosophy of Hinduism), this debate—"Are mystics crazy? Are psychotics really mystics experiencing the truth? Are children mystics?"—is avoided, since the functions of mind are divided differently than in Freudian theory, and since it describes levels of psychological development beyond the healthy ego. To Freud, the concept of "I-ness" was inseparable from the other ego functions. In the Vedantic system, *ahankara*, the sense of "I-ness," is simply one component of the mind, separate from the integration of sense perceptions (*manas*), from the ability to understand and make decisions (*buddhi*), and from the memory function (*chitta*).

The infant is undeveloped in both his/her sense of "I-ness" and executive ego. When we guess what infants experience, we imagine that they do not separate self and world. Piaget and Freud, Steiner and Pearce, all agree on that. When the world is pleasurable, this experience of unity means ecstasy; when the world is painful, it means hell—no way out. And since the world is both, we imagine an unintegrated flipping between the two states, similar to that which we see in psychotic (or "insane") people. The task of the infant is to develop an observing awareness, give up the sense of omnipotence, and accept the limitations of a realistic human "I."

The child's world will be stable enough, we hope, so that s/he will feel the continuity of his/her self through changes without constant fear of annihilation. The more fear there is, the more rigidity, the more clinging to old habits and self-definition.

An excellent book, *Yoga and Psychotherapy*, by Swami Rama, Rudolph Ballantine, M.D., and Swami Ajaya, explores what the authors call the "evolution of consciousness":

> The psychotic and the most advanced mystic seem to lie at opposite extremes of a spectrum which spans the whole of personal evolution. At one end are the most massive of attachments—where pain and pleasure are both excruciatingly exquisite and where identity is fleeting and fragmentary. This is the domain of madness. At the other extreme, attachments have been almost completely shed. There is no more of the alternation of pain and pleasure, only a constant and pervasive joy. Identity has been expanded to the point that every part of the universe is part of the Self. . . . The psychotic has not shed the ego-identity—rather he has never acquired it. His need is to develop the ego, which can later be transcended. This is an indispensable transitional stage—one necessary step on the lad-

der. *Trying to jump over such necessary rungs results in a tragic fall.*

This is the tragedy of some teenagers who look to "spiritual" groups as a substitute for, rather than an addition to, the development of autonomy.

The psychotic has no center:

Further along the path can be found the neurotic who is in many ways a caricature of that state in which most of us find ourselves. He has gradually established that bundle of habits which goes to make up a personality. He has accepted the limitations of I-ness and safely settled into a routine of reinforcing and acting on the habits which sustain him and give him a sense of continuity and solidity. . . . No matter how maladaptive his pattern of habits, no matter how much pain his attachments bring, he is unwilling to let go his familiar self-definition and venture around the next turn in the path of personal growth. . . .

Still further along the path is the mystic who has patiently trained himself not only to live with the uncertainty of the external world but to relish the feeling of constant renewal that its changes bring. He has learned to continuously give up his prior concepts of self and accept a continual process of changing I-ness.

MODELS OF THE SELF

For the benefit of "right-brain" understanding, I present five diagrams of the relationship of the "personal self" to the "higher Self." In Yoga, "consciousness resides in the Self, rather than in the mind. The Self uses the mind as an instrument of knowing, just as one might use a microscope."

In figure 1, there are five levels of being (or "sheaths") around the Self: the outermost is (1) the physical body (the "food sheath"), then (2) *prana*—breath and energy connecting mind and body, (3) mind, (4) intuition, and (5) bliss.

The "chakras" are centers of consciousness linking the sheaths (figure 2). The lowest (anal) is related to survival, the next (genital) to sexuality. Freudian psychology takes its viewpoint about the nature of man from the orientation of the second chakra. The third chakra, at the solar plexus, relates to assertion and power. The heart chakra is the center of emotion and compassion. It is represented by the six-pointed star, the two triangles symbolizing integration of the higher and lower aspect of our nature. The throat chakra represents nurturance, trust, and devotion, receiving grace, and expressing creativity. The seat of intuitive knowledge is at the level of the "third eye," and the highest state—the crown chakra—is the "thousand-petaled lotus," beyond verbal description. Thus there are three lower chakras and three higher, meeting at the heart. Until recently, Western psychology (except for Jung) had no place for the highest two chakras.

Roberto Assagioli, founder of Psychosynthesis, divides the "unconscious" into lower, middle, and higher regions (figure 3). The "lower unconscious" corresponds to Freud's "id," the middle to Freud's "preconscious." Assagioli calls the higher unconscious the "superconscious"—the source of altruistic love, genius, and illumination. The smaller circle of "the field of consciousness" is that part of our personality of which we are directly aware. At its center is the self, which, as in the Yoga model, is witnessing the changing contents of consciousness. The higher Self is above, and unaffected by, the flow of the mind-stream "and the personal conscious self should be considered merely as its reflection, its 'projection' on the field of the personality."

Carl Gustav Jung expressed the paradox of our dual natures with a cross (figure 4). Our "self" is where the lines meet.

The final diagram, figure 5, pictures consciousness as a wave. Points of personal consciousness emerge as crests from the "collective unconscious," which itself is grounded in a transpersonal field.

HOW CAN PARENTS
APPLY THESE THEORIES?

So what are parents to do? What practical application can we make of all these theories? The first thing we can offer a child is to make his/her life as secure as we can, to minimize the outer threats.

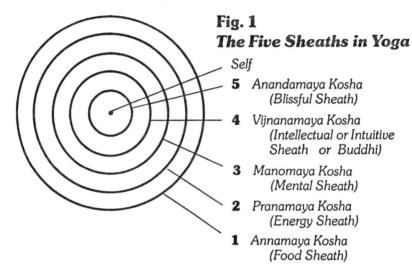

Fig. 1
The Five Sheaths in Yoga

Self

5 Anandamaya Kosha
  (Blissful Sheath)

4 Vijnanamaya Kosha
  (Intellectual or Intuitive
  Sheath   or Buddhi)

3 Manomaya Kosha
  (Mental Sheath)

2 Pranamaya Kosha
  (Energy Sheath)

1 Annamaya Kosha
  (Food Sheath)

Fig. 2
The Chakras

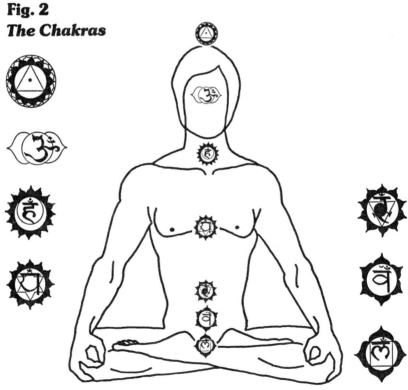

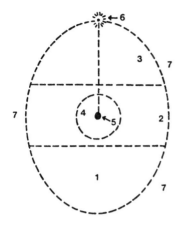

Fig. 3
Psychosynthesis

1. The Lower Unconscious
2. The Middle Unconscious
3. The Higher Unconscious or
    Superconscious
4. The Field of Consciousness
5. The Conscious Self or "I"
6. The Higher Self
7. The Collective Unconscious

Fig. 4
Jung's Cross

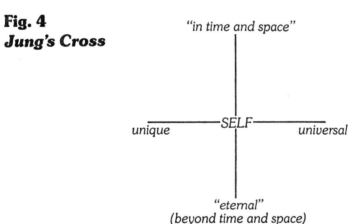

Fig. 5

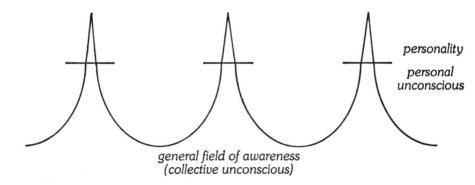

Spiritual life begins after survival needs have been met, which includes not only food and shelter, but needs for love and mastery. As we grow, we learn skills, bridle instincts, and create for ourselves a characteristic way of coping with obstacles that we can call our "personality." This in itself is not a barrier to further growth. What creates the barrier to "transcendence" of the personality is anxiety about survival. The personality that feels itself threatened by overwhelming rage or fear, sexual instincts, or loss of love, creates rigid defenses.

Reducing anxiety means love, discipline, and consistency: love so that our children need not fear its loss; discipline (or "limits") so that our child need not live in constant fear of his/her own animal nature, which might destroy what it loves (children feel safer with parents who can control them until they learn to do it themselves); and consistency so that the children need not live in constant fear of us.

Life provides enough losses and insecurities so that no one grows up without a share of defenses. We spend years relatively helpless and certainly inferior to the "giants" who control our lives. If Freudian theory is accurate, we are inescapably frustrated in our first great passion—for the exclusive possession of our parents. Our drive for autonomy leads us to separate from our mothers, but with that comes the feeling of loss as well.

There must be attachment *and* separation, and a parent's job is to facilitate both. As one mother put it: "The whole job of parenting in a nutshell is to know how to be there when you're needed and not be there when you're not needed." Sometimes it is impossible to tell which is which.

Failure of attachment does not make the separation easier—it makes for a maimed human being. Similarly, it is too easy for some spiritual-minded young people to misunderstand "nonattachment" as not loving, not feeling, or not caring, and to make a virtue of that. Enlightened masters are among the *most* loving people, and may get angry—they simply do not identify their true being with any of these states.

In practical terms, encouraging bonding to the mother's body can begin at birth, with the new childbirth practices that treat both mother and infant as conscious beings for whom the breast feeding and body contact during hours and days after birth are crucial.

Joseph Chilton Pearce says, "The child's intent drives him/her to maintain the parental bond, explore the world, and play in it." That is the same duality: exploring (autonomy) while maintaining the parental bond (attachment). "When intent can express itself freely, no dividing line grows between any of these critical needs." His advice for the parents of a young child is to allow as much exploration as possible, without imposing adult values, so that the child will not limit his/her perceptions to conform to our imposed construction of reality. And above all, he emphasizes again and again, our job is as much as possible to keep the child free of anxiety about survival.

Piaget's theories of cognitive development can be useful as we watch our children actively constructing their own belief systems. Piaget tells us how much "understanding" to expect of children at each age—that, for example, during the period of concrete operations, "it is more important for children to be incorporated into a loving community than to be given abstractions about God's love." And when we say we want them to be good people, they know that means pleasing us, but they don't know what behaviors are "good" in given circumstances. We need to spell that out in concrete detail: "Don't squeeze the kittens so hard that they meow—that means you're hurting them" instead of the vague directive "Be kind to animals." And as one parent said, "Don't make adults out of children. Let them have their (religious) concrete images, even if they're offensive to you."

Books such as those of Arnold Gesell, Frances Ilg, and Louise Bates Ames (*Infant and Child in the Culture of Today* and *The Child from Five to Ten*) which tell exactly what to expect from children at every age can be tremendously helpful to parents. We learn that our two-year-old is not a monster; not to despair when our sweet three-year-old turns four (that pleasant disposition will return next year); that our uncoordinated six-year-old is not permanently disabled. Much bad parenting comes from simple ignorance: expecting a child to perform in some way before s/he is biologically capable of it.

But beware! The stage theories are more culture-bound than the researchers are willing to admit. Stage theories are *not* useful to parents to the extent that they tell us "before a certain age, your child cannot possibly do that." Different studies find variation in the ages at which children move through Piaget's stages. Children at the "egocentric" stage are not supposed to have ability to imagine or care how others feel, but recently, psychologists found that some children under two or three will try to comfort others who appear distressed—as when a toddler offers a weeping parent his bottle as consolation. My personal observation of the *est* Young Person's Training (see chapter 9) shot down several theories I had read about children's limited self-awareness before adolescence, and also makes me seriously question whether "unitary operational thought" comes *after* "formal operations," since I *saw* children six to twelve taking responsibility for constructing their own reality.

The stage development theorists show us that some stages do evolve in their own time, and cannot be rushed. The transpersonal theorists show us that we can help the child stay in touch with early intuitiveness, wonder, and creativity; that it is not necessary to "re-press" the irrational in order to continue to develop our reason. We do not have to be afraid, and we can teach our children not to be afraid, of the very "altered" states of consciousness that reveal a wider horizon.

Children are full of wonder and love as well as aggression and self-seeking. People have puzzled for years how to keep what the Zen Buddhists call "beginner's mind," since it is clear that we limit children's ability to "see" as we teach them the rules of our culture. The children themselves seem eager to learn our rules, to please us and do things the "grown-up" way. Stage theorists say that this is not entirely up to us or the children—that the brain itself is structured to lose "beginner's mind" at least from seven to ten.

Extremists say, "Do away with culture." That is impossible. Culture is like air. We may substitute cultures, fresh air for foul, or pretend it isn't there because we cannot see it; but no one grows up outside of language, history, and the set of relationships with others that we call culture. What we *can* do is point to the unnameable, legitimize for our children their own "intimations of immortality," and share ours. The challenge is not how to do away with culture, but how to help our children remain open to other realities even as they are learning their way around this one.

The world of the preschool child is *analogous* to that of the mystic—alive, and without the concept of space and time as we know it. (Remember, though, that consciousness *before* the concept of space and time develops may not be the same as consciousness that goes *beyond* it). There is enough overlap so that our children can help *us* enter into "beginner's mind"—that state before defenses, concepts, and conditioning insulate us from experiencing directly. What we can do for their spiritual life in the first five years is allow their joyfulness to inspire us, and encourage them to continue to expand their love and wonder even as they enter the age of reason.

CHAPTER 8

How to Answer
Children's Questions
About God and Death

Amelia: Who made God?
Eve: Why don't we kill *people* for their skins?

From the time they are born, children are trying to find out,
"Who am I?" "Where did I come from?" "Where am I going?"
They do not always put these questions into words. When they do,
we "grownups" are often uncomfortable because we are still strug-
gling with the same questions. We cannot ask children to wait for
an answer until we "know." Our silence is interpreted (correctly) by
the child as "I don't want to talk about this" or worse, "You
shouldn't be curious about this." The lines of communication close
off, perhaps forever, leaving the child alone.

Still, it is not easy. As one mother said:

*I've tried to be frank . . . struggle not to talk about God as a man.
. . . I found myself mouthing things I didn't believe in—it was so*

hard to communicate. I didn't know how to talk to my daughter about Jesus or the crucifixion. I was given a lot of that—the nice satisfying answer that wasn't true—and that caused a lot of confusion and suffering in my life. I think it is better to communicate your puzzlement.

Unresolved feelings about our own religious training can add to the difficulty. One Catholic mother finds herself saying, "I'm sorry I can't answer questions. I feel I don't believe in God. Go listen to others and see what they say." She is aware of fighting her feelings, and thus must keep silent. "I don't want to say I think Catholics are idiots. There is too much raw anger under the scars."

The greatest source of difficulty discussing metaphysics, the science of ultimate things, with children is that before the teenage years they do not think in abstractions. As we saw in chapter 7, children understand things they can see, hear, and touch. This, of course, leads to misunderstandings, some hilarious, some troubling.

It helps to understand the stages of a child's thought. Then we may choose to give the concrete explanation that comes closest to our true thinking:

Kids have trouble with the fact that you can't see God. We call it a force, like a large wind.

The stage concept helps us not get upset at any particular notion that children may express. We see how they play with ideas, and how quickly they change. A Rocky Mountain family said:

We've had a lot of stages. At first, God lived up in a canyon. . . . We've had many discussions that God is spirit in all of us and everything. In spite of this, at one point Wendy got very literal about God, Mary, and Joseph, and got confused. The older girls, since they've been learning to read, want to know Bible stories. . . . We are also teaching Sufi stories. Now their interest in the inner life is fading—they want to ride horses. The cycle will come around again.

The children may be much more definite about God than their parents are:

My daughter has a personified view of God as a he, whereas I at this point in my life know God to be the totality—everywhere—

love energy. Heaven, to her, is a place, whereas to me it is a state of existence attainable in the here and now.

My son talks as if he believes in God—gets it completely from his friends. . . . He wanted to go up in the sky and see how "God was working us." I told him some people believed in Heaven, and I didn't, but I didn't know.

It is important to remember that although children speak concretely, like poets, they may be able to use their concrete images to express a deeper reality. They may "know" something that is hard to say in any language.

Our daughter, Eve, when she was five, said, "God is like the wind, the rain, the snow and the moon and the sun . . . and all of those things are all put up in the sky and all of those things create a mixture, and all of those things are God. . . . Well, God's all living things—like God made everything and everybody, from the first dinosaur to the last—God made everything we use, and us."

Her sister, Amelia, then three, said, "God protects you from the scary dark . . . and you can't feel a god and you can't hear it and you can't touch it, and you can't smell him but he's still there . . . and he watches over the big girls and the mommies, too, and the poppies, and he watches over babies so they wouldn't get scared and cry . . . he watches over the big girls . . . what should we have for breakfast?"

One of the advantages of belonging to a traditional religious system is that it provides ready-made answers to the Big Questions of personal identity: Why am I here? What is the meaning of my life? Where was I before I was born, and where will I be when I am dead? It provides answers for our social identity: Who are we as a community? What group do I belong to? And our cosmic identity: What is this universe we live in all about? How was it made? Is it friendly or not? What powers are at work in our lives?

No wonder some parents envy the certainty of the catechism as they search for answers:

Joshua often asks about God. I tell him that I am not sure whether there is a God, and don't believe in it; that many other people believe there is God, or in different gods . . . the kids ask questions, and often they're asking for guidance, especially if they ask twice. I find that hard sometimes—my answers are not as clear-cut and simple as if I did subscribe to some religion. . . .

In spite of this, some parents were able to answer with relative ease:

I told them about the Christian Heaven and Hell, the Buddhist reincarnation, and added, "I really don't know."

I usually respond in terms of value, of love, or in context of history (Bible), or in terms of "some people believe." They don't ask a lot.

The children have asked lots and lots of things—have not told them anything I don't believe. Have told them there is much that I don't know. My husband and I have such a strong sense of consciousness being more than the body that it's natural our kids do, too. They see God as everywhere and within everyone. And the body as a necessary vehicle to be loved, cared for, in order to experience life on earth.

They ask mainly, do we believe in God. I tell them I'm uncertain about what God is, but I believe in something godly in each of us.

Sometimes the questions get really sticky. Amelia wanted to know, "Who made God?" "Who made Dracula?" "How was the first chicken made?" "Who was the great great chicken mother?" She is also grappling, as I am, with the problem of evil: "Did God make poison ivy?" "Did God make ticks?" "Why?"

I have found Benjamin Spock's advice helpful here:

In trying to understand complex matters, children are likely to want to take one small step at a time. If and when their curiosity reaches out further, in a minute or a month, they will ask more questions. So it is well to answer only the question the child has asked, not to volunteer more.

"Where do I come from?" is as much a question about the origins of life as it is about "sex." Explanations about the microscopic egg which they cannot see and the microscopic sperm which they cannot see are deeply unsatisfying and rapidly forgotten by children, not only because they are so removed from children's experience, but also because they really do not explain anything. How life and consciousness emerge from those two little cells is something we don't like to admit to ourselves that we hardly understand at all. Nevertheless, we can only tell them what we know.

The mystery of the origin of consciousness is related to the mystery of the end of human life. Children (like us) are universally anxious about their own personal death and the death of those they love, and turn to their parents for answers. These questions are the hardest of all.

Earl Grollman, in the prologue to an excellent anthology called *Explaining Death to Children* (which includes articles by psychologists and educators from different religions), makes several important points.

Age, he says, is only one of the factors affecting an understanding of death; personality and environment make a big difference. Some two-year-olds will have a concept of death, while some five-year-olds will not. One study found that between the ages of three to five the child may deny death as a regular and final process. S/he thinks it is like sleep; you are dead, then you are alive again, or like when mother and father go away on a trip, and then come back. Between five and nine, children may begin to "accept the idea that a person has died but may not accept it as something that must happen to everyone and particularly to themselves. Around the age of nine, the child recognizes death as an inevitable experience" that will happen to him or her as well.

Grollman's advice to parents focuses on *how* to answer and what *not* to say:

What is said is important, but how it is said has even greater bearing on whether the child will develop anxiety and fears or accept, within his capacity, the fact of death. The understanding of the very young child is, of course, limited. He doesn't ask for or need details. His questions should be answered in a matter-of-fact way, briefly, without too much emotion. Too complicated a reply often confuses the child . . . even if the child does not fully understand the explanations given him, death will be less of a mystery and therefore less frightening to him. . . .

You can give your religious convictions along with the factual: "As far as the physical body is concerned, the parents should make it clear that with death, life stops, the deceased cannot return, and the body is buried. A less explicit explanation is apt to result in more confusion and misinterpretation."

What *not* to say? Something you do not believe. Especially harmful are explanations of death as a "long journey," which makes the child feel abandoned, especially if it is a parent who has deserted him or her without saying good-bye. Saying that to die is to sleep simply makes the child afraid to go to sleep.

Steve Joseph, in *Children in Fear*, believes that many children are paralyzed by anxiety because of notions (usually from religious teaching and/or violent television shows) that death is a punishment for being bad. Since they know they are often "bad," they expect to be killed. Working in a nursery school, he found he could stop the children from acting out their questions (by hitting each other to see what would happen) and help them begin to verbalize them.

He offers the following scientific explanation:

The children learned that the brain controlled the functioning of the entire body. They learned that death occurred when the brain stopped functioning, and then a person could no longer feel or experience anything. Above all, I emphasized that death was not a punishment. Society does not usually allow children to talk about death, but they are allowed to play games which dramatize it, and they do, over and over again. I continually explained to them, though, that their bodies were beautiful organizations of energy, tremendously strong and capable of repairing themselves. . . .

We should encourage children to ask questions about God. They need as much accurate information as we can give them about the various theories of genesis, like the Big Bang theory and Heisenberg's theory of the confluence of gases. After that, we should encourage them to explore and develop their own theories and ideas. Since the promise of the avoidance of death is the cornerstone of religion, we need to discuss death with them openly and try to tell them what we understand about what does and doesn't happen afterward.

As with questions about God and sex, it is always valuable, and sometimes mind-blowing, first to ask children, "What do *you* think?" At worst, they'll say, "I don't know. That's why I asked *you!*" If they do answer, you have a starting place to compare your points of view, give facts, or correct "misconceptions" if that is what the child wants. At best, you may find that your child's poetry expresses what you wanted to say better than you could.

When Eve was six, she said about death, "Nobody knows the whole story. I don't think anybody even knows half of the story. Is that true, Mama?" Her four-year-old sister had a different view. "No, God knows the whole story—how to make people dead, and how to get them alive, and how to make babies and to fix the whole world." (I had never told her that.)

Once when Eve said she kind of wished she were dead, I got worried and asked her what she meant. She told me, "I want to see if I could turn into another animal and be another kind of life—a penguin or a seal." One father told me his son "invented" reincarnation. The boy called it "going around again."

Repeated questions, especially when you have answered them many times, usually mean the child is not asking what s/he *really* wants to know, and you may have to do some sensitive detective work. The child who asks, "What is going to happen to you, Mommy, when you die?" may mean "Who will take care of me?" Earl Grollman suggests, "The best answer may be mostly non-verbal. The parents might hold the youngster close and say, 'All of us hope to go on living together for ages and ages—for a longer time than you can even think of.'"

The parents who were able to explain their beliefs with relative ease follow the general principles of sharing what they think—including the uncertainty, and recognizing the difficulty of the question. They feel free to say, "Nobody can say for sure . . . it's not real simple."

Here is what some parents said:

The children have asked seriously about God and death. Until recently, we lived in Utah, so that they know well their Mormon relatives and many of their beliefs. I have told them that many millions of people believe in God, so it may be true, that it certainly is for many, but that I don't know; that the death of a loved one is wrenching and difficult, can make one angry, but that the person "lives" in our memories—they have become a part of our lives.

They talk about death and growing old and are worried about their Grandma dying. Have told them they go on living even though the physical body dies, that they are eternal beings and that they can unify with anyone in spirit, even those who have left their body. I have not told them anything I don't believe.

On Heaven, we said that Christians believe it is a place they go to in mind, after death. Death is what happens to a leaf in fall—it forms the base for new life.

We have told her that people and animals "go back to God" when they die.

T. (age five) has had many questions regarding death. My answers to her basically focus on the fact that death is the absence of life. We look at dead leaves, plants, animals, and note the differences between these examples and alive things. T. has not viewed a dead person or had a direct experience with family death. I have told her that to me, when a person dies, part of the person continues to live, and this part does not need the old body, but instead finds a new one.

I have told my son, since he first discussed it with me at about age four, that I personally have no concepts about Heaven or a God outside me, but that some other people do and find it comforting.

I shared my beliefs. I believe in a universal consciousness and that death comes when you are ready to rest or to go to a new body. Amy talks about people dying and getting new bodies. Heaven hasn't come up. God—I keep it universal—more a positive universal force. We talk more about Jesus.

In summary, the main points to keep in mind when answering children's questions are:

1. Say only what you believe.
2. Ask them what *they* think. Clarify "misconceptions" if you

want, but don't worry about them. Children's ideas change rapidly.

3. As much as possible, use concrete words that refer to things or situations children can see, hear, smell, or touch. Use teaching *stories*. Save abstract ideas for (roughly) age eleven and after.

4. Keep it short and to the point of what the child has asked. Jenny Green, psychotherapist, says, "The goal is not to answer the question, but to keep them asking."

5. Don't worry if you disregarded rules 2–4. The kids will usually discard the part of your answer that was confusing.

6. Don't say that death is like going to sleep, or a punishment for misdeeds.

7. If the child keeps repeating the same question and doesn't seem satisfied with your answer, s/he is probably looking for reassurance. Try to discover the hidden question that is too frightening to ask directly.

Most of us are not accustomed to talking about our deepest beliefs unless we are part of an organized group. I found from the responses to my questionnaire that many people did not know what their parents believed, and now that the parents were dead, wished they had asked. For many people, speaking about what is (and isn't) sacred to them is a taboo as strong as talking about sex. As with sex information, children's learning will ultimately go far beyond what parents have told them. Yet those children who remember being able to ask freely when they were still intensely curious and somewhat fearful are grateful to their parents for the rest of their lives.

The mother who asked, "How can I *share* my spiritual experiences with my child?" was asking for permission to break the taboo. She was also genuinely perplexed about how to communicate these things to her six-year-old, wondering how much the child would understand.

Don't worry about how much children understand—they will get as much as they can. What is most important is that they will definitely get your intention to share part of your self—something important that you felt. The words to use will come if you tune in to your listeners. Children love "true stories" and "chats" with their parents (until they're teenagers, that is). "Let me tell you about the time . . ." can apply to all kinds of experience. What matters is not so much what you say as your sincere desire to share yourself so that the children get to know you better (and, by seeing what part of your story interests them, you get to know them better).

What matters is that in your chat you are also saying (simply by *doing it*) that it is all right to talk about, think about, and experience these things.

CHAPTER 9

"How Can I Build Character?" Values, Ethics, and Morals

Children should grow up in an atmosphere where people work and laugh. The best you can do for them is to be something yourself.
John Lovejoy Elliott
Leader of Ethical Culture
Society (1868–1942)

He who would do good to another must do it in Minute Particulars. General Good is the plea of the scoundrel, hypocrite, and flatterer. . . .
William Blake

Meno asked Socrates: "Can you tell me, Socrates, whether virtue is acquired by teaching or by practice; or if neither by teaching nor practice, then whether it comes to man by nature, or in what other way?"

Socrates concluded that virtue was a kind of knowledge that

cannot be taught; "that virtue is neither natural nor acquired, but an instinct given by God to the virtuous."

In the twenty-five hundred years or so since this comment, parents, educators, and philosophers have wondered how to build character—and we still don't know. In this chapter, we will look at the question from four viewpoints:

1. The research of psychologists on children's moral development

2. Your own values and how best to communicate them (taking hints from what people remembered about "spiritual teachings from parents")

3. Connections between morality and "religion"

4. How all these are expressed in the day-to-day business of disciplining children

Abraham Maslow has written:

The Supreme Court decisions on prayer in the public schools were seen (mistakenly, as we shall see) by many Americans as a rejection of spiritual values in education. Much of the turmoil was in defense of these higher values and eternal verities rather than of the prayers as such. That is to say, very many people in our society apparently see organized religion as the locus, the source, the custodian and guardian and teacher of the spiritual life. Its methods, its style of teaching, its content are widely and officially accepted as the path, by many as the only path, to the life of righteousness, of purity and virtue, of justice and goodness, etc.

In a footnote, he adds: "As a matter of fact, this identity is so profoundly built into the English language that it is almost impossible to speak of the 'spiritual life' (a distasteful phrase to a scientist, and especially to a psychologist) without using the vocabulary of traditional religion. There just isn't any other satisfactory language yet." I have found the same problem.

RESEARCH ON MORAL DEVELOPMENT

Twentieth-century scientists tend to examine the process of "moral development" by isolating one of several parts: the innate endowment of children, the contents of conscience that come from interaction with parents, the stages of moral reasoning, or the effects of social control. Each group has a piece of the puzzle (although none of these groups says much about parents' values, personalities, or who we are).

Our "Instincts"

Lloyd deMause illustrates in his *History of Childhood* that throughout most of history, children were regarded as innately evil creatures who needed to be tamed. Parents beat and abused their children without guilt, feeling certain that they deserved it. Even Freudian theory assumes that the instincts are basically antisocial. A more recent theory, the "socioanalytic," questions this assumption. Socioanalytic theory assumes that since culture has played a central role in the course of human evolution, we have evolved "a deep, organic need" for our culture. Conformity is normal and deviancy must be explained. Robert Hogan et al. say that "the feeling of belonging to and participating in a viable, ongoing group gives substance to personality and meaning to life."

We met this idea in chapter 1: the need for love and inclusion in a larger whole, *together with* a need for "control" (which can be aggressive). Hogan says: "This suggests a deep conflict built into human nature so that, although we are a group-living species . . . social existence is invariably marked by struggles for status, competition for scarce resources, jealousy and rivalry, as well as affiliation and cooperation." He points out that children ages four to sixteen not only learn in the peer group about rules and fairness, but also develop empathy, learning to be sensitive to each other's "implicit feelings, intentions, needs and expectations."

The Growth of Conscience

Behaviorists contribute a piece to the puzzle when they describe an important form of learning called modeling, in which we (unconsciously) imitate the behavior of people we admire. In Freudian theory, which considers the subjective side of this process, we identify with our parents, in order to resolve emotional conflicts. The primitive superego or conscience first develops to protect us against our own destructive impulses. Then, at five or six, we identify with our parents, not only to protect ourselves against their imagined punishment for our own hostile wishes (the Oedipus complex), but also to assure their continued loving presence in our psyche.

After we "incorporate" our parents, they will henceforth always be part of us—but only part. Whether we call it modeling or identification, the mystery is that no child is a copy of either parent, or of both.

In common usage, "moral values" or ethics refers to those values which have to do with the way people treat each other, with living in society. The larger term "values" can also refer to our standards for our own competence and self-respect.

When I asked adults what spiritual teachings from their parents they remembered, I deliberately did not define "spiritual teachings." By far the majority of people answering the questionnaire remembered examples of character, rather than what their mother or father had said:

The more meaningful teachings were not verbal, but by example. My father wasn't prejudiced about race or religion; he didn't put other people down and make himself feel better. He was very honest and took stands on issues. We would go to museums and stuff as a family. I remember the way my father talked about his relationships with other people at work. When there were conflicts, he was sympathetic and had compassion for others.

In retrospect, I'd have to say my parents' basic sincere honesty and desire to do good stand out most in my mind. Their attempt to live good Christian lives, despite shortcomings, seems to take on new meaning to me now that I am a parent, a husband, etc. I can now look at their example as having positive effects on my way of life.

My parents thought little about spirituality or at least verbalized little. They did/do lead very good lives—and by their example I have learned more about giving, patience, love than through anything verbalized.

People remembered the way their parents met crises:

I think there were certain times when I saw real struggles, strength of character in my parents, compassion. . . . I remember my father consoling my mother when Grandmother died.

I remember their values and the way they conducted their lives. They lived with a great deal of respect and reverence for others. They suffered the loss of a child, which traumatized our lives in some ways, but in others set us on a search for meaning—my parents have become practicing religious Jews only within the last fifteen to twenty years.

Now, obviously, what we remember consciously is not the sum total of our parents' effect on us. The findings from the questionnaire, however, that people remember *example* more than "moralizing," is consistent with the findings from other research. No one has been able to show that a certain belief system leads to a certain kind of behavior. Attempts to predict conduct on the basis of "moral judgment" have been "weak, indeterminate, or nonsignificant." Hartshorne and May, who in 1928 were interested in the results of "character education" in schools, found that no matter what children's moral knowledge was, their conduct varied according to the context of specific situations. Merton Strommen, in 1962, studied a national cross section of almost 3,000 Lutheran senior high school students. He found "religious activity and cognitive beliefs are quite unrelated to much or little involvement in questionable or immoral practices."

From a social psychologist's viewpoint (Hogan et al), morality is "a set of rules that defines a network of reciprocal rights and obligations, prohibits gross acts of malevolence, and specifies the range of persons to whom the rules apply." These rules are rarely well-formulated. They are learned in the "microscopic moments of everyday life." Through constant interaction with parents, we learn our culture's rules for the governing of behavior. This kind of learning goes on outside of conscious awareness.

Social control can be more subtle than laws and police. Our need for other people's attention and approval is strong and largely unconscious. Ignoring children can be a worse punishment than a rebuke or a spanking. My favorite illustration of the power of attention to reinforce behavior is a story told by Edgar Cayce's grandson, Charles Thomas Cayce: Some students of his decided to "condition" his behavior, without his knowledge, by showing great interest in his lectures—asking questions, etc., whenever he nodded his head. They took a ten-minute film of him before and after two weeks of reinforcing the head-nodding. Before the "experiment," he nodded his head five times. After two weeks of reinforcement, he walked in the door nodding his head and never stopped!

Experiments with posthypnotic suggestion also dramatize how much the "reasons" for our behavior lie outside of conscious awareness, and how tirelessly we invent "reasons" for what we do. Imagine you are the hypnotist, and have told a person in a trance that whenever you scratch your ear, he will put his shoes in the oven. You then bring him out of the trance and scratch your ear. He puts his shoes in the oven. If you then ask, "Why did you put your shoes in the oven?" he will hardly ever say, "I don't know . . . that's a silly thing to do." His body may show a little discomfort but his mind will make up a reason: "It's good for shoes to be dried out in the oven now and then." The childhood scripts we have long "forgotten" continue to affect our present behavior like posthypnotic suggestions. And we are creating the scripts for our children.

How to Discipline with Love

What can we do as parents to facilitate our children's "moral development"? One parent wrote in the questionnaire: "Can anybody give ideas on *discipline* from a spiritual, loving, God-filled viewpoint?" Dr. Fitzhugh Dodson, in his book *How to Discipline with Love,* points out that discipline is a process of teaching that goes on all the time. It is much more than "punishment." "Whether you are aware of it or not, every day of your life you are teaching your child either desirable behavior or undesirable behavior, or a combination of both." In his book, he describes many different strategies of teaching, so that you can choose the ones that best suit you and your child.

The evidence is strong: What matters most is warmth and consistency. To be consistent, it helps a parent to think about which rules are most important, to try not to have too many, to make sure that they are enforceable, and then to enforce them. This way we can avoid nagging. The form of punishment is not the issue; you can spank occasionally or not, according to your personal style.

One study of nursery school children showed that if the parents were warm and strict, the children made an effortless accommodation to adult authority. Children of parents who were warm and permissive were self-confident, but sometimes felt they could break the rules and get away with it. Children of cold, strict parents tended to be angry, anxious, and sullenly compliant. The most delinquent children—hostile and rule-defying—had parents who were cold and permissive.

The trouble with discipline techniques that rely heavily on punishment is that they make children very angry. That anger has to go somewhere—and whether children end up hating their parents or hating themselves, it is not a necessary part of learning the rules of living in the world.

The trouble with what psychologists call "loss of love" methods of withdrawing, not speaking, saying "How could you hurt me like that?" or worst of all, threatening to leave, is that children may become obedient, but will be guilt-ridden and anxious, since they feel their parents' love is conditional on their good behavior.

There is another option—connecting up with children's capacity for empathy by explaining a situation so that children understand the consequences to others of what they have caused to happen. This can be done without angry accusations or "blame." Martin Hoffman, after reviewing numerous studies of the effects of a parent's disciplining practice on a child's moral development, concludes that developing empathy works best. "It is this capacity for empathy which provides powerful emotional and cognitive support for the development of moral controls."

Stages of Moral Reasoning

Part of what it means to be self-aware is to realize that our motives for action are never fully conscious. It is always possible to be self-deceived about the causes of our behavior. Lawrence Kohlberg at Harvard has chosen to ignore this and to focus entirely on what *conscious* processes children use when confronted with a moral dilemma. His research on moral development carried further Piaget's early work on the moral judgment of the child.

Kohlberg wanted to abstract moral "cognition," or thinking, from motivation, social influence, and from conduct. He told children stories with a moral dilemma such as the following: Heinz's wife is dying. The local druggist has discovered a cure, but is charging an exorbitant price that Heinz cannot pay. Should Heinz steal the medicine? Kohlberg was interested not in the content of the answer (whether the children said, "Yes, he should steal the drug," or "No, he shouldn't"), but in the process of reasoning they used to reach their conclusions.

Based on the responses to these hypothetical questions, Kohlberg and his associates thought that they had found a universal, unchanging, innate sequence of stages of moral reasoning. The first two stages were:

1. Avoiding punishment (up to age seven)

2. Satisfying personal needs, i.e., "You scratch my back, I'll scratch yours" (ages eight and nine)

In the next two stages, maintaining the expectations of the individual's family, group, or nation is perceived as valuable in its own right, regardless of immediate consequences. The attitude is one of loyalty, as well as conformity. Most adults are in these stages:

3. Acting to please or help others and win approval from the group ("Good Boy/Nice Girl")

4. Respecting authority, fixed rules, and maintaining the social order. Doing one's duty. ("Law and Order")

Stages 5 and 6 become possible only after the dawn of abstract thinking in adolescence. Only a few adults reach stage 6:

5. Respect for the social contract: Principles are gauged according to the highest social good (which could be contrary to the prevailing conventions of law and order).
6. Moral judgments on the basis of universal ethical principles (i.e., the Golden Rule)

According to Kohlberg, we cannot comprehend reasoning at a stage that is more than one stage beyond our own. That explains the uselessness of appealing to a three-year-old's sense of principled justice.

It is important to be aware of his work because so much research on this subject is derivative of Kohlberg even though he himself has changed his position. As we have seen, people's intellectual analysis of a *story* may not have much to do with their actual conduct. This was dramatized by an experiment by Randy Gerson and William Damon in which they challenged children age four to ten with a real moral situation and a hypothetical one. The children, who had been making bracelets together, were given candy bars to distribute among themselves "fairly." The children who were given *real* candy bars kept them for themselves, and defended that choice with their moral reasoning. The children who were given *cardboard* candy bars (the hypothetical situation) distributed them to the "deserving"—that is, to those who had made the most bracelets, or who were neediest—and showed a higher stage of moral reasoning. The experimenters decided that the children changed their reasoning to allow them to "more easily justify their self-serving objectives."

Psychologist Eleanor Ruma-Blofson studied the difference in components of conscience between delinquents and nondelinquents. She found *no* differences in the cognitive or intellectual component. The difference that *did* predict behavior was in emotional development—the experience of guilt.

Another major criticism of the cognitive theory is that although children in general do progress from waiting to be caught to internalizing the "voice of conscience," the details of the stages are class-, sex-, and culture-bound. Not all cultures emphasize the sacred right of individuals the way ours does; some give more importance to the good of the collective.

Kohlberg himself has moved from studying individual moral development to that of the group, working hard to create a "just community" in a Massachusetts high school. He now says that though his abstractions may be necessary for certain research purposes, "it is not a sufficient guide to the moral educator, who deals with concrete morality in a school world in which value content as well as structure, behavior as well as reasoning must be dealt with. In this context, the educator must be a socializer, teaching value content and behavior, not merely a Socratic facilitator of development. . . . This is true by necessity in a world in which children engage in stealing, cheating and aggression."

DISCOVER YOUR VALUES

In your family, *you* are the socializer, teaching value content and behavior. Do you know what your values are?

Milton Rokeach, in *The Nature of Human Values,* distinguishes between "moral values" and "self-actualization values." Moral values have to do mainly with relationships with other people: being helpful, loving, forgiving. When we violate them, we feel pangs of guilt for doing wrong. "Competence" or "self-actualization" values, such as being imaginative or self-reliant, lead instead to feelings of inadequacy and shame when we fail to live up to them.

He defines a value as a belief that a specific mode of conduct or end state of existence is preferable to another. The "terminal values" concern preferred end states of existence, such as Salvation versus Wisdom versus Happiness. I found these highly abstract and therefore of limited usefulness. In the Value Survey (see the following material), you are asked to rank eighteen "instrumental values" or preferred modes of conduct. This is not easy to do, because all are "good." In the process of forcing yourself to rank them from one to eighteen, you have an opportunity to confront which modes of conduct are, in fact, most important to you (and therefore which you will be most likely to reinforce in your children).   Rokeach found that even when people rapidly and casually numbered the items and insisted they had been "guessing," the responses were more meaningful than the people themselves knew because they were consistent on retesting. The following material has a list of eighteen "instrumental values." Rank them for yourself (one, the most important; two, the next, and so on) and then I will give you an opportunity to compare *your* values with Rokeach's research results from members of different religious groups. The disadvantage of having to fit yourself into preset categories is offset by the advantage of being able to compare your responses with the general population, since the Value Survey has been used nationally in the United States.

Notice two striking items on this survey: First, *all* Americans (Protestant, Catholic, or Jewish) rated "honest" number one. Second, being "loving" was rated tenth or lower. As Rokeach says, "There is no evidence from the national sample that being loving and helpful are distinctively Christian values."

On the other hand, John Biersdorf, who describes the beliefs of new, vital religious groups of all traditions in his book *Hunger for Experience,* found that being honest *and* loving were the values most important to the people in his study.

VALUE SURVEY

RANK FROM 1 TO 18:

A. Ambitious	_____	J. Imaginative	_____
B. Broad-minded	_____	K. Independent	_____
C. Capable	_____	L. Intellectual	_____
D. Cheerful	_____	M. Logical	_____
E. Clean	_____	N. Loving	_____
F. Courageous	_____	O. Obedient	_____
G. Forgiving	_____	P. Polite	_____
H. Helpful	_____	Q. Responsible	_____
I. Honest	_____	R. Self-controlled	_____

COMPARISONS WITH
RANKINGS OF NATIONAL SAMPLE
(The Number = The Rank Number)

Value	Protestants	Roman Catholics	Jews
A. Ambitious	2	2	6
B. Broad-minded	5	6	2
C. Capable	11	8	5
D. Cheerful	12	10	10
E. Clean	8	9	11
F. Courageous	6	5	7
G. Forgiving	4	4	15
H. Helpful	7	7	9
I. Honest	1	1	1
J. Imaginative	18	18	17
K. Independent	14	14	3
L. Intellectual	16	17	8
M. Logical	17	15	12
N. Loving	10	11	13
O. Obedient	15	16	18
P. Polite	13	13	16
Q. Responsible	3	3	4
R. Self-controlled	9	12	14

From *The Value Survey* by Milton Rokeach, which is reproduced with permission of Halgren Tests, 873 Persimmon Avenue, Sunnyvale, CA. 94087. © 1967 by Milton Rokeach.

Also note that "imaginative" is way down on the national list.

Even after we know what our values are, they may conflict in a given situation, such as the classic dilemma in which we must choose between honesty and betraying a friend. Religious faith does not protect us from the agony of such decisions. Ronald Goldman, the Protestant religious educator whose views were discussed in chapter 7, explains this:

It is a common view that religion and morals are closely related, morals stemming directly from the values believed in an accepted religious faith. If, for example, we believe in God and this belief involves the value of love for God and our fellow men, we would expect a person's behaviour to be more sensitive to the needs of others, to be more considerate, that is more consistent with the command that we should love one another. There is a sense in which this is true, because a relationship with God should provide a moral purpose and a moral power to implement it. An essential part of Christian belief is that what makes a man a human being is his moral dilemma, and his need to be redeemed or saved from his own dual nature.

Yet to use religion directly as a means of teaching moral values is to start the wrong way round. We start with the nature of the world we live in, the nature of human life, the nature of God and what kind of relationship he has with us. The center of this is the fact of love. From this fact stems the whole of the life, teaching and redemptive life and death of Christ. In this sense, Augustine's saying, "Love God and do as you like" is good morality, for if the implication of love is followed, then all that we do will be consistent with love.

The situation is often confused by what, in my view, is misnamed Christian Ethics. There is a Christian ethic, which is the law of love, but there is no system of ethics laying down specific commands for each situation or human problem we encounter. Taken merely at the social level, there is no Christian moral specific about war, divorce, family planning, or race relations, much though some of us would like such practical directives about these problems. Christians disagree among themselves on all these issues, and many more, because they have to interpret the meaning of the law of love in each situation. . . .

Discussing Values in the Family

Sidney Simon, who with Louis Raths and others originated Values Clarification, points out that conflicting values are unavoidable for the youth of today who are offered one set by parents, another by their peer group, others at school and at church, and still others from movies, magazines and television. He feels that presenting our own values in word and deed—that is, moralizing and modeling—are not enough, because children need a way to make sense of these conflicting messages.

Values Clarification emphasizes the *process* of valuing, rather than the content. This process includes *choosing* one's beliefs and behaviors freely, after considering the alternatives and the consequences; it includes *prizing* and cherishing them (with public affirmation) and *acting* consistently on one's beliefs.

Helping Your Child Learn Right from Wrong by Sidney Simon and Sally Olds presents a series of "strategies" or games that families can play to help us look at "what we want out of life, and what we're putting into it." Simon and his co-workers say that we can help children to think clearly about the choices they make; we can teach them to explore options, consider the consequences of their decisions, and to see whether they really are living according to what they say they value.

Parents who avoid the whole issue, who leave the children to "make up their own minds," are actually setting an example of not committing themselves: "Children rightly interpret such a lack of parental involvement in their lives as a lack of caring. They learn a values lesson—not to commit themselves to anything."

One parent trying to remember spiritual teachings recalled: *There were no conversations in my household about spiritual values. I would go to my mother and say, "I'm so worried about the atomic bomb," and she would say, "Hush, hush, don't think about those things." I don't really think they taught me anything—they always had the school do it.*

Values Clarification strategies have been much used in schools because they are one way of addressing the problem of moral education without imposing values with which parents might violently disagree. One criticism is that because the games are not "in context," they become "just another game." The child learns from the role model of the "facilitator" that values choices aren't really that important since the teacher seems willing to let them decide whatever they choose, and then go on to another game.

On the other hand, parents who find it hard to initiate discussions about values and ethics may find the structured "strategies" or games just what they need. As a Sunday school director said, "Anything that gets you to sit down with your kids to talk about something serious cannot go wrong. It helps create a climate that is hard to achieve in the busyness of the usual day."

Another structured format helping parents and children to talk is the Parent Participation TV workshop, started by Gloria Kirschner. In these workshops, often held in schools, churches, or community centers, parents are learning how to watch television with their children and use the viewing experience to open communications between the generations.

One of my most cherished teachings from my father was a book he gave me when I was thirteen. This book, by Stuart Chase, is called *Guides to Straight Thinking*. Using the principles of general semantics, Chase helps young people spot the common logical fallacies used in everyday arguments and especially in propaganda. As Sidney Simon says, "Too often the important choices in life are made on the basis of peer pressure, unthinking submission to authority, or the power of propaganda."

Dr. Spock recommends that

in addition to setting their children a good example of their ethical standards, [parents] occasionally discuss their own spiritual beliefs with them—not suddenly, out of the blue, but when conversation is brought near such topics by world or neighborhood or family events.

The reason I mention this is that often the reaction of agnostics and atheists against established religion makes them shy away from even referring to any spiritual beliefs. Even the word "spiritual" may make them a bit suspicious, as if it might be a disguise for religion. But spiritual only means feelings of a positive kind as opposed to material things—feelings such as love for others, dedication to one's family and community, courage, the response to music and scenery. All but the most materialistic among us hold to strong spiritual values and beliefs, even if we never speak of them, and our children absorb them gradually and silently by living with us. But to hear them spoken of and to discuss them with us helps children to clarify spiritual beliefs and values, to select those aspects that have the most meaning and to adopt them as their own.

People answering the questionnaire did remember some wise words from their parents:
My father told me to respect myself and everyone else.

Nothing specific from a religious source—just a basic teaching that each human being has a life of his/her own and attempts should be made to understand them even if they seem to be very different from oneself.

Nothing transcendental. Basically humanitarian: be good to yourself. Be good to others. Don't do anything to others you wouldn't want them to do to you. Be honest—above all, with yourself.

Hypocrisy or preaching without example was remembered with bitterness:
They talked it more than they lived it. When my sister was dating a Chinese boy, they were hysterical.

Several parents emphasized the importance of intellectual discussions:
Teach acceptance of others' right to other beliefs . . . a critical consciousness. . . . Give children a full opportunity to understand your convictions. Model your own convictions to them in everyday behavior.

Religious or spiritual education for children needs to be understood as an intellectual digestion of ethical and moral norms of conduct. Experience alone without philosophical comprehension is no better than theory without parallel experience.

It can be embarrassing when the kids actually *learn* what we have been trying to teach. Recently, after I yelled at her, Eve (age 6) handed me a note. On it she had written: "MOM REMEMBER THE GOLDEN RULE."

MORALITY
WITHOUT THEOLOGY

The practice of a moral life is itself a form of spirituality for many people: people joining together to support each other in their efforts to reach a common goal, a vision of a better life for all people, based on a perception of the oneness of all human life.

Humanists refer to our "higher self" —what we can become or manifest when we use our personality for a goal that goes beyond it—whose fruits we may never see. We all know people like this, often dedicated to social reform, guided by an "immaterial" principle: justice. These people may think of themselves as "political," not spiritual; yet they may devote their lives to selfless, loving service.

Many philosophers have recognized this, and some call themselves "religious." Since the eighteenth century, some of the names given to members of this tradition have been Freethinkers, Rationalists, Free Religionists, Deists, Natural Religionists, Humanists, and Ethical Culturists. This group includes some Reform Jews, Unitarians, and Universalists. They share the view that one can have as a highest goal the human effort to improve the human condition, embodying this in a life of loving devotion to humankind. They have demonstrated that a complete system of ethics can be developed without making any unprovable assumptions about the existence or nonexistence of God.

These philosophies and religions are connected to the rise of science and rationalism in the eighteenth century, although the ideas have been present in many other cultures. They are critical of affirmations of faith that go beyond the possibility of verification— and do not believe in the evidence of things unseen. Kant maintained that "the right way is not from divine grace to virtue, but from virtue to the divine grace." This represented the revolt of reason and reasonable people against centuries of dogmatism (as in a sense we are now witnessing some revolt against two centuries of "reasonableness" isolated from emotions, body intuition and imagination).

Although the humanist tradition offers a way of spirituality for many people, a practice of loving service devoted to an ideal of unity, it specifically chooses to ignore "unseen realities."

Abraham Maslow describes what these traditions omit:

> They make no basic place in their systems for the mysterious, the unknown, the unknowable, the dangerous-to-know, or the ineffable. They pass by entirely the old, rich literature on the mystical experiences. The inexact, illogical, the metaphorical, the mythic, the symbolic, the contradictory or conflicted, the ambiguous, the ambivalent are all considered to be "lower" or "not good," i.e., something to be "improved" toward pure rationality and logic. . . . Any religion, liberal or orthodox, theistic or nontheistic, must be not only intellectually credible and morally worthy of respect, but it must also be emotionally satisfying (and I include here the transcendent emotions as well).

If people manifest both "original sin" (that is, the will of the "little self" to satisfy its own desires at any cost) and "original innocence" (the will to expand the "little self" by experiencing the Self, the greater whole of which we are a part)—then humanism can work for those who, in William James's words, are once-born, who, from the beginning seem able to work for the good of others. It is a hard path for those who in James's terms feel there is "something wrong" with their own natures that keeps them from doing what they know to be right, for those in need of grace. Ethical Culture offers the support of a "just community" but no means of training the consciousness via meditation, prayer, or other techniques for *transformation* of the personality. On the other hand, the humanists make it clear that we do not need to live in fear of God's judgment or hope of heavenly reward to lead a moral life.

OTHER SOURCES
OF SPIRITUAL TEACHING

Fortunately for those who feel intimidated by the responsibility of "building character," parents are not the only influences. One father reminds us: "I have known people whom I felt were spiritually inclined and whose background had nothing to indicate that that would happen, or encourage it." Our children will find other sources of "spiritual teaching." Parents answering the questionnaire remembered siblings, grandparents, wives, husbands, teachers, ministers, and friends, as well as books and nature:

I was inspired by the way my brother lived and died. He lost his arm at twenty-seven from cancer, and took it as the biggest challenge life was going to throw him.

My maternal grandmother was a strong, positive influence on me, teaching me about plants, herbs, stars, love, truth, and goodness. She was a very wise woman.

My father's mother had an important part in my teaching. She went on evening walks with me in the summer and we talked of God, Jesus, being kind and good to people. The Golden Rule and being kind to old people were important.

My father practiced justice in his business; community sharing in his work as a volunteer fire chief; compassion in his acting as a sponsor for a teen just out of prison. My mother is a sharer . . . basically a very loving person. From them I get a sense of goodness rather than any teaching which is verbalized. Other sources: religious sisters in high school who were warm, energetic and caring teachers. After that it is a matter of a long list of human beings from Plato to Elie Wiesel who share their human searching for spiritual meaning through books and through life. This includes close friends.

My parents taught me kindness and givingness—that's more of an ethical than spiritual (per se) teaching. I don't know. Not much of Christianity is meaningful anymore. It says love all and is instead extremely separatist. I've been much influenced by a man named Charya Bernard who taught in Hawaii; also, Ram Dass, Krishna- murti, Vimala Thakar, and a man named Bill Wannall (channeling) and most recently, Seth.

My parents did not understand spirituality and communicated nothing meaningful in direct terms, although they were honest peo- ple who professed to want peace and love while seeking security. I recall no one as an inspiration until my wife, who exemplifies the qualities of love, patience, and nonattachment I identify with true spirituality. Bhagwan Rajneesh's writings make my heart sing and the teachings of Lao-tse, Chuang-tse, and Jesus have at different times given me strength and awareness.

Several parents felt that permission to explore religion for them- selves was a form of "spiritual teaching":

I grew up never doubting that I was loved. I think perhaps this was the greatest "spiritual" teaching that I could have had. We, as children, were not subjected at home to time-slot ritualistic training in "spiritual" matters, as opposed to normal everyday activities. However, by precept and example, we were taught (by osmosis, I think) to be individualistic; skeptical of conventional wisdom; free- thinking; curious; and reverent. To what extent these teachings were effective is, I suppose, a matter of question. However, I am very grateful for my background with my parents—especially my mother, who articulated her outlook more. Inherent within the background was the "permission" to explore without a sense of guilt other modes of religious expression than the traditional. Many answers to my personal questions about life have come through exploring non-Western religious outlooks.

I think the openness of my parents to explore and learn comes first to me. This taught me early to question and deal with uncer- tainty. It taught me that we don't always get final sure answers. There are some issues that we can never know about. But it also taught me to develop a base of strength so that no questions or doubts will shatter my peace of mind. I see adults around me tied in knots, emotionally, about whether God is dead, Jesus' shroud has been found, etc., etc.

Where moral teaching intersects with spiritual teaching is not only in the *content* of the values being taught, but perhaps most of all in the attitude of the educator.

In "The Education of the Buddhist Child," Rev. Roshi Jiyu-Kennett, Abbess of Shasta Abbey, in California, writes:

The Buddhist teacher, if he is a real teacher, says, "This child knows all, as indeed I know all, but he cannot yet express it and I can only express it partially. Therefore, he and I are on the same road. I have been going it for a little longer than he has and I will try to go at the speed he is going so that he may catch up with me, and perhaps, be able to surpass me—who knows?" So it is the duty of the Buddhist teacher to get his egocentric self out of the way to a very, very great extent so that the education of the child may be a free and beautiful thing, untrammeled by "Look at what I have achieved in my educating of this child!" It is the child that does the educating of itself by using its experiences to fall back on later; the child that makes the running; and the child that matters—we are all children in the Buddha Nature. When we say, as teachers, "I know, and you do not," we are really saying, "Our Buddha Nature is better than your Buddha Nature"; thus, is set up duality, self, fear, and inadequacy. If, on the other hand, we say, "Your Buddha Nature and our Buddha Nature are one but there is a difference between us because you are smaller than us and we are older than you; therefore we have run a little farther but we will come back to help you run as far," the difference in our attitude of mind, the difference in the attitude of the child to learning, is phenomenal.

. . . Even the stupidest child is fully accepted as having the Buddha Nature; it is embraced within the Buddha Mind and never made to feel inferior. "There are some Buddhas that are tall, some short, some fat, some thin, some bright, some stupid," say the scriptures. Unless you can see the Buddha in the little child who comes to you with his "silly" story . . . unless you can see the Buddha in the little boy with his hand in the *cookie jar and unless you can see the Buddha when you spank him—and spank him with love and cherish him in your heart whilst doing it—you will not be able to educate the Buddhist child.*

The power of the *est* Young Person's Training for children from six to twelve derives from the ability of the trainers never to lose sight of what Roshi Kennett calls the Buddha Nature, which *est* would call the Being of each child, or more simply, who we are.

I assisted at a four-day Young Person's Training at which the trainer was Phyllis Allen. Many times I was moved to tears as I saw the children move beyond the limits of what I thought was possible for them. I was stuck in my stereotypes; Phyllis wasn't. The training is not about "teaching morality"; it is (exactly like the adult training) about transforming the way we view ourselves in the world, to see that we are responsible for creating our own experience, that we are "cause in the matter." This is difficult for children to see because we mostly reinforce their "kid act," i.e., "I'm not responsible—I'm only a child." Their response to a world in which grownups make the rules is to become adept at avoiding "blame." (We continue this as adults with mental maneuvers to avoid taking responsibility, to evade feelings of guilt.)

Phyllis won't buy any of that. She gives the children an opportunity to see that although the world is certainly full of rules, they are in a position to agree or not to keeping certain rules, and to observe the consequences of keeping or breaking these agreements. Phyllis can do what is so hard for a parent to do, namely, deliver harsh truths from a *place of no judgments.* Where she may say, "This is not 'bad'—it is simply what you are doing. Take a look at it," I, as a parent, want to say (in a horrified tone), "Look at what you're doing!" Yet, as I watched Phyllis in action, it became clearer that part of a parent's job is to be as impartial and predictable as gravity in enforcing important rules. A person doesn't get to disobey gravity by complaining or being miserable about it.

The Young Person's Training is open only to children who live with at least one parent who has taken the *est* training who can support them in keeping agreements. Ultimately it is up to us to demonstrate our understanding that the children are intelligent, responsible beings like ourselves.

WHAT ARE PARENTS TO DO?

Be warm, empathic, discipline with love, and foster empathy in the kids. We can all think of incidents from history (e.g., the Inquisition) in which individuals who were cruel seemed more deficient in compassion and empathy than in moral reasoning.

Find a "just community" to support yourself and your children in the struggle to live according to what you value. Think about that when you are looking at schools, or Sunday schools.

Understand what your own values are so that you can verbalize them, and use incidents from "the morality of everyday life" — including television—as springboards for discussion.

Teach children how to think clearly, so they can clarify their own values and see the consequences of their actions.

If possible, make use of a training such as *est* that helps you and your children reach an awareness that all of us are at all times 100 percent responsible for our experiences.

And while you are doing all this, relax and realize that the children will soon have to find their own way.

CHAPTER 10

Mixed Marriages:
How Can Parents from
Different Traditions
Best Share Them with
Their Children?

Meditate, regardless of your religious affiliation, because no worthwhile creed could possibly prohibit meditation on the Self. . . . You will become aware of the omnipresence of the Lord and dance in the ecstasy of pure love at all hours. . . . Thus your own house will become sacred, your household work your worship, and your daily life your religion. The husband and the wife will consider each other divine. Muktananda exhorts you to meditate for this objective.

Swami Muktananda
The Play of Consciousness

The purpose of this book as a whole is to look at the spiritual *experience* of parents and children independent of traditional religious labels. Experience cannot be measured. Almost everything I could find on the subject of "mixed" or "interfaith" marriages was written with an underlying *quantitative* concern: how many children of these marriages are going to leave the faith? My interest throughout this book has been more in quality than in quantity, in "What was it like?" rather than "How many . . . ?" I wanted to find out what spiritual life is like for parents in mixed marriages and for their children, without pre-judging that it would be "bad."

The overarching, unanswerable question is: How do we get to be who we are? Some of the *answerable* questions I have explored, using the data from my questionnaire and from other people's research, are: What is the effect of a mixed marriage on the couple and their children? What suggestions do parents and others have for dealing with differences in religious background?

Although I made no attempt to be comprehensive (for example, I did not ask questions about race or social class) some interesting statistical findings did emerge from the parent group who volunteered to answer my questionnaire, and I will use them to examine some relationships between people's religious backgrounds and their present lives.

For example, although eighty-six percent of the respondents described their "religion now" as something other than simply Protestant, Catholic, or Jewish, 42 percent of these considered themselves more spiritual than their parents, 34 percent the same, and only 12 percent less so. (Twelve percent of the questionnaires could not be categorized in this way.) These findings seriously question the common assumption that to leave organized religion means to "lose your faith." Almost three-fourths of the respondents considered themselves at least as spiritual as their parents, if not more so.

The other striking finding was that 47 percent of the people answering the questionnaire were, or had been, in mixed marriages (according to the parents' religion). The composition of the mixed marriages was:

Protestant-Jewish	36%
Protestant-Catholic	33%
Catholic-Jewish	12%
Protestant-None	6%
Catholic-Humanist (or None)	6%

Protestant-Hindu   3%
Protestant-"Spiritual"   3%

THE EFFECTS
OF MIXED MARRIAGES
ON THE COUPLE

J. Richard Udry, in *The Social Context of Marriage,* points out that whereas religious leaders used to argue against interfaith marriages on the grounds that it would lead one away from *religion,* in American society the young couple is now warned not to marry outside the church because it is bad for their *marriage.* Presumably that is a more frightening idea.

The facts, however, are difficult to interpret. Sociologists measure marital *stability* (and instability) by the incidence of divorce and separation. Marital *satisfaction* is measured differently—by questionnaires asking about marital happiness. Statistical pictures of marital "stability" do not necessarily mean successful marriages. Landis, in 1963, found that people who were indifferent to religion tended to end unhappy marriages in divorce, while the devout tended to continue in unhappy marriages. Landis concluded then that organized religion is the strongest opponent of divorce, and religious convictions discourage divorce.

Analysis of data from the 1970 National Fertility Study by Bumpass and Sweet, controlling all variables except religious differences, showed, as we would expect, that interfaith marriages were more *unstable* than homogamous marriages. ("Homogamous" is used by social scientists to describe a marriage in which both partners come from the same—here, religious—background.) Interestingly, among the homogamous marriages, Jews were the most stable, Catholics intermediate, and Protestants the least.

In a 1961 study of marital *adjustment,* or happiness, Heiss found that intermarriage lowered marital adjustment *slightly* for Catholics and Jews, but not at all for Protestants. Several older studies did *not* find any significant effects of interfaith marriages on marital happiness.

Sixty-six percent of my respondents (who are not a random sample; they volunteered to answer the questionnaire) were still married, as opposed to separated or divorced. This is roughly the national average. *More* of the couples in mixed marriages were still married (73 percent) than couples in homogamous marriages (61 percent). This finding, though not statistically significant, was surprising.

When I looked to see whether the partners in these mixed marriages held similar beliefs (which I called "true attitude" as opposed to the traditional religious label), I found that 60 percent of them did. Their true attitudes toward religion, however, had no statistically significant relationship to whether the couples were still together. But in the homogamous marriages, significantly more of those partners who shared the same true attitude were still together.

Roughly 10 percent of the sample had parents who were in mixed marriages. Half of this group had themselves married a partner from a different religious background, but two-thirds of the group described their spouse's true attitude as the same.

WHO ARE THE RESPONDENTS?

The ages of the people who answered the questionnaire ranged from twenty to sixty-eight. The largest group, over half, were in their thirties. Roughly one-fourth were from twenty-one to thirty and the rest were evenly divided between forty-one to fifty and fifty-one to sixty.

Over half live in Eastern cities or suburbs, probably because that is where I am located. Twenty percent live in the West (mostly California) and the rest were evenly distributed among New England, the South, and the Midwest. Over half live in cities, roughly one-third in suburbs, and the rest in rural areas.

Women outnumbered men, 2.8 to 1. One can only speculate about the reasons for this. Partly it is because 44 percent of the women are single parents, raising their children without men.

In chapter 1, I describe how people's answers to the question

"What religion do you consider yourself now?" fell into four main groups. Sixty-six percent of the respondents were broadly "spiritual"; 16 percent were "religious" (i.e., traditionally Protestant, Catholic, or Jewish); 13 percent were "Humanist"; and 5 percent were "none." The large "spiritual" group had four subgroups: "spiritual—no labels" (55 percent of the total "spiritual" group); "spiritual-Christian" (23 percent); "spiritual–new group" (16 percent); and "spiritual-Jewish" (6 percent). Although there was no statistically significant relationship between respondents' religion now and whether they were still married, I could not help marveling that *all* (100 percent) of the "spiritual-Christian" couples were still together. People in the other "spiritual" subgroups broke up their marriages as often as the national average.

There is no question that the more similar in background we are to our mates, the easier we will find it to communicate, the more likely we are to understand each other without the need of explanations. Psychologists have shown that much, if not most, communication is nonverbal—which includes not only gestures and facial expression but assumptions about what needs to be said and how it should be said. In one respondent's family, parents and children, brothers and sisters, shout at each other all the time; these lively "discussions" are normal. In her husband's family, this behavior is considered at best uncouth and aggressive, at worst "crazy." He thinks so, too (when he is annoyed). (On another level he enjoys the free flow of feelings, since he did choose her to be his wife.)

The fact is that in America *most* of us are members of several different ethnic groups, if we define ethnic group as "a collection of people considered both by themselves and by other people to have in common one or more of the following characteristics:

Religion;
Racial origin;
National origin;
Language and cultural traditions."

This definition from the *Handbook of Social Psychology* concludes: "It is a hopeless task to specify the boundaries of any ethnic group exactly."

In addition to our holding different assumptions by virtue of belonging to different "ethnic groups," we also must consider the different cultural styles that go with different "socioeconomic groups," or, more simply, social class. Two white, English-speaking Protestants whose ancestors came from England may not have much in common if one is in an upper-class Boston "Brahmin" and the other a working-class southerner.

Seen in this perspective, differences in religious background are only one of many variables that can make a marriage "mixed." When true attitudes toward religious belief are concerned, many homogamous marriages are "mixed."

Joseph Campbell says that "even where a single deity is worshipped, the varieties of religious experience represented by the worshippers may differ to such an extent that it is only from the most superficial sociological point of view that they can be said to share the same religion. They are held together sociologically by their god, or gods, yet psychologically are on different planes."

The opposite is also true. Parents from " mixed marriages" can have the same attitudes. Laura, age twenty-three, is a Presbyterian married to a Jew. Speaking of their eight-month-old daughter, she says:

We have yet to work this out, but we have talked about this. We would like to expose her to both Christian and Jewish practices at home, primarily the holidays. I would like Amy to be exposed to many different religions by meeting people and by attending their ceremonies. If she knows they exist, eventually she may express an interest to learn about them in depth and perhaps even join up with one. I do not feel she needs a religion; I do feel she needs to develop a feeling about God. We will share with her our feelings and thoughts about God and she will be exposed to prayer at mealtime, perhaps before going to sleep at night.

Laura's religion now is "no named, organized religion; maybe Life is the best name." Her husband "does not practice any religion. He has a personal relationship with God and does not disbelieve in Christ."

A forty-year-old woman from a Catholic background whose religion now is "none—though hold a humanistic philosophy" is married to a Jewish man. In her family:

We celebrate all major holidays of Christianity and Judaism—sometimes with one parent, sometimes both. We focus a great deal of energy on providing humanistic and ethical communities for the kids to participate in (schools, community meetings, social protest events, etc.). I do not worry that they are missing something. We read the Old and New Testament, books that deal with ethics and values. Their school experiences focus on the same. We've selected the schools for that reason.

One couple (the wife's background Methodist and the husband's Catholic) answered the questionnaire separately. He defines his religion now in this way: "I consider myself to be a child of God and a brother to all humanity, and Christian in consciousness." She calls herself "a Universal Christian—that is, I believe in the God within and try to love all people and recognize their God within." They have two daughters, ages three and one. The wife says:

We make sure our three-year-old thanks God for the things given us and calls on the Lord or the Angels when she needs help from them. She loves to look at pictures in the Bible and hear some stories about Jesus and his work done here on earth. She says a prayer at dinnertime usually by herself but sometimes we all add a little to it. Nothing is pushed on her but we try to make her understand how to live in love by practicing it and showing her. She knows we have to help one another do this.

Her husband echoes the same thoughts: "I feel that these ways of sharing we have found provide much love and nourishment to us parents as well as to the children."

THE EFFECT
OF MIXED MARRIAGES ON
THE CHILDREN

Research on offspring of mixed marriages has mostly been written by churchmen who, no matter how hard they try to be "objective," obviously view with alarm the findings that the children are indeed statistically more likely to leave the ranks of churchgoers. Their interest is usually in conversion rates of spouses or children, and the children's participation in the researcher's religious community.

Most of the "research" has been theoretical (speculating on the *causes* of mixed marriage and/or predicting the dire consequences that *should* follow) rather than empirical (studying the consequences of mixed marriage on real children when they reach adulthood). The only objective psychological study I could find was by James Frideres (1973), who measured the effects of Jewish-Christian intermarriages with regard to Jewish identity, alienation, self-esteem, and anxiety. He found that young children from the mixed marriages did have a lower religious and ethnic identity than their homogamous counterparts, although this difference became smaller after age sixteen. On the other hand, there were *no* differences in "alienation" or "anxiety" reported by the two groups of children. Children nine to fifteen from mixed marriages scored lower on self-esteem scales, but this difference disappeared after age sixteen. Frideres concluded that his data gave no support to the common view that children from mixed marriages are more psychologically unstable than children from homogamous marriages.

JEWISH INTERMARRIAGE

Mixed marriages involving Jews (of which two out of three are a Jewish husband with a non-Jewish wife) represent a special situation because of the deep-seated sociological prejudice against Jews. Anti-Semitism sees (and usually rejects) the man or woman of Jewish origin as Jewish regardless of his or her religious conviction. The Nazis killed Jewish converts to Christianity along with other "Hebrews." Conversely, centuries of persecution have created in many Jews a deep distrust of the "Gentiles."

Jewish religion is so mixed with ethnic history that staying Jewish is seen as a matter of survival of a people, rather than a matter of belief. The holocaust of World War II demonstrated the struggle for survival to be a present reality in spite of twentieth-century hopes for a "modern" world of progress, tolerance, and rationality.

In this context it is understandable how Jewish authors lament each child lost to the tribe, and how even nonreligious Jews may experience guilt about accepting Christian beliefs, since this involves betrayal of their martyred ancestors.

Louis Berman (1968) and Albert Gordon (1964) are both Jewish authors who choose to emphasize the disasters possible in Jewish-Christian marriages. They draw their data from personal observation of friends, couples seen in rabbinical counseling, novels, and some previous research. Their assumption is that intermarriage is neurotically motivated. The best they have to say is a summary by Berman of research findings indicating that "intermarriage is less likely to be neurotically motivated for partners who share a secular point of view. There are people who have, to all intents, left their faith long before they contemplate a mixed marriage. The marriage then becomes an incidental and not the crucial factor in the separation from their religious background. . . . One might say that the shorter the religious distance [by this he means true attitude] in a mixed marriage, the less likelihood of finding neurotic factors operating." Marriage between a Unitarian and a Reform Jew involves less "religious distance" than marriage between a Catholic and an Orthodox Jew, for example. Gordon observes that in a successful intermarriage at least one partner is only a nominal member of a religious group.

The other problem heightened in Jewish intermarriages because of anti-Semitism is the opposition of the couple's parents, as well as rejection by society. Bishop James Pike writes: The plain truth is that many who are distressed about the possibilities of a mixed marriage . . . have only a secondary interest in the religious problem that may be involved—and in fact . . . there may be none involved. But the concern is often about the prospective crossing of the lines of social groupings within our culture—a division which is of course not a matter of race, but one of sociological origin." He points out that "a young man of Jewish extraction who has never entered a synagogue and a woman from a 'Christian family' who has been an agnostic since college, and has not been to church for five years, is not a 'mixed marriage' at all. It is a contemplated marriage between two modern young secularists, which stands on about the same religious footing as marriage between a lapsed Presbyterian and a lapsed Methodist."

If neither side of the family really accepts the child as one of its own, s/he is in a sort of limbo. Belonging to two cultures is undeniably more confusing to a young child than belonging to one, but this is an experience any immigrant child, or one living in another country, has. Whether it becomes enriching or pathological depends mostly on two factors: the amount of unconditional warmth and support at home, a secure center from which the child is free to develop his/her own cultural mix, and the amount of rejection s/he meets outside the family. A middle-class white Cuban immigrant in Florida may feel more secure than a middle-class black Jamaican immigrant, no matter how loving their families, because of society's barriers.

SOME PRACTICAL SUGGESTIONS

Over parental opposition and social prejudice we do not have much control. What parents in mixed marriages *can* do is create a climate in which the child is not torn between conflicting loyalties, and does not feel that s/he has to choose. Children need to identify with both parents because they love both.

Bishop Pike, in *If You Marry Outside Your Faith,* has the most balanced view of anyone I've read, although his suggestions apply more to parents who belong to two different churches than to families in which one or both are unchurched.

He strongly discourages the "peaceful" solution of silence about religious matters in the household. "This is all the more devastating; the possibility of the child's developing a sense of the relevance of religion to life as a whole becomes virtually nil."

His suggestion is that the couple should assess what they are religiously entirely apart from the faith of their parents or their own past attitudes, and then, on a fifty-fifty basis, each study the other's position. Here are some of the highlights of his fourteen-point "Guide to interfaith sharing":

Stress common ground; seek to translate concepts and practices into the other person's religious terminology so that agreement on substance can be made evident—where such is honestly the case.

Whatever faith the children are being brought up in, see to it that they gain as favorable an impression as possible of the faith of the other party, that they see the points in common, that they know which differences are nonessential and which are essential. And encourage them to respect the sincerity of the different religious allegiances.

Lay off certain points which have shown themselves to be creative of tension and misunderstandings; do not keep going over and over the same ground.

Actually put the theological and ethical insights of your tradition to work, in the discussion of family problems and decisions about future plans. This is the best way to commend them.

If your religious worship and interest bring you joy and excite your enthusiasm (and if they do not you had better find another Church yourself), let this show itself; and it will be hard for even the most rigorous separatist and "exclusivist" in religion not to concede that "there are diversities of gifts, but the same Spirit. And there are differences of administrations, but the same Lord" [I Corinthians 12:4–5].

Linda is a thirty-five-year-old mother of a ten- and a six-year-old. Of her husband, whose religion is "none," she says, "He has become interested in my spiritual pursuits as long as I don't push it." Her background is Presbyterian, and she tentatively calls her own religion "World." She says:

I feel that the togetherness of our family is very important and that would be interfered with if parts of us went to church. I occasionally worry that my children will miss learning moral senses and not have some foundation to come from. Most of the time I don't believe they are missing anything and derive greater benefit out of being in a relaxed family on a Sunday morning than rushing off somewhere. I feel good about how I "turned out" and therefore feel perhaps my children could benefit from the same upbringing. On the other hand, my present beliefs are so different from my own Sunday school time that I would not feel comfortable sending them. I am thinking of sending the ten-year-old to Self Realization (Yogananda) summer school this year for some sort of formal information.

A mother whose parents were Quakers and who is herself "sympathetic to Quaker" is married to a Jewish atheist who says, "I do partake of the spirit, but not of a defined Godhead" and expresses his spirituality in art. To the question "Do you worry that your children are missing something?" he says, "No," but his wife says, "Yes, but no solutions."

Even when the spouse's background and attitudes are basically the same, the husband is often more "rational," the wife more "spiritual." Here is how two couples answer "Do you worry your children are missing something?"

The first husband says:

Yes. Possibility of lack of social acceptance by not having an accepted "name brand" religion. Lack of understanding of religions of world. I would like to have my child have an understanding of the world's major religions and if she wishes she may participate in any spiritual (religious) activities.

His wife says of their one-year-old:

Sharing food, reading quietly, singing her to sleep and generally teaching her how to be with others and letting her be by herself have been her "religious education." We have close friends who are also "unchurched" and so she won't feel she's missing something. She may go to a Sufi school in our neighborhood (or may not go to school at all). We still celebrate Christmas, Thanksgiving, and so forth and the ritual involved there may be sufficient. Usually, we all participate in unifying activities—her birth, at home, with family was the first of such times.

[How would you go about practicing a spiritual daily life?] Sharing in the preparation and taking in of food . . . keeping my patience when it's hard to—knowing that she has no need of my anger, and making bedtime stories the gateway to dreams . . . there will be more as time goes on, I know.

The next couple are both humanists. The wife is from a Catholic, the husband from a Lutheran background. She says:

I worry that they might be missing some good understanding of the various religions of the world and how at the final common denominator we are all human beings—we have found no satisfactory solution in terms of organized programs. We do the best we can at home on a daily basis including extensive conversations as well as letting them attend religious functions with friends—followed by discussions. These are infrequent but good learning processes.

He says: "Do I worry? Not really. We think they get ethical education at home."

PREDICTING HOW SPIRITUAL YOUR CHILD WILL BE

How do we get to be what religion we are? It is certainly quite mysterious, and not entirely a question of following in our parents' lead. As noted earlier, many of the respondents became more spiritual than their parents. I looked at the data to see if there was any clear-cut relationship between the respondents' religion now and the true attitudes of their parents.

Here are some people's descriptions of their mother's or father's religion and what I called a "nonreligious" true attitude:

"Jewish: Utilitarian use of synagogue for social life and identification with a group."

"Methodist: Indifferent."

"Presbyterian: Agnostic."

"Episcopal: Avoided church as much as possible."

"Dutch Reformed: The church represented the status thing in town, and not the spiritual life."

"Presbyterian: I don't think he has ever given it much thought one way or another. Goes to church because he thinks he 'should.' Can't stand people there or the sermons."

Other parents were clearly "religious":

"Mormon: To my knowledge, she never doubted any basic tenet of the Mormon religion. Her intellectual understanding of it and her faith have deepened with her age."

"Lutheran: Mother—serious, but liberal. Father—Lutheran, very serious and fundamentalist."
"Catholic: Always seemed to uphold dogma and principles to the utmost."
"Jewish: Strong sense of religion. Lights candles on Fridays and keeps kosher house."

If one parent was religious and the other nonreligious, I called the parents' attitudes "mixed."

As I had expected, significantly more people in the "spiritual" group came from homes in which the parents' attitude was nonreligious or mixed. However, as I had *not* expected, the spiritual people now in mixed marriages were evenly divided between *religious* and nonreligious parental homes, with many fewer from mixed-attitude homes, although the numbers were too small to be statistically significant.

Protestant parents of the spiritual group were equally divided between religious, nonreligious, or mixed attitudes. The Jewish parents were all nonreligious. The Catholic parents were more religious than mixed, and none were nonreligious.

None of these data gives us any clear-cut way of predicting a child's attitudes from the parents'.

It was interesting to ask what happened to brothers and sisters in the same family. In one Catholic family, of the four siblings, two are humanists, one Catholic, one "nothing." Another humanist from a Protestant religious home has four Protestant siblings.

A sixty-year-old mother from a Protestant background who describes herself as "religious with a mystical outlook" described what four of her five sons were doing:

The eldest was active in anti–Vietnam War efforts—went to Canada to live in defiance of the draft. He is now active with UN subcommittee work—has a broad interest in international affairs, particularly where there is oppression. I believe that he would be termed pantheistic. Deep love of nature. The second son is a high school teacher with interest in science and astronomy. Calls himself "nonreligious." One of the identical twins decries the fact that he was not given "spiritual instruction" at home as a child. He, too, is a nature-lover, a skilled rock-climber, and is currently enrolled in a conservative Baptist seminary, expecting to become a missionary. His twin brother is a whimsical, self-styled "hippie" who readily credits me with being the source of all his "radical ideas" (of which he is proud) and says "of course" all his sense of right and wrong came from his upbringing and that he considers himself very spiritually trained and oriented! He is, also, enthralled with nature, and is very politically astute. The youngest, 22, another nature-boy, last week helped deliver his first-born son. An unconventional exercise perhaps, as he and the child's mother are in a "love" marriage rather than a legal one. As is noticeable, there is a great deal of variance in life-styles. I hope that some of the courage and freedom to be themselves has come from the home situation in which they grew up. I consider integrity to be a "high" spiritual value.

No matter what we do, we cannot be sure we will be happy with our child's spiritual life. As parents, we cannot help fear that if our children's ways are too different from ours, they will become strangers to us. Anthropologists say that in no culture is a child expected to choose his or her own religion. Even when, as in the United States, we do expect our sons and daughters to choose their own mates, most parents expect their children to follow the "faith of their fathers."

Just as the data do not "explain" the way our beliefs have evolved from those of our parents, so we must be prepared for our children's beliefs to differ from ours. We all know examples of prodigal sons (or daughters), and conversely, of materialistic parents whose children seek something other than money or fame.

As one Sunday school principal said:

Of the children in the same family, one has a great yen to become a responsible person, the other one's totally irresponsible. Where does that come from? Same parents. Same schools, same religious training . . . and yet they're different. I'm not sure it's all that doable. It's almost out of our control. Maybe that's why it's religious, spiritual, rather than psychologic.

CHAPTER 11

Religion and
Psychological Health

Parents want to know, "Are children from the most spiritually advanced home any different from anyone else?" Another version of this question is "Will the children suffer identity problems if we don't belong to one organized religious group?" Data to help answer these questions come from the work of psychologists and sociologists studying "religion and psychological health" and from the responses of parents answering the questionnaire.

There has been a great deal of research and very few findings. There are simply too many variables involved. How do you measure "spiritual advancement" or even "religious faith"? Behavior that is measurable, like churchgoing, is often misleading—people go to church for many reasons. It is almost as difficult to define or measure "psychological health" outside of gross differences such as whether one has ever been in a mental hospital.

Observations of real people can lead us to bewildering conclu-

sions. Gregory Zilboorg says, "I am skeptical about the tendency
... to connect mental health and religious life. If you are ill men-
tally, you cannot be a halfway decent street cleaner any more than
lead a proper religious life; yet, capital criminals may have a religious life of considerable depth and neurotics can achieve sainthood. I feel like warning myself to beware when emphasis is laid on
the fact that religious life promotes mental health, and good old
mental health promotes religious life."

William James notes that a neurotic temperament (his word,
used at the time, was "psychopathic") may even be an aid to
religious experience:

> In the [neurotic] temperament, we have the emotionality
> which is the sine qua non of moral perception; we have the
> intensity and tendency to emphasis which are the essence of
> practical moral vigor; and we have the love of metaphysics and
> mysticism which carry one's interests beyond the surface of the
> sensible world. What, then, is more natural than that this tem-
> perament should introduce one to regions of religious truth, to
> corners of the universe, which your robust Philistine type of
> nervous system, forever offering its biceps to be felt, thumping
> at its breast, and thanking Heaven that it hasn't a single morbid
> fiber in its composition, would be sure to hide forever from its
> self-satisfied possessors? If there were such a thing as inspiration
> from a higher realm, it might well be that [the neurotic] temper-
> ament would furnish the chief condition of the requisite recep-
> tivity. And having said this much, I think that I may let the
> matter of religion and neuroticism drop.

Yet James himself describes saintliness, the "ripe fruits of religion in a character," as having these features:

1. A feeling of being in a wider life than that of this world's
selfish little interests; and a conviction, not merely intellectual,
but as it were sensible, of the existence of an Ideal Power. . . .

2. A sense of the friendly continuity of the Ideal Power with
our own life, and a willing self-surrender to its control.

3. An immense elation and freedom, as the outlines of the
confining selfhood melt down.

4. A shifting of the emotional centre towards loving and harmonious affections. . . .

How does this state of love and harmony, of sainthood or enlightenment, fit with the equally described neuroticism of the seekers? The writers are describing the goal; we are on the path. We start where we are. Any practice, be it Rolfing, psychotherapy, or a spiritual discipline, can take us further along our personal evolutionary road, but it cannot guarantee that we will get to a certain place. Moreover, many spiritual teachers have described the "dark night of the soul" that has its own place on the path. Ira Progoff says simply, "It is not the high points that are real, any more than the low points. What is important is the *continuity*."

One mother wrote on the questionnaire:

After taking the est training at age thirty-three, I had the strongest mystical experience of my life. I actually experienced being the eternal being I am and being God. . . . This has definitely had a lasting influence. . . . I seem to be getting more and more of an attitude of wanting to serve my fellow man. I am more willing to let God's will be done than ever before, but lots of fear of the unknown keeps coming up. Doubts also.

There is no way a researcher can create a situation in which we all begin on the same starting line. We can only serve as our own controls. The researcher who samples the travelers passing his station on the road may think, "A motley bunch!" The travelers, on the other hand, might reply, "You should have seen us two miles back!"

Though there are many dramatic examples of people who have achieved peace of mind and/or a new zest for living after a spiritual peak experience, a religious conversion, or a training such as *est,* they are always subject to the scientist's doubt of spiritual healing: "Yes, but it might have happened anyway."

Therefore, it comes as no surprise that the research evidence is sketchy and inconclusive. No one has been able to correlate a person's religious belief with his or her psychological health as a whole. The only positive finding has been that authoritarian personalities tend to be religious conservatives, and vice versa. Even in these cases, *how* beliefs are held—whether rigidly or flexibly—must be distinguished from *what* people believe.

Attempts to correlate positive personality traits, such as feelings of security or self-esteem among college women, with religious group identity (as Protestant, Catholic, Jew) have failed.

One of the most ambitious research projects was the 1954 Midtown Manhattan mental health study, which surveyed a sample of the population of Manhattan with psychiatric interviews. Sixteen hundred adults were assigned to four groups according to psychiatric symptoms: the categories were "impaired," "moderate" symptoms, "mild" symptoms, or "well."

The major finding was that the subjects in the lower socioeconomic classes were more likely to be impaired, to have serious mental illnesses (psychoses that put people in hospitals and cause them to act "crazy"). When socioeconomic class was held constant, Protestant and Catholic differences were minor. Jewish subjects, on the other hand, were less frequently categorized as either "impaired" or "well," and therefore represented a relatively higher percentage in the "neurotic" group with mild or moderate symptoms.

The Midtown study also asked the question "How important would you say belief in religion was to your parents? Very important? Somewhat important? Not at all?" The researchers then rated the subjects' mental health in relation to the religiousness of their parents. The results are complex, so I reproduce the entire table (for Protestants only of lower and middle socioeconomic groups).

Table 2: Parental Religiousness as Judged by Subjects

Mental-Health Category	Very Important	Somewhat Important	Not Important at All
Well	21%	22%	13%
Mild-moderate	51%	60%	50%
Impaired	28%	17%	38%

The data were interpreted as follows: If you are Protestant, lower and middle class, you are more likely to be "impaired" if religion was either very important or not at all important to your parents. Your chances are better if religion was "somewhat important" to them. On the other hand, although not statistically significant, there is a trend for the "well" group to have religious parents.

Our minds cannot grasp the whole complex pattern of heredity (or karma) interacting with environment (we are our children's environment and they are ours). We try to simplify by analyzing this pattern into its parts—our children's temperaments or our behavior.

Good parenting is made easier by a good "fit" of the parent's temperament with the child's. An active baby can drive a quiet parent crazy, and vice versa, as pediatrician T. Berry Brazelton shows in his classic *Infants and Mothers.* Psychologists studying newborns have finally confirmed what mothers have always known: that babies are individuals. Some temperamental differences show up in the first hours—in the vigor with which newborns suck, in their arousal patterns, in their sensitivity to noise and bright light.

Wise parenting or spiritual guidance works with these differences. Rudolf Steiner, for example, described four "juvenile temperaments" that emerged by age five or six. The "sanguine" child is cheerful, responsive, and attention-seeking; the "phlegmatic" child nonresponsive; the "choleric," ebullient and impulsive; and the "melancholic," sensitive and withdrawn. He regarded these as physiologically determined behavioral characteristics which are *not* necessarily connected with the true individuality of the child that will emerge after adolescence. A wise parent or teacher works *with* the requirements of these temperaments. Any attempt to "eradicate" them causes them to persist.

Frances Wickes agrees that it is destructive to try to change a child's innate psychological type. Unlike Steiner, she believes these attitudes *do* remain with us through life. In *The Inner World of Childhood,* she describes the Jungian types: The 'introverted' child whose interest flows toward the inner world of *subjective* realities and values, and the 'extroverted' child whose interest goes out to the *objective* world of persons and things. Our extroverted society often undervalues introverted children, viewing their withdrawal as retreat or morbid introspection. The introvert, on the other hand, views the extrovert as lost in the material world, with no inner light to guide.

In some children, these interests are balanced, and in every case we can work toward balance—encouraging the introvert to make relationships with people and strive for tangible achievements, and encouraging the extrovert to reflect on inner meanings. We can respect the virtues of each temperament: the friendliness, quick responsiveness, and assertiveness of the extrovert; the depth and originality of the introvert. Jung found a further division between these two types, on the basis of whether the psychological function of thinking, feeling, sensation, or intuition predominated.

The development of personality is not a barrier to spiritual goals —it is the route. The loving child/adult will find a sense of meaning through devotion; the thinker will puzzle over paradoxes, perhaps scientific, perhaps those of sacred texts; the doer will dedicate his/her actions to serving people or "God."

Our children are born with their own personalities, which will affect both their "psychological health" and the kind of religion they are drawn to. Some kinds of children seem to prove theories of original innocence; others demonstrate "original sin."

William James pointed out that people's spiritual histories generally fall into two lines of development. One type of person is the "once-born," who seems to have been gifted with grace from childhood. Sunny, cheerful, and loving as children, such people simply expand the sphere of their love as they pass through the stages of child development. This is the "blessed" child who seems to need some socialization, but not "religion." As s/he grows, his or her confidence in the goodness of the universe can actually inspire or even convert a cynical adult. These are the children who take their parents to church. Evil does not shake their faith. James notes that the once-born gravitate toward or invent those philosophies that see evil as an illusion.

The other kind of person has a sense of "original sin" from childhood. Such people's lives are a struggle to come to terms with the evil they experience in themselves and the world around them. At times the "struggle" may not be evident and they look as though they are pursuing only pleasure, power, or self-indulgence, but periodically this grows stale, and they long for "something more." This kind of person needs to be "born again," to go through an experience of unworthiness, and to give up the illusion of control, making space for an experience of perfect love and/or forgiveness that feels as if it comes from the outside. Some Protestant groups emphasize the necessity of this rebirth; other Protestants as well as Catholics (Roman and Orthodox) and Jews expect a gradual growth in spiritual love, knowledge, and service to others without the need for a crisis, a sudden ecstatic transformation. Ideally, the child's temperament will "fit" the parents' religion.

As some of us struggle to become more "integrated," "sane," "whole," "actualized," "enlightened," or whatever you want to call it, we discover that the work is not to "change" ourselves, but rather to be with the experience of our lives in a new way. Psychological "health" takes on a new meaning.

What Chögyam Trungpa, the Tibetan Buddhist Rinpoche, writes is as true for our children as for ourselves:

No one can really change your personality absolutely. No one can turn you completely upside down and inside out. The existing material, that which is already there, must be used. You must accept yourself as you are, instead of as you would like to be, which means giving up self-deception and wishful thinking. Your whole make-up and personality characteristics must be recognized, accepted, and then you might find some inspiration.

CHAPTER 12

Girls and the Goddess

To Whom It May Concern:
What am I doing here? It is very simple. Your world is a
mess. . . .
But what's a mother to do? I'm here to bring it all back together
again. I'll come and straighten things out for you. I will choose an
image here to do my work. To do your work. I shall spray your
dusty corners with Lysol so you will find knowledge, stitch up those
parts of your soul which have lost each other so that man knows
what is womanly in him and woman knows what is manly in her.
You hate, screw, war, starve and die without knowing me. . . .
Somehow, I will distribute the wonders of my baking to you, to
heal and balance and restore to you the powers that once were
yours in the antique. I have always been the connection between
heaven and earth, between man and woman, between thought and
act, between everything. If your philosophers insist the world is a

dichotomy, tell them that two plus two don't make four unless something brings them together. The connection has been lost. But I'm back. Don't worry. I am going to give you the secrets this time. You are not ready, but then you may never be and whatever will I do with them then? I must warn you that I am jealous and selfish. However, I am really all that you have. I am one and my name is one and there shall be no one before me. I will forgive you anything, though, if you will love me. Cordially yours, I remain,

Your Mother/Harlot/Maiden/Wife
(The Queen of Heaven)
P.S. Call me Ishtar.
from Call Me Ishtar *by Rhoda Lerman*

"Consciousness raising" in women's groups means becoming aware of the pervasive effect of sexism, so woven into the texture of our lives since birth that it is invisible, unconscious. As women in a patriarchal culture we begin to see that our power is either feared or devalued. We have internalized many of society's views of ourselves: the "sex roles" defining our proper feelings and behavior, the "dirtiness" of our sexuality outside of marriage and childbearing, and our "nonexistence" in the making of history.

A raised consciousness begins to notice how traditional religions have deeply betrayed women. The Jewish and Christian traditions have been so male-dominated that even many women are convinced that God intended them to be second-class citizens.

In Western culture, the Source itself, the Godhead, the Numinous Element, when given a visible symbol, is generally viewed as male. Even if theologians tell us that God is not male, the symbols convey their own meaning. As Carol Christ points out, women and girls "can never have the experience that is freely available to every man and boy in her culture, of having her full sexual identity affirmed as being in the image and likeness of God." The laughter provoked by jokes in which God is called "She" reveal just how unthinkable that is for us. We may deny "His" existence, but to imagine "Her" is extraordinarily difficult. Although at higher or mystical levels of consciousness, God is neither male nor female, women as well as men need symbols along the path. Rita Gross, a Jewish theologian, asks, "If we do not mean God is male when we use masculine pronouns and imagery, then why should there be any objections to using female imagery and pronouns as well?"

The answer, in part, is political. Mary Daly says, "If God in 'his' heaven is a father ruling 'his' people, then it is in the 'nature' of things and according to divine plan and the order of the universe that society be male dominated." When women internalize these religious symbols, in which we are subordinated and inferior, then we function as our own internal police and keep ourselves in line. Myths whose sources are far from consciousness are continuously feeding us self-hatred, no matter how much we may change the details of our daily lives.

To undo the damage, women are embarking on a spiritual quest for wholeness. One way is to turn our imaginations away, temporarily, from contemporary society, back and inward to discover images from places and times where it has been otherwise. This exploration leads us to the prepatriarchal traditions. Merlin Stone writes, "In the beginning, people prayed to the Creatress of Life, the Mistress of Heaven. At the very dawn of religion, God was a woman. Do you remember?"

Joseph Campbell, whose four-volume series *The Masks of God* traces the development of mythologies throughout the world, writes:

> There can be no doubt that in the very earliest ages of human history the magical force and wonder of the female was no less a marvel than the universe itself; and this gave to woman a prodigious power, which it has been one of the chief concerns of the masculine part of the population to break, control, and employ to its own ends. It is, in fact, most remarkable how many primitive hunting races have the legend of a still more primitive age than their own, in which the women were the sole possessors of the magical art. . . .
>
> The mystery of the woman is no less a mystery than death. Childbirth is no less a mystery; nor the flow of the mother's milk, nor the menstrual cycle—in its accord with the moon. . . . Woman, as the magical door from the other world, through

which lives enter into this, stands naturally in counterpoise to the door of death, through which they leave. . . .

In the neolithic village stage [at the beginning of agriculture] of this development and dispersal, the focal figure of all mythology and worship was the bountiful goddess Earth, as the mother and nourisher of life and receiver of the dead for rebirth. In the earliest period of her cult (perhaps 7500–3500 B.C. in the Levant [the middle East]) such a mother-goddess may have been thought of only as a local patroness of fertility, as many anthropologists suppose. However, in the temples even of the first of the higher civilizations (Sumer, around 3500–2340 B.C.) the Great Goddess of highest concern was certainly much more than that. She was already, as she is now in the Orient, a metaphysical symbol: the arch personification of the power of Space, Time, and Matter, within whose bound all beings arise and die: the substance of their bodies, configurator of their lives and thoughts, and receiver of their dead. And everything having form or name—including God personified as good or evil, merciful or wrathful—was her child, within her womb.

Toward the close of the age of Bronze and, more strongly, with the dawn of the Age of Iron (around 1250 B.C. in the Levant) the old cosmology and mythologies of the goddess mother were radically transformed, reinterpreted, and in large measure even suppressed, by those suddenly intrusive patriarchal warrior tribesmen whose traditions have come down to us chiefly in the Old and New Testaments and in the myths of Greece. . . .

The Bible and Greek myths are full of textual evidence of this violent suppression of the old ways. Merlin Stone's book *When God Was a Woman* is a beautifully documented account of how the suppression of "idolatry" in biblical traditions meant the suppression of female imagery and authority. Any image—Jesus and the Virgin, as well as Astarte and Demeter—can be subject to idolatrous use. It does not mean that they cannot also signify the forces of transcendence and the unity of life.

Adrienne Rich, in *Of Woman Born*, observes, "The Yahwists

savagely repressed the cults of Astarte . . . and denounced all worship of the Goddess as 'an abomination.' The Mother Goddess is gradually devalued and rejected; the human woman finds her scope and dignity increasingly reduced. Patriarchal man impregnates 'his' wife and expects her to deliver 'his' child; her elemental power is perceived more and more as a service she renders, a function she performs."

Joseph Campbell continues:

> For it is now perfectly clear that before the violent entry of the late Bronze and early Iron age nomadic Aryan cattle-herders from the north and Semitic sheep-and-goat herders from the south into the old cult sites of the ancient world, there had prevailed in that world an essentially organic, vegetal, non-heroic view of the nature and necessities of life that was completely repugnant to those lion hearts for whom not the patient toil of earth but the battle spear and its plunder were the source of both wealth and joy. In the older mother myths and rites the light and darker aspects of the mixed thing that is life had been honored equally and together, whereas in the later, male-oriented, patriarchal myths, all that is good and noble was attributed to the new, heroic master gods, leaving to the native nature powers the character only of darkness—to which, also, a negative moral judgement was now added. For, as a great body of evidence shows, the social as well as mythic orders of the two contrasting ways of life were opposed. Where the goddess had been venerated . . . women as her representatives had been accorded a paramount position in society as well as in cult. . . . And opposed to such, without quarter, is the order of the Patriarchy, with an ardor of righteous eloquence and a fury of fire and sword.

From those beginnings we can trace the dualism of the Judeo-Christian-Greek tradition, in which the (male) virtues of soul, spirit, rationality, and transcendence must overcome the dark forces of (female) body, flesh, matter, nature, and immanence. God is set over, and in opposition to, "the world." Rosemary Reuther, a Catholic theologian, describes the consequences as "a world-destroying spirituality that projects upon the female of the race all its abhorrence, hostility, and fear of the bodily powers from which it has arisen and from which it wishes to be independent." Every woman who has been pregnant has had an experience that contradicts this dualism between "me" and "not-me," for the growing baby is both. The new women's spirituality not only recalls to women the human capacities of intellect and will, but also expands "I-ness" to include the unconscious, the body, and nature, so that men and women can live in harmony with each other and the natural world.

THE FEMINIST RELIGIOUS REFORMERS

Women critical of patriarchal religion take two main paths: that of the "reformers" who work within their traditional religious heritage, and that of the "revolutionaries" who are creating new forms.

The reformers point out that women were centrally important in the life of the Buddha, and in the early Christian church, but the organizations which crystallized around the teachings became more like the patriarchal cultures in which they originated. Women were among the first followers of Jesus and were the first witnesses to the Resurrection; they were prophets, apostles, and full participants in the missionary work of the early Christian community. Before the official gospels of the New Testament were selected, there were secret Christian gospels, rejected as Gnostic heresies, in which God was imagined as father and mother, male and female, in which the feminine principle of God was called Source or Silence, Grace and Wisdom. The Holy Spirit, usually considered male because the Greek word for spirit, *pneuma*, is a "masculine" noun, was interpreted as female from the feminine Hebrew word *ruah*. Some feminist theologians suppose that the fact that women played important roles in the Gnostic Christian groups—healing, teaching, baptizing, prophesying, and even acting as bishops—may have been an important factor in the suppression of these groups as heretic.

Anne M. Squire, a member of the United Church of Canada, summarizes the Judeo-Christian position of women:

Biblical women were, with a few notable exceptions, seen as non-persons, honoured as wives and mothers but always seen in relationship to the man and categorized as whores or harlots if they did not fit into the traditional slot. Women were protected but without rights, discriminated against in law, especially in matters of divorce or inheritance. They were always subordinate to the male and dependent upon him. For much of their lives they were considered unclean and thus excluded or exempted from religious duties. . . .

In Judaism, the Talmud pictures women as "important in terms of family life but dependent upon men and excluded from formal education and restricted in rights. . . .

In Christian circles after a brief promise of equality through the liberating gospel of Jesus, women were pictured in the early church in polar terms, either as the unreachable virgin or as the source of temptation and evil. "You are the devil's gateway" was Tertullian's way of summing up the attitude toward women. All women were considered weaker than men not only physically but intellectually and morally as well."

Anne Squire continues to find hope in the "liberating word" of Genesis 1:27, "So God created man in his own image, in the image of God created he him; male and female created he them"; and Galatians 3:26–28, "For ye are all the children of God by faith in Christ Jesus. For as many of you as have been baptized into Christ have put on Christ. There is neither Jew nor Greek, there is neither bond nor free, there is neither male nor female: for ye are all one in Christ Jesus."

She recommends to religious educators that they bring a feminist perspective to Bible studies and church history, eliminate sexism from the curriculum, avoid masculine pronouns to refer to men and women (substitute "humans" or "everyone" or "we"). Say, "Children of God" instead of sons of God, write new prayers, and above all, involve women in the total life of the church. Women in all religions are fighting their traditional exclusion from positions of spiritual authority, for their right to be rabbis and priests.

Jewish reformers look to the Kabbalistic teaching that says that the cause of exile and suffering is the alienation of God from a feminine principle called the *Shekhinah,* the Divine Presence. Jewish feminists publish a magazine, *Lilith,* have written a new Passover Haggadah which celebrates the foremothers as well as the forefathers, have invented new rituals to bring infant girls into the covenant with God as well as infant boys (who are initiated by means of the *brit,* or circumcision), and have written new prayers praising God with the words "Blessed is She. . . . I will exalt Her."

The reformers believe that religions are constantly evolving and changing. They feel they are simply taking the next step in this evolution without contradicting the core teachings. Elisabeth Fiorenza, a Roman Catholic theologian, points out that the cult of Mary grew in proportion to the gradual repatriarchalization of the Christian God and of Jesus Christ. She says:

> *Feminist spirituality proclaims wholeness, healing love, and spiritual power not as hierarchical, as power over, but as power for, enabling or transforming power. It proclaims the* Goddess *as the source of this power, as the enabling context of human lives, and of a nonhierarchical, nonauthoritarian, noncompetitive community. . . . Being a woman, living in sisterhood under the aegis of the Goddess, brings us in touch with the creative, healing, life-giving power at the heart of the world. In my opinion the Goddess of radical feminist spirituality is not so very different from the God whom Jesus preached, and whom he called "father."*

The reformers, then, feel that the creation of feminine symbols is consistent with their faith. In the words of Mary Daly, "Authentic faith . . . accepts the relativity of all symbols and recognizes that fixation upon any of them as absolute in itself is idolatrous." Needless to say, many "fundamentalists" disagree.

NEW SPIRITUAL FORMS

Another group of women feel a deepening alienation from the biblical tradition. In the words of Carol Christ: "We will no longer be content to read ourselves sidewise into stories in which the daughters do not exist." Some turn to the European tradition of Wicca or the Craft, while others are working to create new forms of spiritual practice, through female imagery and symbolism, "getting in touch with our bodies and nature," and the stories and rituals that grow out of community with other women.

For some, the Goddess is a divine female who can be invoked in prayer and ritual, for others she is symbol of the life, death, and rebirth energy in nature and culture, in personal and communal life. Merlin Stone explains:

What has been happening is the experiencing, and at times the reporting of these personal or group experiences: how it feels to regard the Ultimate Life Force in our own image—as females; how it feels to openly embrace and to share our own contemplations and intuitive knowledge about the role of women on this planet; how it feels to gain a sense of direction, a motivating energy, a strength, a courage—somehow intuited as coming from a cosmic female energy force that fuels and refuels us in our struggle against all human oppression and planetary destruction.

Some say they find this force within themselves; others regard it as external. Some feel it in the ocean, the moon, a tree, the flight of a bird or in the constant stream of coincidences (or noncoincidences) that occur in our lives. Some find access to it in the lighting of a candle, chanting, meditating . . . alone or with other women.

She points out that the Goddess symbolizes much more than even the fertile Mother. Many women regard the Goddess as *all* the phases of the moon: the virgin huntress, complete unto herself; the Mother; and as she wanes, the old "wise woman," who in the Middle Ages became the evil "witch." We have lost the archetype of the wise woman. Contemporary women are expected to get depressed after the menopause. When they can no longer bear children, their "lives are over." Merlin Stone tells us that this was not always so:

The Celtic Cerridwen was the Goddess of Intelligence and Knowledge in the pre-Christian legends of Ireland. The priest-

*esses of the Goddess Gaia provided the wisdom of divine rev-
elation at pre-Greek sanctuaries, while the Greek Demeter and
the Egyptian Isis were both invoked as lawgivers and sage dis-
pensers of righteous wisdom, counsel, and justice. The Egyptian
Goddess Maat represented the very order, rhythm and truth of
the Universe. Ishtar of Mesopotamia was referred to as the Di-
rectress of People, the Prophetess, the Lady of Vision, while the
archaeological records of the city of Nimrud, where Ishtar was
worshipped, revealed that women served as judges and magis-
trates in the courts of law.*

She suggests that if we dated our calendar from the beginning
of agriculture 10,000 years ago, we would find it easier to include
the Goddess worshippers (who were, after all, our ancestors) in our
religious identity along with the religious identity of our more immediate ancestry (the last two, three, or five thousand years).

I strongly recommend the anthology *Womanspirit Rising*, edited
by Carol Christ and Judith Plaskow, and an issue of *Heresies* magazine titled *The Great Goddess* for those who wish to explore this
area further.

I have always wondered why so many women, as well as men,
support patriarchal antiwoman attitudes. Dorothy Dinnerstein gives
a convincing answer in her book *The Mermaid and the Minotaur*.
She says that male dominion over females, and female acceptance
of that dominion, reflects our terror of sinking back wholly into the
helplessness of infancy. We fear the power of our first caretaker,
who has always been female. We fear not only her life-and-death
control, but also her power to foster or forbid our emerging autonomy. Hers is

*the earliest and profoundest prototype of absolute power. It
emanates, at the outset, from a boundless, all-embracing presence. We live by its grace while our lives are most fragile. . . .
Power of this kind . . . is far too potent and dangerous a force
to be allowed free sway in adult life. . . . The essential fact about
paternal authority, the fact that makes both sexes accept it as a
model for the ruling of the world, is that it is under prevailing
conditions a sanctuary from maternal authority.*

Her elegant arguments, which are much too extensive to be easily summarized, include an analysis of why it is difficult for everyone to see woman as fully human. At first, we knew her as an embodiment of "global and inchoate, all-embracing qualities. . . . The mother is first experienced by every one of us as an 'It' while the father, who is a much more peripheral presence at the beginning, becomes a significant figure only after the concept of an independent outside 'I' has begun to be established. It would be strange if this early difference did not carry over, on a pre-rational level of feeling, into adult life."

This observation also explains why so many people (including Freud) have feared and devalued the mystical sense of union—it is too close to the feared early experience. Others make it acceptable by relating it to a "male" God.

In addition to our fear, we also feel rage. In our infancy, mother was the source of bliss and the source of despair; it was she who "mysteriously withheld food, who . . . mysteriously allowed loneliness, terror and pain to continue." We blamed her for what we now "know" to be inevitable frustrations of life, and in the prerational parts of our mind, we continue to blame her. We all keep from infancy the assumption that woman (mother) "exists as a natural resource, as an asset to be owned and harnessed, harvested and mined, with no fellow-feeling for her depletion and no responsibility for her conservation or replenishment," says Dinnerstein.

What do women want? Dinnerstein says plainly, "What women want is to stop serving as scapegoats . . . for human resentment of the human condition." She thinks this will happen only when men as well as women participate in the physical care of infants and young children, so that the dynamics described above will not be directed at only one sex. Modern technology has made this possible for the first time in human evolution.

Women's restriction to the home by continuous pregnancy and lactation throughout a short life is no longer a biological necessity. Childbearing now occupies only a small percentage of women's adult years. Physical size and strength for work outside the home is now largely irrelevant, and as Dinnerstein points out, male "aggressiveness" is now more dangerous than protective, since our enemies are each other and not wild animals. Yet society continues what she calls the present "sexual arrangement" of dividing responsibility, opportunity, and privilege between male and female humans, distorting "our species' stance toward itself and nature."

Here we meet again the point made in chapter 1: that each human being feels simultaneously the "self-assertive tendency" for autonomy, freedom, and mastery, and the "integrative tendency" to transcend the boundaries of the self, to be part of a greater whole. We all need both, but our culture values the first, which it assigns to men, and fears the second, which it assigns to women.

Dinnerstein adds, "One reason why it is harder for men than for women to achieve real critical perspective on our gender arrangements is that mother-raised man's self-respect rests too heavily on the belief that he is better than woman and has successfully put her in her proper place; in other words, that he has outgrown her initial power over him. The thought that the arrangement has in some way maimed him too—that it does not represent an unequivocal triumph over her, that it is not wholly to his advantage—is too threatening to be voluntarily entertained." Among the disadvantages are men's need to imagine themselves more in control of nature than they really are, and often a "general constriction of the emotional flow between the man and his world."

Until the "arrangement" changes, until babies and toddlers are "dominated" by both sexes, so that we can find new unconscious defenses against early fear and rage, what can we do? How can we help our daughters value themselves and our sons value their own "integrative" needs? Part of the answer, as in psychotherapy, is to make the unconscious conscious, to become aware of how patriarchal society increases the difficulty of these developmental tasks.

Psychologists of all schools agree that it is easier for the son to separate from his biological continuity with the mother because he can identify with his father. What isn't so readily noticed is how society makes the daughter's already difficulty task much harder: to identify with her mother, she must accept an inferior position, and she must not resent her mother for transmitting society's expectations!

We can use the symbol of the Goddess psychologically, to reach into the unconscious for the maternal strength and love that were as much a part of our early experience as her fearful power.

It is remarkable that our culture provides no celebration of a proud ongoing mother-daughter relationship. There are proud virgins, the saints, and a model for mother-father-son in Mary-God-Jesus, but where are the mother and daughter?

In the Eleusinian mysteries of ancient Greece, the mother-daughter relationship became a metaphor for human spiritual survival. In this myth, Demeter, Goddess of the harvest, Queen of the grain, loves her daughter so much that she descends to the Land of the Dead to search for her when the daughter—Kore or Persephone—has been raped and abducted by the Lord of the Underworld. All crops wither and die. Spring never comes when Demeter is gone.

Adrienne Rich notes:

When her daughter is restored to her—for nine months of the year only—she restores fruitfulness and life to the land for those months. But the Homeric hymn tells us that Demeter's supreme gift to humanity, in her rejoicing at Kore's return, was not the return of vegetation, but the founding of the sacred ceremonies at Eleusis . . . the most forbidden and secret of classical civilization, never acted on the stage, open only to initiates who underwent long purification beforehand. . . . The role played by the Mysteries of Eleusis in ancient spirituality has been compared to that of the passion and resurrection of Christ. But in the resurrection celebrated by the Mysteries, it is a mother whose wrath catalyzes the miracle, a daughter who rises from the underworld.

The deep meaning of the myth of Demeter and Kore is a teaching about eternal life within the cycle of birth and death. At a superficial level the story provides a model of a mother willing to fight a powerful male to save her daughter—quite the opposite of our stories about bad mother figures who lock their daughters away from men (Rapunzel), insist they marry for wealth and social position, or eliminate them from the competition (Snow White). We are much more familiar with the Witch than with images of the good mother. Only a few come to mind: the fairy godmother in "Cinderella," Glinda the Good in *The Wizard of Oz.*

Not only do our myths deemphasize the good mother; our society makes it harder to *be* a good mother. If a large part of the mother's role has been restricting the growing girl's assertiveness and training her in passivity, the daughter's resentment is justified: "Be a little lady!" "Girls don't do that!" "Don't be too smart, aggressive, adventurous—no man will want you!"

Adrienne Rich notes:

> For much as she may act as the coequal provider or matriarch within her own family, every mother must deliver her children over within a few years of their birth to the patriarchal system of education, of law, of religion, of sexual codes; she is, in fact, expected to prepare them to enter that system without rebelliousness or "maladjustment" and to perpetuate it in their own adult lives.

Too often the mother herself has internalized self-hating sexual attitudes and transmits these to her daughter as the most effective way of keeping her a virgin until marriage. At a superficial level, this led to girls being discouraged from the full use of their bodies. They were supposed to be pretty but not strong, not to be a "tomboy" interested in active sports.

The Freudian concept of penis envy is rooted in the fear and repression of female sexuality. Freudian psychoanalysis teaches that girls feel inferior for not having a penis, and resent their mothers, who also "lack" a penis, and didn't give them one.

The Womanspirit movement, affirming femaleness, is reclaiming images, myths, and practices that *celebrate* the wonder and mystery of women's bodies.

I once had an argument with a (female) psychoanalyst, who said, "The little boy and the little girl look at the girl's genitals and see . . . nothing. How can they not be afraid?" My answer is that they see "nothing" because that is what their own mother saw, and hers before her. She was not supposed to see, touch, or feel anything there. Our language does not even have a female equivalent for the word "phallic." When one of our daughters was three, she constructed a "penis" out of a cardboard paper towel roll and paraded around with it, saying, "Look at my penis!" She then proceeded to make a soft, flowerlike vulva out of tissue paper and paraded around with *that,* saying, "Look at my vulva!" If she feels "penis envy," it will be envy of the respect, freedom, and privileges given every man and boy in our culture.

The daughter who has internalized our cultural devaluation of women will blame her mother not, as Freud said, because she lacks a penis, but partly because she has *witnessed* her mother devaluing herself. Perhaps her mother has been full of bitterness and resentment, and perhaps not, but in either case she has been unable to provide the example of a whole person for which the daughter yearns.

Perhaps mothers of today can be better models. In addition, we can tell the old stories, and make up new ones, that speak to the Goddess power, that provide for the psyche the organizing images of strong maiden, good mother, and wise "witch."

When I was a child my introduction to the Goddess was in the form of Wonder Woman comics, which I loved as my daughters do now. Wonder Woman (otherwise known as Princess Diana) begins life on Paradise Island, where no men are allowed. Her mother is Queen Hyppolita, Queen of the beautiful Amazons. Aphrodite and Athena come frequently to advise and instruct. The best of these comics have been reissued as a paperback book (see "Resources").

For one Catholic feminist the lives of the Saints provided a model of nonconforming women who chose to follow their own spiritual path, with supreme courage. More and more children's books are being published about the inspirational lives of real women throughout history.

To me, even more important than examples from history are those visionary works of fiction or poetry that allow us to imagine old/new worlds in which women are strong and self-reliant, in which the Goddess comes back, or, best of all, worlds in which men and women live together without sexism. My favorite adult books are a prose poem by Monique Wittig, *Les Guérillères;* a very funny novel by Rhoda Lerman, *Call Me Ishtar,* in which the Mother Goddess is managing a rock band; and several of the novels and stories of

Ursula Le Guin, particularly *The Left Hand of Darkness* and *The Dispossessed.*

The Feminist Press publishes a book and tapes of fairy tales in which girls are the heroines (see "Resources"). My daughters love them. Merlin Stone is compiling Goddess and heroine myths from all cultures for adults. She writes in a letter:

Now that I have become so familiar with the many legends and images of women as wise, just, strong, compassionate and more, it all seems even stranger that anyone could regard having a daughter as less fulfilling than having a son. . . . I find it astonishing that all this material exists in various archaeology and anthropology books but that so little is known to even the most educated people today. . . . It is truly my hope that once others have become familiar with the stories they will want to take the information and use it as "archetypal imagery" in writing novels, short stories, plays, painting, etc. (time to retire the themes of Romeo and Juliet and Adam and Eve).

Let us hope that the next generation will not be limited to Wonder Woman.

PART FOUR:

Adolescence and After

CHAPTER 13

How Do People
Find Meaning in Life?

The struggle for economic security provided a purpose in life for many parents who were raising children in a time of economic depression. These children, now affluent adults, cannot find a sense of purpose in simply making more money. As Abraham Maslow said, "Affluence itself throws into the clearest, coldest light the spiritual, ethical, philosophical hunger of mankind. This is so because striving for something one lacks inevitably makes one feel that life has a meaning and that life is worthwhile. But when one lacks nothing, and has nothing to strive for, then . . . ?" In Maslow's hierarchy of needs, after physical needs have been met, we satisfy our needs for love-belongingness, esteem, self-actualization, and transcendence.

Psychotherapy and religion both attempt to help individuals satisfy their spiritual hunger. Jung said, "A psycho-neurosis must be understood as the suffering of a human being who has not discovered what life means for him." Selfhood, in Jungian terms, is in essence a religious matter. What Jung called the process of individuation, in which we come to grips with unconscious parts of our personality, involved recapitulating in the psyche "the enduring motifs of religious salvation."

One of the parents who answered the questionnaire reported her experience in Jungian therapy:

So at forty, I startd therapy with a Jungian—a guy named Roger Woolger in Burlington. I showed him a print of a woodcut I had done of a giant bird with a mandala eye hovering over a naked female—and he said, "Hmmm . . . maybe you're concerned with your spiritual development." And I said, "Huh?" and went home to ponder that one, and of course I realized he was right on. And since then, it feels a fairly continuous process—at times slow, at times breathtakingly fast, painful and joyful, terrifying and reassuring—of first of all "owning" my spiritual nature in the face of all my highly rational conditioning and secondly, exploring the new territory and making the linkages to those parts of my past I kept behind that wall.

One understanding I've gained is that it is impossible to separate the problems and strengths of the important human relationship from the relationship of the spiritual. Making peace with my parents' ghosts, ending the war with them, giving up the anger and pain are as much a part of the process of finding God as using prayer and meditation—and vice versa.

Roberto Assagioli, founder of Psychosynthesis, and Victor Frankl are other psychotherapists whose schools deal centrally with the question of finding meaning.

Victor Frankl writes:

Let us now consider what we can do if a patient asks what is the meaning of life?

I doubt whether a doctor can answer this question in general terms. For the meaning of life differs from man to man, from day to day, and from hour to hour. What matters, therefore, is not the meaning of life in general but rather the specific meaning of a person's life at a given moment. To put the question in general terms would be comparable to the question posed to a chess champion, "Tell me, master, what is the best move in the world?" There simply is no such thing as the best or even a good move apart from a particular situation in a game and the particular personality of one's opponent. The same holds for human existence. One should not search for an abstract meaning of life. Everyone has his own specific vocation or mission in life; everyone must carry out a concrete assignment that demands fulfillment. Therein he cannot be replaced, nor can his life be repeated. Thus, everyone's task is as unique as his specific opportunity to implement it.

As each situation in life represents a challenge to man and presents a problem for him to solve, the question of the meaning of life may actually be reversed. Ultimately, man should not ask what the meaning of his life is, but rather must recognize that it be he who is asked. In a word, each man is questioned by life, and he can only answer to life by answering for his own life; to life he can only respond by being responsible. Thus, logotherapy sees in responsibleness the very essence of human existence.

A traditional religious perspective is not the only way of finding meaning and purpose in life. When I asked parents: "How meaningful do you find life now on a scale from 1 to 3, if 1 is very meaningful and 3 is not at all?" Ninety percent said: "1. Life is very meaningful," and they told why. Freud's criteria of mental health was the ability to love and to work. Others have added to play creatively, and to take responsibility for the larger community. Parents' answers expressed all of these and more.

One group found their meaning in life itself:

The sense of being alive, having perceptions, feelings, making decisions, using my intelligence, creating, moving, acting.

Life simply has it. Meaninglessness seems a meaningless concept. Life always has "meaning" and individuals can be more or less in contact with it.

Others listed more concretely what mattered most in their lives:

My child, the natural world, my family and friends and myself —all of which are a source of continuing joy and amazement to me.

The children, my lover, my work—the sense that I'm doing what I want to and doing it well.

All of it: people, relationships, challenges, art, music, poetry, philosophy.

To feel a lot: birth, death, love, friends, husband, art. . . .

Many others emphasized the sense of connectedness as an important part of life's meaning:

The awareness of myself as a part in a whole, with a responsibility to the rest as well as the knowledge that I am what I am because of the rest. We are interdependent. Every interaction can be mutually beneficial.

An awareness as an adult that the universe is connected and what I do makes a difference.

I trust existence. I am learning to flow with life rather than viewing the living process as a series of obstacles to overcome. I know that I am connected with all other things.

Sense of imbeddedness and interconnection of family, work, social movements. . . .

Out of this comes a sense of challenge or purpose:

We're living in a most incredible time when we have opportunities to correct things that have gone wrong in all of us—for the unity of humanity.

The fact that I know it is up to me. I have been given everything I need to live a full life, but it is up to me to decide how to conduct myself in ways conducive to growth. Simultaneously, I recognize that there are forces beyond me which propel me.

My understanding that my life is purposeful in a self-developmental sense (in the Eastern sense of karma). I also have a splendid husband, two great kids, and live in a great spot in the mountains.

Only a few specifically mentioned consciousness, or God:

A sense of interrelationship with other people and with nature and therefore with the creative energy of "God"—or vice versa.

A belief that I'm here to learn, to grow, to develop greater consciousness, to achieve sometime a realization of my oneness with God that I know is—also I have a sense of being here to help others gain tools to sharpen their awareness of inner (and outer) divinity and of their part, which can become conscious, of life on this planet.

The "believer" group of churchgoing psychology students who answered the questionnaire in class were more likely to use the word "God": "Living my life for God." "Communion with God." "The God I serve."

What of the 10 percent who rated their lives less than "very" meaningful? Only one person said, "3. My life has no meaning right now." Her husband added: "or lack of meaning" to the questionnaire and rated "2 plus." They were both depressed at the time because they couldn't find work.

One woman answered, "1 for now, 3 for eternity" and explained: "This lifetime is quite meaningful because I am beginning to see where I can contribute best to life on earth and am able to actually accomplish some dreams, visions. Three for eternity because my life seems only a drop in the sea of the Eternal, a moment in all time, a flash in the Universe."

One woman who answered "2" found meaning in "the challenges, goals, purposes, and even the disappointments and disillusions of my everyday life."

A good summary of the connection between life's activities and spirituality was given by one mother (who rated her life 1):

A strong sense that with each moment I am creating my life and helping share in the creation of lives that are growing around me. Activity yields meaning. Receptivity also opens the meaning of life as a gift-process. I lose my sense of meaning when I succumb to passivity, which feels very different to me than receptivity. Passivity equals thinking that my life is made by what happens around me. More concretely, my meaning-sense is worked out through my marriage, my friendships, my professional work (this last is really a struggle for me right now). Coming to the sense of what life's meaning is and actively working at creating it is probably what I'd call my spiritual life.

A sense of meaning does not have to include the *knowledge* of the "purpose of life." Like bees, as we gather our pollen and make our honey, we may not know that we are also pollinating flowers.

Jacob Needleman was brave enough to answer when a magazine interviewer asked him, "What is the purpose of life?":

*Well, that is a great question. I have been asking that question
since I took Philosophy One at Harvard University! I asked that
question, and I remember very clearly being put down and
snickered at. It was a "naive question." You must remember
that attitude from your own college days: "That is not a philosophy question; go to a psychiatrist for that."*

*Years later I found that the state I was in when I asked that
question was itself a beginning of the answer. It was a state of
openness, of hunger, of need in all my parts that was really
closer to what I am than when I started finding all of the pat
answers of the philosophy professors.*

*This is not exactly a direct answer to your question, but I
think our own lives and history show us that we don't know the
answer to that question. Western, modern thought says,
"Therefore we can't find the answer." After my own studies, I
say it means we can't find the answer in the state we are in. It is
a question which requires of us another state. So in order to
answer the question, we have to be trying at that same time for
what they call a "greater state of presence, or consciousness."
In that state we can be sensitive to laws and energies in the
universe, so that the answer becomes clear. It may not be intellectually formulated right away.*

*It is like a five-year-old asking, "What is the purpose of man
and woman?"*

CHAPTER 14

Adolescence
and Other Spiritual Crises

We shall not cease from exploration
And the end of all our exploring
Will be to arrive where we started
And know the place for the first time.

> T. S. Eliot
> Four Quartets

Adolescence is an age of spiritual hunger and a quest for meaning, as well as a time of tremendous physical and emotional
changes. This is accepted by theorists who doubt that *children* have
genuine religious experience. So much has been written about the
spiritual life of teenagers that I can cover the subject only briefly.

With the developing power of abstract thought, the adolescent
for the first time can ponder intangibles such as life and purpose.
Havighurst and Keating, summarizing research on this age group in

"The Religion of Youth," note that "adults tend to miss the critical areas of youth's concerns by overestimating their anxiety about family and sexual activities and underestimating their concerns about faith, values, and life goals."

Johanna Klink says:

There are many children who during their twelfth year or thereabouts undergo an experience of faith which is decisive for their further development. The experience of being meaningfully related to the whole of existence is almost always first recognized in the condition of being cast loose. It is no accident that it occurs at the age at which a more or less stable period of life is passing into another. Adolescence is such a period to the utmost degree. At this stage a person looks for new landmarks, suppressed urges come to the surface, and former certainties disappear.

Psychosynthesis teaches that adolescence can best be understood if we consider the child to be experiencing a surge of spiritual energy from the higher self at the same time that s/he is dealing with new rushes of sexual energy.

Recent scientific support of that idea comes from research on brain development. Paul MacLean notes that the prefrontal cortical circuits that connect with the part of the limbic system responsible for parental care do not come into full operation until the hormonal changes of adolescence occur. He suggests that this may be a critical period for the development of altruism and empathy, and recommends that adolescents be given the responsibility for ministering to human suffering.

The inflow of "spiritual energy" can take many forms. It is at adolescence that the poetic sensibility of the preschooler, tempered by the information and skills gathered in the school ages, flowers into disciplined creativity. Herman T. Epstein, studying brain growth, found that human brain growth occurs primarily during the age intervals of three to ten months, two to four years, six to eight, ten to twelve or thirteen, and fourteen to sixteen or seventeen. All these intervals correlate with the classical leaps of intellectual development described by Piaget (see chapter 7) *except* ages fourteen to seventeen. Epstein suggests that the fourteen-to-seventeen spurt might represent the growth of potential for creative thought, "problem finding" as opposed to problem solving. He proposes saving new intellectual challenges for the periods of brain growth spurts and providing a wide variety of direct life experiences and facts to learn during the plateau phases. (He also guesses that Head Start programs for three-and-a-half to five-year-olds may have failed because of an accidental choice of exactly the wrong age for brain stimulation; it should have been earlier or later!)

The teenager dealing with new spiritual energy may begin to doubt what s/he passively accepted as a child, and reject the teaching of institutional religion. Or s/he may experience a conversion, and be "born again," as an adult with conscious choice.

Edwin Starbuck, who in 1899 was among the first to study the psychology of religion, concluded that conversion was a natural event of adolescence. E. T. Clark, in 1929, and G. W. Allport in 1948 found that about 7 percent of the college population had experienced sudden conversion. The 1960s brought an even greater demand for immediate, powerful, and deep religious experience.

I have chosen to say little about traditional religious conversions because they have a great deal to do with the group dynamic. I have been focusing on spiritual experiences independent of religious group identity. Yet, as Walter Clark says, "The line between mysticism and conversion is hard to draw for the reason that mystical perception or rebirth will bring conversion along with it."

Teenagers are particularly likely to have dramatic experiences.

Sometimes the experience refers to God the power within. Parents recalled:

When I was thirteen I felt very miserable at school, trying unsuccessfully all the time to get into the clique of popular girls. One night, I had a dream in which "God" or my guardian angel appeared to me with The Answer to my life's problems. The Answer, without words, encouraged me to "Be yourself." It worked. I remember everything was different in school the next day—I no longer cared to try to make certain girls like me, and I soon found my own circle of friends.

When I was nineteen, I was totally at loose ends, traveling and finally going to where some good friends were. While coming out of a treacherous mountain canyon, I "saw" a banner across the canyon which said, "Your heart holds all the answers." I felt centered, confident and magnificent. It has most certainly had a lasting influence. I began looking within for connection and beauty, love and confidence.

One mother remembers:

When I was about fourteen or fifteen I had what I guess could be called an "illumination experience." It was Easter morning. I was quite distraught at my parents not allowing me to go to a Love-in that day. I remember waking up and turning the radio on beside my bed. It was 8:00 and the next hour of music was devoted to contemporary songs along the Easter theme. I found the music very inspiring and uplifting. As if I was being directed by a higher force, at 9 I turned the radio off, got out of bed and lit a candle and began to sob for apparently no reason. When I stopped crying I was aware that I was experiencing a consciousness that was very alien; it was spiritual instead of physical. It was as though I had been given "new eyes" or a new perception of life. I felt so detached but light, joyous, and ethereal. The oneness of all life was so clear to me. The strangeness of the experience was outweighed by the pure joy I was experiencing. This experience of another reality lasted the whole day. Ever since that time, Easter has had a very special significance for me. As a result of the experience I gained faith and hope that there was something beautiful and real to strive for and believe in in this life. That was the beginning of my search to the answers concerning life's deeper meaning and purpose.

Robert Jay Lifton has said:

A hunger for transcendence is central to our age. And the success the cults have had depends no less on their indoctrination procedures than on the quality of transcendence they have promised. They can offer the most intense form of "community high." This consists of an immediate sense of being surrounded by a caring, loving group in sharp contrast to the rootlessness and confusion one has known. More than that, cults provide communal forms of ecstasy—psychic states so intense that time and death disappear.

For the young, these cult experiences can have some of the psychological function of initiation rites in primitive societies— including the sense of being confronted, threatened and challenged, and then ecstatically united with a new group. One of the reasons why cults have helped many people kick drug habits is that they have substituted for them alternative forms of transcendence that can themselves be habit-forming or even addictive. But their success in doing so reflects the impoverishment of opportunities for transcendence in our culture at large.

What can we do as parents to help channel the teenager's spiritual energies? As usual, the most important thing is simply to recognize and respect their quest. This is the age where many of the exercises described in chapters 3 and 6 may help the adolescent find the sacred in everyday life, without having to join a cult or make a pilgrimage to India. If they are very lucky, they may find it in school.

Paula Klimek and Jack Canfield, of the Institute for Wholistic Education, have become convinced that during sixth, seventh, and eighth grade one is at "a very special age to make contact with one's "potential." They have devised several classroom techniques to help young people recognize and affirm their inner awakening, and contact inner wisdom. One of these is the "life purpose fantasy."

They prepare for this exercise by several weeks of building a classroom environment of trust and mutual support, teaching basic imaging and centering techniques, and practice with guided fantasies. Then they discuss what is meant by the term "life purpose." The students' pre-session comments are usually very career-related, much different from the post-session comments.

On the day of the session they ask the kids to get into a comfortable position with their spines straight, either sitting up or lying down. Then they ask them to close their eyes and become relaxed, being aware of the rhythm of their inhalation and exhalation. To begin the fantasy, they say:

We are about to review your life. You will begin to experience yourself going backwards in time. Begin by thinking about this day. Go back to when you woke up this morning. . . . What have you done all day? . . . Now look back at the past week . . . the past month . . . the past year. . . . Review the significant events of this time. . . . What did you look like? . . . Who were you with? Where have you been? . . . Try not to get caught up in any particular event or to be judgmental. Allow your life to pass by as if you were watching a movie. . . . Now go back to your previous grade. . . . To your elementary grades. . . . To the primary grades. . . . To the time you first entered school. . . . To being a young child. . . . A two-year-old. . . . A baby. . . . To the time of your birth and the time you were in your mother's womb. . . . And now go back to the time before your conception. You are about to meet a special guide, your own special guide. A guide to whom you may ask what the purpose of your life is. . . . Meet this guide and pose your question. . . . Feel your guide's unconditional love and strength and beauty. . . . Let whatever happens happen. . . . Communicate with your guide in whatever way possible. . . . Listen to your guide's response. . . . Notice what you are experiencing. . . . Now ask your guide for a gift to represent your purpose, your essence, your unique gifts, your genius. . . . Now you must begin your journey back. Say farewell to your guide knowing you may visit your guide at any time. . . . Begin to make your journey back bringing with you both your life purpose and the gift from your experience. Make your journey through time, through your birth, your infancy, your childhood, and finally to the present moment in this room. When you are ready, open your eyes, remain silent and draw and write about your experience.

The drawings contained many archetypal symbols such as light, rainbows, the sun, mountains, meadows, flowers, and animals. One young man wrote, "When I met my guide and asked my question, he gave me a great big smile and held my hands. It was like he was saying, 'it's real neat. Try it. It's a great thing to be a person.' He gave me a sense of wanting to be just by holding my hands. . . . When I was leaving, I looked back. It seemed as though he was saying, 'It's O.K. Go ahead,' just by looking at me. We met in a place full of nothingness."

There is always a danger that teenagers will seek intense "spiritual" experience as a "high," as an end in itself. Anna Mow, a Protestant, says, "Many people forget about growing up after they are born again." Abraham Maslow, the humanistic psychologist, has a similar warning, as he watched young people turn to drugs, magic, the occult, and the exotic in their impatient search for *more* peak experiences:

> To take up residence on the high plateau of Unitive consciousness . . . tends to be a lifelong effort. It should not be confused with the Thursday evening turnon that many youngsters think of as the path to transcendence. . . . The "spiritual disciplines," both the classical ones and the new ones that keep on being discovered these days, all take time, work, discipline, study, commitment. . . . The great lesson from the true mystics, from the Zen monks, and now also from the Humanistic and Transpersonal psychologists—is that the sacred is in the ordinary, that it is to be found in one's daily life, in one's neighbors, friends, and family.

In the Jungian view, we are "reborn" whenever there is the death of an old attitude and the birth of a new consciousness. The spiritual "crisis" of the adolescent is programmed by biological necessity: death of the dependent child attitudes, rebirth as a psychological adult. It may not be the last of such crises. The parents who answered my questionnaire reported doubts, conversions, and mystical experiences happening throughout their lives.

Piaget's and Freud's theories of development stop at adolescence. Many others do not. Erik Erikson was the first psychoanalyst to look at the "psychosocial" stages of our lives. He viewed the task of adolescence as that of establishing an identity. Once that is completed, we face the challenge of intimacy, a loving relationship with a mate. After intimacy comes generativity, our nurturance of the next generation and our contribution to the world. And finally, in old age, comes either the wisdom of "integrity" or, if we fail that stage, despair. Gail Sheehy in *Passages* dramatized the research of Roger Gould, Daniel Levinson, and others on the stages of adult life. We are never free from the pressure to continue growing as our lives move on.

James Fowler, of the Candler School of Theology, attempts to bring together the cognitive stages of Piaget's theory, Kohlberg's stages of moral development (which we met in chapter 9), and Erikson's psychosocial stages into a comprehensive theory of "faith development."

I have avoided using the word "faith" in this book because to me, the word is simply overloaded with the idea of "belief in God." Fowler, however, uses the word "faith" in the same sense that we have used "spiritual": as a form of knowing, a way of being in relation to what he calls "an ultimate environment."

Although Fowler has been criticized for establishing his stages first, and then fitting people into them (as well as for his extraordinary use of jargon), I include my version of his noble effort at a grand synthesis to give you an opportunity to ponder what stage you're at.

The twists and turns that parents reported were part of their *adult* spiritual growth are far too varied to summarize, and would only be misleading. What matters is that you trust *your own* process.

Jung introduces his autobiography, *Memories, Dreams, Reflections,* by saying:

My life is a story of the self-realization of the unconscious. . . . I cannot employ the language of science to trace this process of growth in myself, for I cannot experience myself as a scientific problem. . . .

Thus it is that I have now undertaken, in my eighty-third year, to tell my personal myth. I can only make direct statements, only "tell stories." Whether or not the stories are "true" is not the problem. The only question is whether what I tell is my fable, my truth.

TABLE 3: FAITH: THE STRUCTURAL-DEVELOPMENTAL APPROACH

Age	Piaget (Cognitive)	Kohlberg (Moral) Stage	Erikson (Psychosocial) (Psychoanalytic)	Fowler (Faith) Stage
0	Sensorimotor	The Good is what I want and like	Trust vs. Mistrust (oral)	
2	Preoperational	(1) "Punishment-Reward"— Something is wrong if you are punished, right if you are not.	Autonomy vs. Shame & Doubt (anal) Initiative vs. Guilt (phallic)	(1) (Age 4–7) "Intuitive-Projective" A collage of images and beliefs given by trusted others, mixed with child's own experience and imaginative construction.
6–7	Concrete Operations	(2) "Instrumental hedonism and reciprocity"— You scratch my back, I'll scratch yours.	Industry vs. Inferiority (school age—latency)	(2) (Age 7–11 or 12) "Mythic-Literal" Private world of fantasy and wonder; symbols must refer to something specific. Dramatic narrative and myth used to communicate transcendent meaning.
11–12	Formal Operations	(3) Interpersonal relations of mutuality—fulfilling the expectations of others. Keeping agreements and keeping peace. "Good boy . . . nice girl"	Identity vs. Identity confusion	(3) (adolescent or adult) "Synthetic-Conventional" Structuring the world and ultimate environment by the expectations and judgments of others. Interpersonal focus.
Adulthood		(4) "Law and Order"— Doing one's duty, with a recognition of authority and fixed rules; maintaining the social order.	Intimacy vs. Isolation Generativity vs. Stagnation	(4) (after 18) "Individuating-Reflexive" Constructing one's own explicit system. High degree of self-consciousness. (5) (after 30) "Paradoxical-Consolidative" Truth is apprehended from a variety of viewpoints.
		(5) "Social Contract"; Principled Higher Law— Avoiding violating the rights of others, and a recognition of personal values and opinions		
Old age		(6) Universal ethical principles	Integrity vs. Despair	(6) (maybe never) "Universalizing" Becoming an incarnation of the principles of love and justice.

Conclusion

Like love, like wrath, like hope, ambition, jealousy, like every other instinctive eagerness and impulse, [religious feeling] adds to life an enchantment which is not rationally or logically deducible from anything else. . . . A new zest. . . . An assurance of safety and a temper of peace, and, in relation to others, a preponderance of loving affections.

William James
The Varieties of Religious Experience

People asked, when they heard about my research, "What have you found?" What I found, and wished to share in this book, was reassurance that in fact we *have* been attending to our children's spiritual development even if we do not give sermons every night and a home Sunday school on weekends. As we have heard again and again, from psychologists, educators, and people remembering their own childhoods, it is not *verbal* lessons that impress children. We have already been teaching by the example of our love and respect, our compassion, our wisdom, and even our struggle with negative states when we feel all these virtues have disappeared.

I found that in addition to our *example,* our children will remember shared *activities.* I hope that *you* have found ideas for activities that will work for *your* family, whether these are formal "religious" activities (chapter 4), "homemade" family rituals and celebrations (chapter 5), ways to develop inner wisdom (chapters 3 and 6), discussions about "important things" (chapters 8 and 9), or new stories to tell (chapter 10).

Hearing so many other parents expose their own spiritual needs, their sometimes fumbling search, and their breakthroughs into clarity, can, like good group therapy, give us the confidence to experiment. Reading about the experiences of others helps us overcome our reluctance to communicate our own deepest thoughts to our children. When we do, the children can inspire us. I have included questions we can ask to discover more about our children's inner life. Parents repeatedly affirmed: "We are all growing together, learning from each other. The challenge is to keep the channels open."

One mother, Sara, says:

In some aspects, I see myself and my husband as being ahead on the spiritual path, pointing out a direction. I feel our example as growing beings is most important. In other ways, I feel it's important to respect the unique spiritual strivings in our son. . . . Having walked into the forest on my path makes me want to take Mark into the forest too, of course—to introduce him to the ideas and experiences that I think are important parts of life—prayer, awareness of God, deepened awareness of the spiritual interconnection between all things. Parenting here means sometimes leading, sometimes following, sometimes walking with and sometimes letting go . . . and being sensitive to which is needed when.

Some of the parents who answered the questionnaire are already, like Sara, "in the forest." Others who long ago rejected institutional religion are only now wondering about other ways to help themselves and their children find a source of comfort and guidance, and awareness of themselves as meaningfully related to the whole of existence.

William James says, "Religion, whatever it is, is a man's total reaction upon life. . . . To get at |total reactions| you must go behind the foregound of existence and reach down to that curious sense of the whole residual cosmos as an everlasting presence, intimate or alien, terrible or amusing, lovable or odious, which in some degree everyone possesses."

We want our children's relationship to the cosmos to be intimate, not alien. In seeking this, we have explored the traditional ways of religious education, the new, secular ways of transpersonal education, and the personal ways of meditation, prayer, and mystical experience. We have learned how the "spiritual self" grows through the harmonious integration of our physical, emotional, and imaginative, as well as intellectual, selves (chapters 3 and 7). Parents can use their understanding of child development (chapter 7) to help the child's intuitive "beginner's mind" grow into adult intuition without sacrificing the growth of the rational mind and successful functioning in the world.

We have seen how modern physics and consciousness research has brought experiences and mystical teachings that used to be considered "supernatural" into the realm of the natural (chapter 1).

We have seen that religious teaching is not necessary for the development of moral character, spirituality, psychological health, or a sense of life's meaning (chapters 9, 10, 11, and 13). Yet, where there is no organized religion, parents have to find their own symbols and invent their own forms. This always carries uncertainty, and requires energy and creativeness.

Most important of all, we have found assurance that there is no one *right* way. Each family is unique, and each has had a different story to tell, like crystals scattering a beam of white light into rainbows. The variety of spiritual paths can be as dazzling and bewildering as the variety of life itself. There are many forms. I hope that reading this book has helped you respect and clarify your own process: the search for a Way that is "right" for you and your children.

There is more at stake than a personal quest. The life on our planet depends on our awareness that we are all part of one another and always have been. For millennia we did not have to face that fact because there was enough land and few enough people so that much of the time we could simply stay out of one another's way. When we didn't, many people were killed, but not the whole planet. As our growing population and technology continues to consume the planet's resources and destroy land, air, and water, there is a real danger that we might end everything, if not for ourselves, then for our children's children. We may be manifestations of "God," but what is manifest can be made unmanifest. "God" can surely create new manifestations if the old ones don't work out.

Joseph Campbell has written (looking at the astronaut's photograph of our blue-green planet):

> *The mystical theme of the space age is this: the world, as we know it, is coming to an end. The world as the center of the universe, the world divided from the heavens, the world bound by horizons in which love is reserved for members of the in-group—that is the world that is passing away. . . . the exclusivism of there being only one way in which we can be saved, the idea that there is a single religious group that is in sole possession of the truth, that is the world as we know it that must pass away. What is the Kingdom? It lies in our realization of the ubiquity of the divine presence in our neighbors, in our enemies, in all of us.*

Campbell sees the search for "roots" and recent nationalistic movements as reactions against this. The notion of one world is very frightening. It means we have to give up what we know, what we are comfortable with. It requires an enormous amount of cortical control of territorial instincts lodged in the most ancient nuclei of our brains. It requires transformation.

This transformation of human nature, or "salvation," or "enlightenment," has always been the concern of the spiritual life.

William James puts it this way:

> *The individual, so far as he suffers from his wrongness and criticizes it, is to that extend consciously beyond it, and in at*

least possible touch with something higher, if anything higher exists. Along with the wrong part there is thus a better part of him, even though it may be but a most helpless germ. With which part he should identify his real being is by no means obvious at this stage; but when stage 2 (the stage of solution or salvation) arrives (remember that for some men it arrives suddenly, for others gradually, while others again practically enjoy it all their life), the man identifies his real being with the germinal higher part of himself; and does so in the following way. He becomes conscious that this higher part is conterminous and continuous with a MORE of the same quality, which is operative in the universe outside of him, and which he can keep in working touch with, and in a fashion get on board of and save himself when all his lower being has gone to pieces in the wreck.

. . . It seems to me that all [religious] phenomena are accurately describable in these very simple general terms. They allow for the divided self and the struggle; they involve the change of personal centre and the surrender of the lower self; they express the appearance of exteriority of the helping power and yet account for our sense of union with it; and they fully justify our feelings of security and joy.

As parents, we cannot "transform" our children, but to the extent that we can train our own consciousness, we can support its unfolding in our children. As one mother said, "They carry within them the seed; all I do is provide the nourishment, the soil for it to grow, hopefully to its potential."

Resources

References

The following are works cited in the text.

Angyal, Andras. *Neurosis and Treatment: A Holistic Theory.* New York: John Wiley and Sons, 1965.

Aronfreed, Justin. "Moral Development from the Standpoint of a General Psychological Theory." In *Moral Development and Behavior,* edited by Thomas Lickona. New York: Holt, Rinehart and Winston, 1976.

Assagioli, Roberto. *Psychosynthesis: A Manual of Principles and Techniques.* New York: Hobbs, Dorman and Co., Inc., 1965.

————. *The Act of Will.* New York: Penguin (Esalen), 1976.

Bateson, Gregory. *Steps to an Ecology of Mind.* New York: Ballantine, 1977.

de Beauport, Elaine. "Matters of Consequence." *Dromenon* 1, no. 5–6 (Feb. 1979), pp. 22–29.

Becker, Russell. "Religion and Psychological Health." In *Research on Religious Development,* edited by Merton Strommen. New York: Hawthorn Books, 1971, chap. 10.

Beebe, Robin. "The Links Grow in the Bronx." *Dromenon* 1, no. 5–6 (Feb. 1979), pp. 30–31.

Berends, Polly Berrien. *Whole Child, Whole Parent.* New York: Harper & Row (Harper's Magazine Press), 1975.

Berman, Louis A. *Jews and Intermarriage: A Study in Personality and Culture.* New York: Thomas Yoseloff, 1968.

Bhagavad-Gita: The Song of God. Translated by Swami Prabhavananda and Christopher Isherwood. New York: New American Library (Mentor), 1961 (1944).

Biersdorf, John. *Hunger for Experience: The Growing Edge of Religion in America.* New York: Seabury Press, 1975.

Brazelton, T. Berry. *Infants and Mothers: Differences in Development.* New York: Delacorte Press, 1972.

Buber, Martin. *Tales of the Hasidim: Early Masters.* New York: Schocken Books, 1961 (1947).

Buckler, Francis. *Children and God.* Denville, N.J.: Dimension Books, 1972.

Bumpass, Larry L., and Sweet, James A. "Differentials in Marital Instability: 1970." *American Sociological Review,* 37 (1972), pp. 754–66.

Campbell, Joseph. *The Masks of God: Occidental Mythology.* Vol. 3. New York: Viking Press, 1964.

Canfield, Jack, and Paula Klimek. *The Inner Classroom: Teaching with Guided Fantasy.* Englewood Cliffs, N.J.: Prentice-Hall, 1980.

———. *Teaching Students to Love Themselves.* Englewood Cliffs, N.J.: Prentice-Hall, 1980.

Caprio, Betsy. *Experiments in Prayer.* Notre Dame, Indiana: Ave Maria Press, 1978.

Carrington, Patricia. *Freedom in Meditation.* New York: Doubleday (Anchor Press), 1977.

Chall, Jeanne, and Mirsky, Allan F., eds. *Education and the Brain.* Chicago: University of Chicago Press, 1978.

Chase, Stuart. *Guides to Straight Thinking.* New York: Harper & Bros., 1956.

Christ, Carol. "Spiritual Quest and Women's Experience." In *Womanspirit Rising: A Feminist Reader in Religion.* Edited by Carol Christ and Judith Plaskow. San Francisco: Harper & Row, 1979.

———. "Why Women Need the Goddess." In *Womanspirit Rising.*

Clark, Walter H. "Intense Religious Experience." In *Research on Religious Development,* edited by Merton Strommen. New York: Hawthorn Books, 1971.

Daly, Mary. "After the Death of God the Father." In *Womanspirit Rising.*

Dean, Stanley R., ed. *Psychiatry and Mysticism.* Chicago: Nelson-Hall, 1975.

de Chardin, Teilhard. *The Phenomenon of Man.* New York: Harper & Row (Torchbooks), 1965 (1955).

de Mause, Lloyd, ed. *The History of Childhood.* New York: The Psychohistory Press, 1974.

Dinnerstein, Dorothy. *The Mermaid and The Minotaur: Sexual Arrangements and Human Malaise.* New York: Harper & Row (Colophon), 1977.

Dobrin, Arthur. *The God Within.* New York: Ethica Press, 1977.

Dodson, Fitzhugh. *How to Discipline with Love.* New York: New American Library (Signet), 1978.

———. *How to Parent.* New York: New American Library (Signet), 1971.

Donin, Rabbi Hayim Halevy. *To Raise a Jewish Child: A Guide for Parents.* New York: Basic Books, 1977.

Ehrenwald, Jan. "The Non-Euclidian Mind: A Neurophysiological Model of Psi Phenomena." In *Psychiatry and Mysticism,* edited by Stanley R. Dean. Chicago: Nelson-Hall, 1975.

Eliot, T. S. *The Complete Poems and Plays.* New York: Harcourt Brace, 1952.

Elkind, David. "The Development of Religious Understanding in Children and Adolescents." In *Research on Religious Development,* edited by Merton Strommen. New York: Hawthorn Books, 1971.

Elkind, David, and Sally Elkind. "Varieties of Religious Experience in Young Adolescents." *Journal for the Scientific Study of Religion* 2 (1962): 102–12.

Epstein, Herman T. "Growth Spurts During Brain Development: Implications for Educational Policy and Practice." In *Education and the Brain,* edited by Jeanne Chall and Allan F. Mirsky. Chicago: University of Chicago Press, 1978.

Faraday, Ann. *The Dream Game.* New York: Harper & Row, 1974.

Fargues, Maria. *How to Teach Religion.* New York: Paulist Press, 1968.

Fiorenza, Elisabeth. "Women in the Early Christian Movement." In *Womanspirit Rising*.
———. "Feminist Spirituality, Christian Identity, and Catholic Vision." In *Womanspirit Rising*.
Fowler, James, and Sam Keen. *Life Maps*. Waco, Tex.: Word Books, 1978.
Frankl, Viktor E. *Man's Search for Meaning*. New York: Simon & Schuster (Pocket Books), 1977 (1959).
Frideres, James S. "Offspring of Jewish Intermarriage: A Note." *Jewish Social Studies* 35 (April 1973): 149–56.
Gerson, Randy P., and William Damon. "Moral Understanding and Children's Conduct." In *New Directions for Child Development* 2 (1978): 41–61.
Gesell, Arnold, Frances L. Ilg, and Louise Bates Ames. *Infant and Child in the Culture of Today*. Rev. ed. New York: Harper & Row, 1974.
———. *The Child from Five to Ten*. New York: Harper & Row, 1977.
Ginott, Dr. Haim G. *Between Parent and Child*. New York: Avon, 1969.
Goldman, Ronald. *Readiness for Religion: A Basis for Developmental Religious Education*. New York: Seabury Press, 1970.
———. *Religious Thinking from Childhood to Adolescence*. New York: Seabury Press, 1968.
Goldstein, Joseph. *The Experience of Insight: A Natural Unfolding*. Santa Cruz, Calif.: Unity Press, 1976.
Goleman, Daniel. *The Varieties of the Meditative Experience*. New York: E. P. Dutton, 1977.
Gordon, Albert J. *Intermarriage*. Boston: Beacon Press, 1964.
Greeley, Andrew. *Ecstasy as a Way of Knowing*. Englewood Cliffs, N.J.: Prentice Hall, 1974.
———. *The Sociology of the Paranormal: A Reconnaissance*. Series no. 90-023. Vol. 3. Beverly Hills, Calif.: Sage Publications, 1975.
Greenberg, Irving. "From Modernity to Post-Modernity: Community and the Revitalization of Traditional Religion." *Religious Education* 73, no. 4 (1978), pp. 449–70.
Grollman, Earl A., ed. *Explaining Death to Children*. Boston: Beacon Press, 1969.
Gross, Rita. "Female God Language in a Jewish Context." In *Womanspirit Rising*.
Group for the Advancement of Psychiatry. *Mysticism: Spiritual Quest or Psychic Disorder?* New York: Group for the Advancement of Psychiatry, 1976.
Harms, Ernest. "The Development of Religious Experience in Children." *American Journal of Sociology* 50, no. 2 (1944): 112–22.
Havighurst, Robert J., and Barry Keating. "The Religion of Youth." In *Research on Religious Development*, edited by Merton Strommen. New York: Hawthorn Books, 1971.
Heiss, Jerold S. "Interfaith Marriage and Marital Outcomes." *Marriage and Family Living* 23 (1961), pp. 228–233.
Hendricks, Gay, and Russel Wills. *The Centering Book: Awareness Activities for Children, Parents, and Teachers*. Englewood Cliffs, N.J.: Prentice-Hall (A Spectrum Book), 1975.
Hendricks, Gay, and Thomas B. Roberts. *The Second Centering Book*. Englewood Cliffs, N.J.: Prentice-Hall (A Spectrum Book), 1977.
Hendricks, Gay, and James Fadiman, eds. *Transpersonal Education: A Curriculum for Feeling and Being*. Englewood Cliffs, N.J.: Prentice-Hall, 1976.
Hennesy, Thomas C., ed. *Values and Moral Development*. New York: Paulist Press, 1976.
Hoffman, Martin. "Development of Internal Moral Standards in Children." In *Research on Religious Development*, edited by Merton Strommen. New York: Hawthorn Books, 1971.
Hogan, Robert, John A. Johnson, and Nicholas P. Emler. "A Socioanalytic Theory of Moral Development." *New Directions for Child Development* 2 (1978): 1–19.
Houston, Jean. "Consider the Stradivarius." *Dromenon* 1, no. 5–6 (Feb. 1979), pp. 40–42.
Huxley, Aldous. *The Doors of Perception*. New York: Harper and Bros., 1954.
———. *Island*. New York: Harper & Row, 1972 (1962).
James, William. *The Varieties of Religious Experience*. New York: Macmillan (Collier Books), 1961 (1902).
Joseph, Stephen M. *Children in Fear*. New York: Holt, Rinehart & Winston, 1974.

Jung, C. G. *Memories, Dreams, Reflections.* New York: Random House (Vintage), 1965.
———. *Modern Man in Search of a Soul.* New York: Harcourt, Brace (Harvest), 1957 (1933).
Jung, C. G. "The Psychology of the Child Archetype." In *Psyche & Symbol,* edited by Violet S. de Laszlo. New York: Doubleday (Anchor), 1958.
Kennedy, Joseph. "Earthrise: The Dawning of a New Spiritual Awareness." *New York Times Magazine,* April 15, 1979, pp. 14 ff.
Kennett, Jiyu (Roshi). "The Education of the Buddhist Child." *Journal of the Zen Mission Society* 5 (December 1974).
Klingberg, Greta. "A Study of Religious Experience in Children from 9 to 13 Years of Age." *Religious Education* 54 (1959): 211–216.
Klink, Johanna L. *Your Child and Religion.* Richmond, VA.: John Knox, 1972.
Koestler, Arthur. *Janus.* New York: Random House, 1978.
Kohlberg, Lawrence. "Revisions in the Theory and Practice of Moral Development." *New Directions for Child Development* 2 (1978): 83–89.
Koplowitz, Herbert. *Unitary Operations: A Projection Beyond Piaget's Formal Operations Stage.* Unpublished manuscript, 1978.
Landis, Judson T. "Social Correlates of Divorce or Non-Divorce Among the Unhappily Married." *Marriage and Family Living* 25 (1963), pp. 178–80.
Larsen, Earnest, and Patricia Galvin. *Will Religion Make Sense to Your Child?* Liguori, Mo.: Liguorian Books, 1970.
Laski, Marghanita. *Ecstasy: A Study of Some Secular and Religious Experiences.* Bloomington, Ind.: Indiana University Press, 1961.
Lee, R. S. *Your Growing Child and Religion.* New York: Macmillan, 1970.
Lerman, Rhoda. *Call Me Ishtar.* New York: Holt, Rinehart & Winston, 1977 (1973).
LeShan, Lawrence. *How to Meditate.* New York: Bantam Books, 1975.
Lifton, Robert Jay, and Eric Olson. *Living and Dying.* New York: Bantam, 1974.
———. "The Appeal of the Death Trip." *The New York Times Magazine,* January 7, 1979, pp. 26 ff.
Little, Sara. "Belief and Behavior." *Religious Education* 73, no. 4 (1978): 398–409.
Long, Diane, David Elkind, and Bernard Apilka. "The Child's Conception of Prayer." *Journal for the Scientific Study of Religion* 6 (1967): 101–109.
Loukes, Harold. *Friends and Their Children: A Study in Quaker Education.* Philadelphia: Religious Society of Friends, 1967.
Maclean, Paul D. "A Mind of Three Minds: Educating the Triune Brain." In *Education and the Brain,* edited by Jeanne Chall and Allan F. Mirsky. Chicago: University of Chicago Press, 1978.
Maslow, Abraham J. *Religion, Values and Peak-Experiences.* New York: Penguin Books, 1977 (1964).
———. *Toward a Psychology of Being.* New York: Van Nostrand Reinhold (Insight), 1968.
Masters, Robert, and Jean Houston. *Mind Games: The Guide to Inner Space.* New York: Viking Press, 1972.
Miller, Randolph Crump. *Your Child's Religion: A Practical Guide for Concerned Parents.* New York: Hawthorn Books, 1962.
Mow, Anna B. *Your Child from Birth to Rebirth.* Grand Rapids, Mich.: Zondervan, 1975 (1963).
Muktananda, Swami Paramahansa. *Play of Consciousness.* Shree Gurudev Siddha Yoga Ashram, 1974.
Murdock, Maureen H. "Meditation with Young Children." *Journal of Transpersonal Psychology,* vol. 10, no. 1 1978, pp. 29–44.
Naranjo, Claudio, and Robert Ornstein. *On the Psychology of Meditation.* New York: Viking Press, 1971.

"New Directions for Child Development: #2." *Moral Development*, edited by William Damon. San Francisco: Jossey-Bass 1978.

Ornstein, Robert E. *The Psychology of Consciousness*. New York: Penguin Books (Pelican), 1975.

Parker, William R., and Elaine St. Johns. *Prayer Can Change Your Life*. New York: Cornerstone Library Publications, 1957.

Pearce, Joseph Chilton. *Magical Child*. New York: E. P. Dutton, 1977.

Piaget, Jean. *The Construction of Reality in the Child*. New York: Ballantine Books, 1971.

——. *The Child's Conception of the World*. Totowa, N.J.: Littlefield, Adams, 1976.

——. *The Language and Thought of the Child*. Cleveland, Ohio: World Publishing Company (Meridian), 1955.

Pike, Bishop James A. *If You Marry Outside Your Faith*. New York: Harper Bros., 1962 (1954).

Pitts, V. Peter. "Drawing the Invisible: Children's Conceptualizations of God." *Character Potential: A Record of Research* 8, no. 1 (Nov. 1976).

——. *The God Concept in the Child: A Bibliography*. Schnectady, New York: Character Research Press, 1977.

Plato. *Meno*. Translated by Benjamin Jowett. New York: The Liberal Arts Press, 1949.

Princeton Religion Research Center and the Gallup Organization, Inc. *The Unchurched American*. Princeton, N.J., 1978.

Ram Dass. *The Only Dance There Is*. New York: Doubleday (Anchor), 1974.

Progoff, Ira. *At A Journal Workshop*. New York: Dialogue House Library, 1975.

Rama, Swami, Rudolph Ballentine, M.D., and Swami Ajaya (Allan Weinstock, Ph.D.). *Yoga and Psychotherapy: The Evolution of Consciousness*. Glenview, Illinois: Himalayan Institute, 1976.

Reuther, Rosemary Radford, "Motherearth and the Megamachine: A Theology of Liberation in a Feminine, Somatic, and Ecological Perspective." In *Womanspirit Rising*.

Rich, Adrienne. *Of Woman Born: Motherhood as Experience and Institution*. New York: W. W. Norton, 1976.

Rokeach, Milton. *The Nature of Human Values*. New York: Free Press, 1973.

Rolf, Ida P., and Rosemary Feitis. *Ida Rolf Talks About Rolfing and Physical Reality*. New York: Harper & Row, 1978.

Roll, W. G. "ESP and America's Occult Upsurge." In *Psychiatry and Mysticism*, edited by Stanley R. Dean: Chicago: Nelson-Hall, 1975.

Rozman, Deborah. *Meditating with Children: The Art of Concentration and Centering*. Boulder Creek, Calif: University of the Trees Press, 1976.

——. *Meditation for Children*. Millbrae, Calif.: Celestial Arts, 1976.

Ruma, Eleanor. "The Relationship Between Moral Judgment, Guilt, and Behavior in Normal and Delinquent Adolescents." Doctoral dissertation, Ohio State University, 1967.

Sawin, Margaret M. *Family Enrichment with Family Clusters*. Valley Forge, Pa.: Judson Press, 1979.

Sheehy, Gail. *Passages: Predictable Crises of Adult Life*. New York: Bantam Books, 1977.

Siegel, Richard, Michael Strassfeld, and Sharon Strassfeld. *The First Jewish Catalogue: A Do-It-Yourself Kit*. Philadelphia: The Jewish Publication Society of America, 1973.

Simon, Sidney B., and Sally Wendkos Olds. *Helping Your Child Learn Right from Wrong: A Guide to Values Clarification*. New York: Simon and Shuster, 1976.

Simon, Sidney B., Leland W. Howe, and Howard Kirschenbaum. *Values Clarification: A Handbook of Practical Strategies for Teachers and Students*. New York: Hart, 1978.

Singer, Dororthy G., and Tracey A. Revenson. *A Piaget Primer: How a Child Thinks*. New York: International Universities Press, 1978.

Smith, Huston. *The Religions of Man*. New York: Harper & Row, 1965 (1958).

Spock, Benjamin. "What to Tell Your Child About God." *Redbook Magazine*, August 1978.

Squire, Anne M. "Women and Spirituality." *Religious Education* 73, no. 3 (May-June 1978): 324–35.

Srole, Leo, Thomas, Langner, et al. *Mental Health in the Metropolis: The Midtown Manhattan Study.* New York: Harper & Row (Torchbooks), 1977.

Starbuck, E. D. *The Psychology of Religion.* New York: Scribner, 1900.

Steiner, Rudolf. *The Kingdom of Childhood.* London: Rudolf Steiner Press, 1964.

————. *Ancient Mirrors of Womanhood: Our Goddess and Heroine Heritage.* New York: New Sibylline Books, 1979.

Stone, Merlin. *When God Was a Woman.* New York: Dial Press, 1976.

Strassfeld, Sharon, and Strassfeld, Michael, ed. *The Second Jewish Catalog.* Philadelphia: Jewish Publication Society of America, 1976.

Strommen, Merton, ed. *Research on Religious Development: A Comprehensive Handbook.* New York: Hawthorn Books, 1971.

Targan, Judith. "Jewish Education." In *The Second Jewish Catalogue.* Edited by Sharon Strassfeld and Michael Strassfeld, pp. 176–210. Philadelphia: Jewish Publication Society of America, 1976.

Traherne, Thomas. *Centuries of Meditations.* In *Seventeenth Century Verse and Prose,* vol. 2, 1660–1700, edited by White, Helen; Wallerstein, Ruth; and Quintana, Ricardo. New York: Macmillan, 1952.

Trungpa, Chogyam. *Cutting Through Spiritual Materialism.* Berkeley: Shambhala, 1973.

Udry, J. Richard. *The Social Context of Marriage.* New York: J. B. Lippincott, 1974.

Underhill, Evelyn. *Mysticism.* New York: American Library, 1955.

Vaughan, Frances E. *Awakening Intuition.* New York: Doubleday (Anchor), 1974.

The Way of a Pilgrim and *The Pilgrim Continues His Way.* New York: Ballantine, 1974.

Waldoks, Moshe. "As the Jew Turns: A Guide to Baalei Teshubah" *The Second Jewish Catalogue.* Edited by Sharon Strassfeld and Michael Strassfeld, pp. 253–264. Philadelphia: Jewish Publication Society of America, 1976.

Weil, Andrew. *The Natural Mind: A New Way of Looking at Drugs and the Higher Consciousness.* Boston: Houghton Mifflin, 1972.

Westerhoff, John H. III. *Will Our Children Have Faith?* New York: Seabury Press, 1976.

Wickes, Frances G. *The Inner World of Childhood.* Englewood Cliffs, N.J.: Prentice-Hall (Spectrum), 1978 (1927).

Williams, Herman, and Ella Greene. *Attitude Education: A Research Curriculum Developed by the Union College Character Research Project.* Schenectady, N.Y.: Character Research Press, 1975.

Wittig, Monique. *Les Guerilleres.* New York: Viking Press, 1971.

Young, Samuel H. *Psychic Children.* New York: Doubleday, 1977.

Zilboorg, Gregory. *Religion, Science and Mental Health.* New York: New York University Press, 1959.

OTHER RESOURCES FOR PARENTS

Chapter 2

The Journal of Transpersonal Psychology, published by the Transpersonal Institute, P.O. Box 4437, Stanford, CA 94305. Studies of meditation, transcendence, spiritual and religious paths, aspects of consciousness.

The Highest State of Consciousness, edited by John White. New York: Doubleday (Anchor) 1972. A collection of interesting essays.

Searchlight Seminars. P.O. Box 1437, Orinda, CA 94563. Tapes of Pascal Kaplan's ChildQuest Conference: "Discovering the Psychic and Spiritual Life of Children."

Chapter 3

Jean Houston: New Ways of Being workshops, % Drs. Jean Houston and Robert Masters, Foundation for Mind Research, Box 600, Pomona, NY 10970, or subscribe to *Dromenon: A Journal of New Ways of Being,* G.P.O. Box 2244, New York, NY 10011

A Guide to Resources in Humanistic and Transpersonal Education, published by Jack Canfield at the Institute for Wholistic Education, Box 575, Amherst, MA 01002. More about Jack's work is discussed in chapter 14.

Rolfing. For more information contact the Rolf Institute, Box 1868, Boulder, CO 80306

Chapter 4

Unitarian Universalist Association, 25 Beacon Street, Boston, MA 02108, has a catalogue of Education Resources.

Union College Character Research Project, % Character Research Press, 207 State Street, Schnectady, N.Y. 12305, produces the "Attitude Education" curriculum and other materials.

Sawin, Margaret M. *Family Enrichment with Family Clusters.* Dr. Sawin's book lists addresses for many kinds of family growth groups, both religious and "human potential," as well as curricula published by churches for parents to use at home. (Write Family Clustering, Inc., P.O. Box 18074, Rochester, NY 14618.

Shalom Curriculum (United Church), 1505 Race St., Philadelphia, Pa. 19102

Chapter 5

The GreenBlade. Edited by Sam Mackintosh, Box 322, Haddonfield, NJ 08033

Chapter 6

A Course in Miracles. Write to: Foundation for Inner Peace, P.O. Box 635, Tiburon, CA 94920.

Chapter 7

The following are useful books about Rudolf Steiner's theories applied to children..

Frommer, Eva A. *Voyage Through Childhood into the Adult World.* Elmsford, N.Y.: Pergamon Press, 1969.

Spock, Marjory. *Teaching as a Lively Art.* New York: Anthroposophic Press, 1978.

Steiner, Rudolf. *The Education of the Child.* London: Rudolf Steiner Press 1975 (1927).

Chapter 9

Parent Participation T.V. Workshops, % Teachers Guides to Television, 699 Madison Avenue, New York, N.Y. 10021.

est (an educational corporation), 765 California Street, San Francisco, CA 94108. Write or call this central office at (415) 391-9911 to find the *est* center nearest you.

New York Society for Ethical Culture (Publications), 2 West 64 St. New York, NY 10023.

Chapter 10

Heresies: A Feminist Publication on Art and Politics, P.O. Box 766. Canal Street Station, New York, NY 10013

Stone, Merlin. *Ancient Mirrors of Womanhood: Our Goddess and Heroine Heritage.* Vol. 1. New Sibylline Books, Inc. Box 266, Village Station, New York, NY 10014.

Spretnak, Charlene. *Lost Goddesses of Early Greece.* Moor Books, P.O. Box 9223, Berkeley, CA 94709. Single copies available from Women In Distribution (WIND), P.O. Box 8858, Washington, D.C. 20003.

Tatterhood and other tales: Stories of Magic and Adventure, edited by Ethel Johnston Phelps. The Feminist Press, Box 334, Old Westbury, NY 11568.

Wonder Woman, New York: Holt, Rinehart & Winston (A Ms. Book), 1972.

Miller, Jean Baker. *Toward a New Psychology of Women.* Boston: Beacon Press, 1976. Jean Baker Miller has also edited an excellent collection of essays: *Psychoanalysis and Women* (Baltimore: Penguin Books), 1973.

General

Inner Development: *The Yes! Bookshop Guide* by Cris Popenoe. 654-page annotated bibliography and catalogue. Yes! Bookshop, 1035 31st St. N.W. Washington, DC 20007. cost: $9.95

Spiritual Community Guide: The New Consciousness Source Book. Includes schools, preschool through higher education, and spiritual growth centers. Updated yearly. P.O. Box 1080, San Rafael, CA 94902.

Our Ultimate Investment. "A nonprofit organization for the nurturing of the possible human" was started by Laura Huxley with projects to enhance health and relationships from conception through to the first five years of life. "Caressing centers" provide an opportunity for older aunts to hold babies and develop a grandparent-grandchild relationship for babies to receive love and for busy parents to get some rest. 5615 W. Pico Blvd., Los Angeles, CA 90019.

INDEX